W**O**RLD UPSIDE D**O**WN

Celebrating
30 Years of Publishing
in India

Praise for *World Upside Down*

'Sujan Chinoy's book—*World Upside Down*—vividly describes a world in flux in which India, a rising power, must contend with unprecedented geopolitical challenges and crises. A veteran diplomat of high distinction, Chinoy is an acknowledged expert on the complex international relations and security-related issues of India's extended neighbourhood including the Indo-Pacific region. Chinoy is a highly respected China specialist. His four-year stint in the National Security Council Secretariat, his experience of assignments in Quad countries and his continuing activities as director general of India's Institute for Defence Studies and Analyses lend special importance and high authority to this book.'

—M.K. Rasgotra, former Foreign Secretary of India

'In this collection of his most recent writings, *World Upside Down*, Ambassador Sujan Chinoy offers readers a deep dive into the tectonic shifts taking place in the current geopolitical landscape. The author brings to the subject his rich diplomatic experience dealing with China and Japan and his current vantage point as the head of one of India's most prestigious think tanks. The book provides an indispensable reference work for scholars and practitioners alike providing a rare and lucid perspective that is uniquely Indian.'

—Shyam Saran, Former Foreign Secretary of India

'Sujan Chinoy's *World Upside Down* not only portrays the dramatic changes confronting India in the contemporary international system but the adroitness with which New Delhi has responded to advance its interests. A collection of essays by one of India's most prominent experts on China, this volume is a striking reminder of how artful diplomacy will be essential for the success of India's grand strategy amid the persistent challenges surrounding it.'

—Ashley J. Tellis, Tata Chair for Strategic Affairs, Carnegie Endowment for International Peace, Washington, D.C.

'As the international system changes rapidly and moves in unexpected directions, Chinoy's *World Upside Down* offers deep insights into the shifting geopolitical terrain. Chinoy deploys his long experience in the higher levels of government to throw light at India's efforts at reorienting its foreign and security policies.'

—C. Raja Mohan, Asia Society Policy Institute, Delhi

WORLD UPSIDE DOWN

INDIA RECALIBRATES ITS GEOPOLITICS

SUJAN CHINOY

HarperCollins *Publishers* India

First published in India by HarperCollins *Publishers* 2023
4th Floor, Tower A, Building No. 10, DLF Cyber City,
DLF Phase II, Gurugram, Haryana – 122002
www.harpercollins.co.in

2 4 6 8 10 9 7 5 3 1

P-ISBN: 978-93-5699-310-5
E-ISBN: 978-93-5699-305-1

Typeset in 11/15.2 Adobe Garamond at
Manipal Technologies Limited, Manipal

Printed and bound at
Replika Press Pvt. Ltd.

For my late parents, Romesh and Usha Chinoy,
who sacrificed much for my future

Contents

Quadrilateral Sphere

Chinese Checkers

Foreword

When a diplomat compiles his commentary about the state of the world over the last four years, it has a value in itself. It provides a real-time perspective of international relations, rather than a retrospective evaluation. This is even more so when the global order is in turbulence and a broad range of happenings contribute to its volatility. *World Upside Down* has the merit of recognizing what we are going through and seeks to identify its driving factors. The cause and effect can be debated, as indeed the prioritization of contemporary issues. But the bottom line is that we have started to accept that what we have been used to for so long may no longer be tenable.

This endeavour has been organized into broad themes that reflect our changing world. The section Reordering the Strategic Landscape focuses on the impact of the pandemic, which has been as much a challenge to international politics as to public health. It has ignited a serious shift towards re-globalization by focusing on building resilient and reliable supply chains. This development could have significant implications for the Indian economy and polity. The distress of the Global South that was so starkly in evidence has been aggravated by the impact of the Ukraine conflict. That, too, has more than passing consequences for the world order.

Quadrilateral Sphere is the second section, particularly appropriate given its growing salience to world affairs. Direct diplomatic experiences in Japan and Australia have obviously provided insights to the author. But the central point is the one that requires continued emphasis, which is that the earlier constructs have become archaic. We must, therefore, seek explanations by recognizing anachronisms, not by promoting conspiracy theories.

The relationship between India and China has long been a complex one, but in recent times, troubled as well. The section Chinese Checkers serves to highlight the centrality of ensuring peace and tranquility in the border areas for the stability and development of this relationship. The historical references are useful in correcting any tendencies towards political amnesia. At the end of the day, the answer lies in mutual respect, mutual sensitivity and mutual interests.

Navigating India's Neighbourhood section has a particular relevance, given how much the Neighbourhood First policy and SAGAR outlook have progressed in the last decade. Today, India is consciously pursuing a generous and non-reciprocal approach towards its neighbours. At the same time, it has vigorously striven to delegitimize cross-border terrorism by Pakistan. The triumph of the Taliban in Afghanistan is understandably the focus in this section. But as its ramifications unfold, perhaps we ignore basic principles of state behaviour at our peril.

India, today, requires a healthy debate on its foreign policy because only an objective evaluation of the past and present can help chart a course forward. This cannot be reduced to a theological defence of the past or an exercise of scoring points. By presenting a perspective and triggering responses, the author has endeavoured to initiate a process that serves the collective well. The world of policymaking certainly benefits from a larger conversation about India's interests and how they are best served.

Dr S. Jaishankar
Minister of External Affairs, Government of India
7 June 2023

Introduction

The regional and international environment is undergoing rapid change with far-reaching consequences. India's ties with China remain at a low ebb as a result of a bloody clash in the border areas in June 2020 and the subsequent build-up of a large concentration of military forces. Following disengagement in a couple of places in eastern Ladakh, the situation may no longer be tense but it is certainly not normal. Further disengagement at the remaining friction points has proved elusive.

The dialogue between India and China, meanwhile, has continued at multiple levels—political, diplomatic and military, including physical meetings. That is a positive and welcome sign, in keeping with the sentiments expressed by both sides favouring friendly relations.

India's trade with China has risen sharply to touch $135.98 billion in 2022. The balance of trade is still overwhelmingly in China's favour. Perhaps, this is a function of the structural characteristics of the two economies. Perhaps, it is related to other factors, including non-trade and technical barriers to trade. From India's point of view, it would certainly help if China opened up its markets to more imports from India, to redress the imbalance. This would have a positive impact on the political discourse over China in India.

India's complex neighbourhood throws up challenges that are not limited to the disruptions caused by the rise of China as an economic and military power bent on pursuing irredentist claims. Closer home, in Pakistan, the tumultuous political events in April 2022 ended in the ouster of Imran Khan. Prime Minister Shehbaz Sharif will find it hard to keep his coalition government together. In any case, fresh elections are due in August 2023. Uncertainty in Pakistan can only mean that there is less of a chance for any meaningful relationship with India, especially with Pakistan playing up the Kashmir issue internationally and continuing to use terrorism as part of its toolkit to deal with India.

Both Afghanistan and Ukraine have been in the news, one after the other, like a relay. If the return of the Taliban is a watershed moment for Afghanistan and the region, the war in Ukraine has fundamentally reopened the question of European security seventy-seven years after the end of World War II.

The return of the Taliban to the helm has raised questions about the future of Afghanistan. It is a matter that impacts India as well as China, especially if malevolent terrorism and radical ideology take root again and spill over into the region at large.

The Taliban, some claim, is different this time around. But the Afghanistan they have returned to is also different. The people of Afghanistan, especially the younger generation, the minorities and women, have seen and experienced a way of life different to that imposed on the people by the Taliban 1.0. This means that the Taliban have a great deal of adjusting to do. The initial signs suggest quite the contrary. There are frequent news reports of the Taliban regressing and adopting their old retrograde ways, especially in the treatment of women and minorities. This further undermines social stability in Afghanistan and exacerbates the food and other economic scarcities.

On its part, India has reaffirmed its commitment to the people of Afghanistan as distinct from the regime by recently gifting 4,000 metric tons of wheat, besides other humanitarian assistance.

The war in Ukraine has blanked out all else, perhaps unfairly, and perhaps even non-traditional security threats like climate change. It is not as if the world faced no crises before the war broke out in Ukraine, even though one must acknowledge the egregious situation and lament the humanitarian catastrophe. There have been major disruptions in our part of the world as well.

Right from the beginning of the war in Ukraine, India has taken a principled position. India called for an immediate cessation of hostilities and advocated a peaceful resolution of differences through diplomacy and dialogue. Respect for sovereignty and territorial integrity and a rules-based international order are inherent in the Indian position. India has also provided considerable humanitarian assistance to Ukraine.

The Ukraine crisis has demonstrated the many infirmities of the United Nations Security Council (UNSC). The UNSC failed to reach a consensus on condemning Russia for its 'special military operation', which the West deems to be an invasion. Russia, on its part, portrays it as an act of self-defence against the growing expansion of NATO eastwards. Divergent interests of its Permanent Members, especially the US, the UK and France on the one side, and Russia and China on the other side, have created a stasis in the UNSC. It only further underscores the fact that we are today in a world that is neither a bipolar nor a multipolar world as yet. It is a fractured world.

After months of dilatory positions adopted by the Permanent Members, the UNSC adopted a language in its statement of 6 May 2022 that eschews words such as war, conflict and invasion. In fact, in stating that 'the Security Council expresses strong support for the efforts of the Secretary-General in the search for a peaceful solution,' the UNSC is reflecting the key point that India has been consistently making these past months.

The Ukraine crisis has had an impact on energy security and critical supply chains. Its effects on global food security are gradually unfolding. As for the sanctions, they are bound to delay economic recovery at a time when the global priority everywhere is economic growth in order to mitigate the ravages of the pandemic.

The Ukraine crisis has strengthened the trans-Atlantic partnership. It has undone the weakening of ties during the Trump presidency. Europe, initially divided over policy towards Russia, has come together in an unprecedented manner. NATO stands rejuvenated. Russia's actions have also caused consternation in other parts of Europe, as a result of which Finland has been granted NATO membership, while Sweden's application is under consideration. Simultaneously, defence budgets have witnessed hikes in Germany and the Netherlands, to name just a few countries. Redlines in Europe, whether Russian or Western, are many, and increasingly blurred, which compounds the uncertainties in terms of threat perceptions and responses.

The war in Ukraine will definitely impact the Indo-Pacific region. A stronger trans-Atlantic strategic partnership and a stronger, more focused NATO will be capable of dealing more effectively with other challenges as well. Japan is now closely examining three challenges, i.e., China, North Korea and Russia. Japan's diplomatic Bluebook has cited Russia as being in illegal occupation of its northern territories for decades. Interestingly, there are several references to Taiwan, which suggest that the cross-strait situation is a matter of concern to other regional powers.

Japan has revised its national security strategy and decided to double its defence budget. China has been cited as an unprecedented strategic challenge for the country.

The strengthening of alliance partnerships is not restricted to the European theatre. Both the trans-Atlantic and trans-Pacific alliances have been strengthened in recent times. The two theatres are increasingly fused not only because China and Russia are deepening their strategic partnership and conducting joint exercises in the East and South Seas as well as the Pacific Ocean, but also because of the apprehension that China might be emboldened to mount an invasion of Taiwan in the wake of Russia's 'special military operation' in Ukraine.

As for India, its position on the war in Ukraine and its relations with Russia are sui generis. On Ukraine, there is considerable understanding of India's position among Western countries, as recently observed during Prime Minister Modi's interactions with European leaders during his three-nation tour to Germany, Denmark and France. India's relations with Russia are a legacy issue. There is perhaps a better understanding in the West of India's relations with Russia as compared to China's relations with Russia, which are viewed through the prism of geostrategic contestation.

This is an opportune strategic moment that India must seize to make full use of its emerging pole position and its growing value as a 'swing state' in the Indo-Pacific.

This book is largely a compilation of my numerous writings over the last four years coinciding with the sharpening of differences between the United States and China over trade and technology, the Covid-19 pandemic, which left no country unscathed and accelerated major power contestation, the unprecedented tensions between India and China as a result of the bloody conflict in eastern Ladakh, the return of the Taliban following the retreat of US troops from Afghanistan, and the war in Ukraine. Put together, the contents may provide a seamless narrative of emerging geopolitical challenges and my assessment of India's outlook, responses and role in a rapidly evolving world order.

The views expressed are mine, and I take full responsibility for factual inaccuracies in my writings, if any.

To the discerning reader, I would suggest that some of the figures contained in the essays be read in tandem with current updates available today.

Emerging world order

The nation state

The concept of 'Nation State' in Europe emerged in the Treaty of Westphalia. The Treaty was signed in 1648 after a protracted war among the European powers that lasted for eighty years between Spain and the Netherlands and, involved Germany for thirty years. The Treaty created a precedent for national self-determination and the resolution of disputes through peaceful dialogue. Peaceful coexistence, non-interference in the internal affairs of others and balance of power emerged as the central tenets of the Treaty. However, the Treaty was unable to keep peace amidst renewed rivalries among colonial powers in other geographies. In 1871, Otto von Bismarck, the Chancellor of the German Reich, united his country and brought together several parts of Europe. Germany emerged as a powerful and united nation. This included parts of what is today Poland, which was then known as Prussia. Germany was industrialized and militarized by the Kaiser at a relentless pace. In the early part of the twentieth century, the Kaiser sought to exploit Africa for its natural resources, driven by a vision somewhat akin to Imperial Japan's efforts to create a Greater East Asia Co-prosperity Sphere. The Kaiser also sought to build a powerful navy. Germany began a naval rivalry with Great Britain on the high seas. At the beginning of the twentieth century, British warships, called dreadnoughts, were considered the most powerful ships of the time. Armed with large single-calibre guns, they were capable of inflicting devastating blows. The Germans produced their own version of these formidable battleships that ruled the oceans.

When the Great War ended, the major powers signed the Treaty of Versailles in 1919 to keep peace among themselves. In 1920, the League of Nations—seen as a precursor of the United Nations (UN)—was established. However, major powers such as the US did not support the League. Germany and Japan remained dissatisfied and soon, the world saw Berlin and Tokyo simultaneously engaging in rapid militarization. This was ironic because Japan had fought the First World War on the side of the allies.

In the inter-war years, the attempt to forge a new equilibrium failed. The Treaty of Versailles proved ineffective in thwarting an ambitious Germany. Much of the disagreement surrounded the Washington Naval Treaty of 1922, which sought to limit construction of naval warships.

The League of Nations was stillborn since it was not supported by the US because President Woodrow Wilson wanted the universalization of US values without the burden of direct intervention in Europe, let alone Asia. The lack of a sustainable European order eventually led to the rise of Hitler's Third Reich and the Wehrmacht, which invaded many European countries. In Asia, Japan had also begun to militarize and was particularly vulnerable to the interdiction of its energy supply lines in the Pacific, which became the immediate trigger for its bombing of Pearl Harbour in 1941 when the US attempted to block Japan's oil imports.

The Second World War saw two rising powers—Germany and Japan—perish. The British Empire also weakened, and the US took over its mantle in Asia. The war led to the creation of a new structure, balance of power and global equilibrium in which five countries who were allies during the war became permanent members of the United Nations Security Council (UNSC). When the Second World War ended in 1945, the Americans, the Russians, the Chinese, the British and the French were all on the winning side. They had fought the war together and vanquished the Axis Powers, Germany, Japan and Italy.

Stasis at the United Nations

The current global order was established in 1945 at the end of the Second World War with only fifty-one members.

The global structure that emerged in the form of the United Nations and the United Nations Security Council has in theory preserved peace for the last seventy-seven years since there has been no World War after 1945. However, the United Nations system is archaic and does not represent current realities. The privileged permanent members of the Security Council have permitted only cosmetic changes. The non-permanent membership of the Security Council was expanded in 1965 from six to ten with no further additions being made since then.

Today, after decades of decolonization in the 1950s and '60s and the break-up of the Soviet Union and Yugoslavia as well as successful freedom movements in Asia and Africa in the intervening years, the United Nations comprises 193 members.

However, the world has not remained static. The end of the unipolar moment for the US, China's rise and the spread of economic growth and prosperity to countries across Asia have created new power centres.

A growing part of humanity is aspirational and seeks access to the fruits of globalization. This includes countries like India.

There is a crying need to reform the United Nations system and to make it more representative, including at the level of the United Nations Security Council. India is at the forefront of such a demand and is among the most qualified to be seated at the high table, given its global profile, its large and youthful demography, its democratic polity, its economic potential and its responsible participation in global institutions and peacekeeping operations.

World in flux

Today, the world order is undergoing a fundamental transformation. The framework for the world order was established in 1945 after the end of the Second World War. The United Nations and the Bretton Woods institutions emerged to provide stability. The United Nations Security Council was made responsible for matters pertaining to international peace and security; UN-affiliated bodies such as the World Health Organization (WHO), United Nations Educational, Scientific and Cultural Organization (UNESCO), United Nations Children's Fund (UNICEF) and United Nations Industrial Development Organization (UNIDO) focused on health, education and capacity-building programmes, and the World Bank (WB) and the International Monetary Fund (IMF) dealt with loans and developmental finance. As creations of the victors of the World War, they represent more the values and interests of the developed world, and the linkages they have established between access to finance and democracy, human rights, 'good governance' and transparency are often viewed in the Global South as interference in internal affairs.

Four major issues have impacted the existing world order in the past decade more than any other in the previous half-century. These are: (1) the end of the Cold War, and the economic and military rise of

China after the brief interlude of the unipolar decade of the 1990s in which the US was the sole superpower; (2) the ever-deepening political, military and economic chasm between erstwhile strategic partners, the US and China; (3) the Covid-19 pandemic, which has accelerated geostrategic differences in a digital age; and (4) the war in Ukraine, which has raised fundamental questions about the weak foundations of European security.

There are several facets to the emerging uncertainty. Power is fractured. Both states and non-state actors have the means to bridge asymmetries in absolute power quotients and cause disruption to the existing order at multiple levels. Unprecedented advancements in lethal technologies, stand-off weapons, drones, hypersonic missiles and space-based platforms, combined with the disruptive force of artificial intelligence and autonomous weapons systems, support this trend.

International relations are increasingly marked by the 'weaponization' of trade and technology. Hedging and multi-alignment or issue-based partnerships are part of every country's strategic toolkit. Multilateralism, especially centred on the UN, has suffered retrenchment and given way to bilateralism and regionalism.

Meanwhile, traditional and non-traditional security threats such as economic and military competition, climate change and energy and food security have grown in magnitude. The spectre of terrorism, especially cross-border terrorism, continues to challenge peace and prosperity.

Today, globalization is being redefined. Not every country has fully benefited from the rapid integration of the global economy. China has gamed the system. It has used the liberal global trading order to create monopolies and dependencies. Without being a market economy, China has exploited its membership of the World Trade Organization (WTO) since 2001 to become a factory for the world. It has hollowed out domestic manufacturing capacities in many countries by exporting cheaper products with hidden subsidies. It practices its own brand of 'state capitalism'. China has long practiced 'supply chain politics' and 'debt diplomacy'. It has endeavoured both to adjust the existing order, which has facilitated its rise, to suit its objectives, and to create parallel institutions and lending mechanisms to advance its influence.

Asia's geography is also increasingly being redefined by the vision of the Indo-Pacific, which, unlike the Asia-Pacific, is more democratic and representative of the realities and aspirations associated with growth and prosperity in a wider arc that cuts across all the way from the Pacific Rim to the east coast of Africa.

A new global order is in the making. The moot point is that global orders are neither made nor dismantled very easily. It usually takes wars or major economic or cataclysmic disasters to replace an existing order. Since the end of the Second World War, the world has oscillated between bipolarity, unipolarity and multipolarity.

The Cold War

The Cold War between the USSR and the US emerged soon after 1945. Suspicion of communism was part of US mainstream politics even in the 1930s, but the war effort called for a temporary realignment that permitted both the US and the Soviet Union to tackle the two main adversaries, Japan and Germany, in different theatres. Once the Second World War was over, these two superpowers split the world into two blocs. The Cold War weakened the existing global order created by the United Nations. However, it did not change it. The order remained in place even though its edges were fraying.

The Cold War coincided with the independence of a large number of Asian and African states from the colonial yoke. As a result, this period was marked by the further weakening of an already debilitated

Great Britain, which had, in any case, ceded the mantle of the world's pre-eminent great power to the US by the end of the great war.

Meanwhile, in the 1960s, China truly parted ways with the Soviet Union while simultaneously having strained relations with the US. It also tested and acquired its nuclear weapons in 1964. Thereafter, a series of incidents led to fears in Beijing of a full-fledged attack by the Soviet Union, possibly involving both an invasion by Mongolia-based regiments and nuclear weapons. Beijing's apprehensions coincided with deep concern in Washington D.C. In the US calculus, some sort of rebalancing was necessary since the bipolarity of the Cold War had clearly failed to prevent the Soviet Union from rapidly scaling the ladder of scientific and technological innovation and militarization, thereby acquiring an edge in terms of space and nuclear capabilities. The visit of President Richard Nixon to Beijing in 1972 is the reset that changed the global order, given that it played a key role in the subsequent rise of China.

The European Union (EU) too had its own ups and downs during this period. Europe was devastated at the end of the Second World War. The American Marshall Plan helped West Germany get back up on its feet. In time, the reunification of Germany after the fall of the Berlin Wall in 1989 undid the division of the country brought about at the Potsdam Conference in 1945 and the Cold War that followed.

The Europeans also changed their economic cooperation model, from the European Economic Community (EEC) to a more meaningful political and monetary union, which culminated in the creation of the European Union.

On the other end of the spectrum, the Japanese economy also grew and revived through the 1950s and '60s. Initially, it was seen through the prism of a low cost and low quality economy. However, once the Japanese had perfected their manufacturing of cars, electronics and television sets by the mid-1960s, Japan too emerged as an economic powerhouse with a huge favourable balance of trade vis-à-vis the US.

Crucially, the global order that emerged post-1945 included the Republic of China (ROC; not the People's Republic of China that came into being only in 1949). It was the ROC led by Chiang Kai-shek's Kuomintang that became a member of the United Nations Security Council in 1945. Following the end of the civil war in China in 1949, Chiang Kai-Shek fled to the island of Taiwan where he re-established the seat of the government of the Republic of China, which continued to be a member of the United Nations Security Council. It was only in 1971 that the growing tide of international recognition of the People's Republic of China, and the American expediencies of the Cold War led to the exit of the ROC and its replacement in the United Nations Security Council by the People's Republic of China (PRC). Uppermost in the US' calculus was the need to rope in Mao Zedong's People's Republic as part of an external balancing strategy against the Soviet Union. It was the same motivation that informed both sides.

Communist China's entry into the United Nations in 1971 amounted to a tinkering of the global order, but within the existing framework. The PRC also imposed on the US, Japan and others a One China Policy. Things shifted dramatically in China's favour thereafter.

Ironically, in 1971, China came into the United Nations Security Council not because it was a victor in the war but because the Republic of China was booted out. It did not enter the Council because it was a rich country, but because it was a relatively poor but a populous, ideologically driven nuclear weapons power. It was a potentially powerful country with much of the same attributes that India has today.

As for China, it launched the Four Modernizations programme in 1978 to transform agriculture, industry, defence and science and technology. China also implemented it in 'open door policy'. With foreign investments pouring in from the US, Western Europe, Japan and Hong Kong, the Chinese economy grew rapidly throughout the 1980s, albeit inequitably.

The inequality was reflected in growing resentment among a large section of China's labour force, including Chinese students, who were left out of the prosperity that was spreading across China in rural pockets, beginning with the agricultural sector where the market economy had been introduced. It was this resentment that culminated in the 1989 Tiananmen demonstrations, which were crushed militarily by Beijing.

It took only a year or two for a transactional global community to normalize relations with China. This led to China's meteoric rise beginning in the 1990s. By this time, the Soviet Union had disintegrated followed by war and division in the Balkans. A new, yet short-lived unipolar moment emerged for the US in the 1990s.

The collapse of the Soviet Union led to the freeing of several nations in Europe and Central Asia, which were earlier part of the Soviet bloc. Some of the European nations became members of the EU and even joined the North Atlantic Treaty Organization (NATO). Eventually though, Britain's exit from the EU (Brexit), announced in 2016 and implemented in 2020, delivered a strategic blow to the EU.

China's rise

The real launching pad for China's spectacular economic rise was its membership of the WTO in 2001, facilitated by the US, which had already granted Permanent Normal Trade Relations (equivalent to the grant of Most Favoured Nation status) to China in 2000. The US strategy revolved around the naive expectation that if only the Chinese economy were to grow, and that if only China were to start mimicking the consumerism of the West by wearing jeans, visiting McDonald's and drinking Coca-Cola, then China would soon turn democratic. However, this was based on a false appreciation of Chinese culture, including the centralized manner in which a Confucian state like China had evolved over millennia.

After 2001, China's rise has been extraordinarily rapid. It emerged unscathed from the Asian financial crisis of 1999 in which a large number of Asian states were affected. It used this period to put in place currency swap agreements through the Chiang Mai Initiative and create dependencies among Southeast Asian countries. China was also unaffected by the 2006-07 global financial and economic crises that took a huge economic toll on the US and Europe.

Subsequently, a confident China started adopting postures that openly challenged the existing order. However, China has never been interested in fundamentally challenging the existing order, since it is precisely the existing order that has facilitated its rise. China is not keen on throwing the baby out with the bath water, as the saying goes. It wants to reshape the existing world order and its institutions such as the UN, WHO, WTO and such like, to suit its objectives.

In parallel, China has also sought to create new China-led, China-centric structures such as the Asian Infrastructure Investment Bank (AIIB) and the New Development Bank. In both these, China has the support of many other countries, including India, which look to alternatives to the Bretton Woods institutions such as the IMF and the World Bank.

Alternative institutions provide China the means to compete with the influence of Western powers. It has been lending developmental finance without strings attached or without making economic assistance conditional to intrusive demands for good governance and democratization. In this context, Xi Jinping gave a new meaning to the idea of 'Go West' by espousing the Belt and Road Initiative (BRI), a gargantuan global infrastructure development strategy announced in 2013, which aims to promote Chinese investments and technical standards and develop markets for its excess manufacturing capacities. The BRI relies on funding by Chinese financial institutions, unlike the newly created multi-lateral AIIB, which is headquartered in China but counts on the support of India, France, Germany, the UK, Australia and others. Today, the BRI has succeeded in creating 'debt traps' by pumping in easy developmental finance in different parts of the world. China has created dependencies around the world through this strategic programme.

The US, having woken up to the challenge posed by China, has now sought to tackle it headlong. Europe too has realized the perils of China's inroads into the economic and strategic space in the heartland. In the Indo-Pacific, Japan, Australia and several other nations are no longer blind to China's strategies.

In the Indo-Pacific, there is a growing consensus on ensuring a rules-based order and a free and open maritime space. Both the Quadrilateral Security Dialogue and the defence-oriented AUKUS pact are manifestations of new concerns.

The war in Ukraine

Russia's war in Ukraine has upended European security paradigms. The turmoil associated with the departure of US troops from Afghanistan, once live and vivid only a few months ago, is now a distant memory, subordinated to the challenges in European security. Russia's invasion of Ukraine, regardless of reasons, demonstrates that a state with an economy the size of South Korea's, about half that of India's, can mount a massive conventional military invasion of a neighbouring state, the combined opposition of the US and the EU notwithstanding.

Russia's action has highlighted the limits of NATO's reach and resolve in the European theatre. Ukraine has emerged as the fulcrum of a new proxy war between NATO and Russia. The crisis in Europe has raised questions about the role of external powers in a potential conflict in the Indo-Pacific, a region where most Western nations have fewer stakes.

This could not have gone unnoticed in Tokyo, Seoul and Canberra, which are covered by treaty alliances with the US. The sudden spike in the German defence budget is likely to be mirrored by further hikes in defence spending across the Indo-Pacific.

Parallels have also been drawn between Ukraine and Taiwan. Taiwan is naturally apprehensive about the mounting military pressure from across the Taiwan Strait. The US policy of 'strategic ambiguity' may not suffice to reassure Taiwan in the aftermath of events in Ukraine.

Both Ukraine and Taiwan are objects of irredentist claims by bigger powers. The difference is that in the case of Ukraine, there is no US or NATO treaty commitment to its defence. In the case of Taiwan, expectations are different even though the US prefers 'strategic ambiguity'. The mutual defence treaty of 1954, which was terminated in 1979, and the Taiwan Relations Act that replaced it, were necessary but perhaps not sufficient guarantees to ensure Taiwan's security. Crucially, the 1954 treaty covered only the island of Taiwan and the Pescadores Islands (Penghu). That is why the US stood by and watched when China shelled Jinmen and the Matsu islands during the second Taiwan Strait Crisis in 1958. The Taiwan Relations Act, similarly, does not explicitly cover the outlying islands close to the mainland.

The risk to China of ill-considered action in the Taiwan Strait is huge. A war in that theatre, regardless of outcome, would be a major setback for China's globalized economy, prosperity, the 'China Dream' and Xi Jinping's future.

The war in Ukraine has raised questions about efforts to achieve nuclear non-proliferation and disarmament. At the start of the year, the P5 issued a joint statement giving assurances that nuclear weapons, for as long as they continue to exist, should serve defensive purposes, deter aggression and prevent war. Ukraine's fate complicates matters in the run-up to the Tenth Review Conference of the Nuclear Non-proliferation Treaty (NPT) later this year. Ukraine was a de facto nuclear power after its independence in 1991 until it acceded to the NPT in 1994 and gave up the legacy nuclear weapons it had inherited following the break-up of the Soviet Union, ostensibly on the understanding that its sovereignty would not be violated by Russia. Nuclear deterrence will now increasingly be regarded as indispensable by those that possess nuclear weapons, including North Korea, as well as by aspirants such as Iran. Earlier, they had no doubt drawn lessons from Libya's fate, where regime change followed the renunciation of a clandestine nuclear programme.

The Ukraine crisis will cast its shadow on the Indo-Pacific. US preoccupation with European security is a distraction from the real challenge of China. Russia's growing proximity to China will not help matters.

Implications for India

For India, the churning on the global stage makes for difficult choices. Russia is one of India's key strategic partners. China is also one of India's largest trading partners, with trade having risen sharply since the bloody events at Galwan in June 2020. If one combines goods and services, the US is also a very large trading partner. The management of differences with a belligerent and militaristic China is of vital importance. India has done well to make clear to China that its unilateralism is unacceptable and that peace and stability on the borders is a prerequisite for the normal conduct of bilateral relations. India is mindful of the fact that Russia has moved even closer to China in recent years, and that Russia and China support one another in their antipathy towards Western democracies. This has also fostered Russia's negative view of the Indo-Pacific and the Quadrilateral Security Dialogue in which India is a key participant.

The imposition of wide-ranging and unprecedented sanctions against Russia by the US, the UK and the EU, including withdrawal of SWIFT facilities for Russian banking institutions, has put pressure on Russia to turn to China and other friendly nations. This has opened up some opportunities for India to import discounted Russian oil using payment mechanisms that do not involve the US dollar.

India's reliance on Russian defence hardware, though much less than in the past, is still overwhelming. Apart from the jointly produced BrahMos cruise missiles recently contracted for export to the Philippines, India would have to review the indigenous production of the AK-203 assault rifle, the fresh leasing of an 'Akula' nuclear-powered attack submarine as well as future production of Sukhoi Su-30MKI fighter aircraft and T-90MS main battle tanks.

The ongoing crisis in Ukraine has implications for India's defence cooperation with that country, especially the upgrading of its ageing Antonov (AN-32) military transport fleet. Perhaps the trickiest one could be the project with Russia involving four Admiral Grigorovich frigates, to be powered by Ukraine's Zorya-Mashproekt M7N1E gas turbines. Apart from two frigates to be built at the Goa Shipyard Limited (GSL), another two are to be built at Russia's Yantar Shipyard. This requires some deft coordination. There are bound to be delays, given the rift between Russia and Ukraine and the sanctions regime. Likewise, a question mark hovers over whether the Vympel R-27 air-to-air missile for India's Su-30 MKI fighters can be sourced from Ukraine.

India did the right thing by abstaining on numerous resolutions at the United Nations, taking into account the need for stable relations with the Russian Federation and the priority it attached to Operation Ganga, aimed at securing the safe evacuation of the thousands of Indian students who were stranded in war-torn Ukraine. India has acted on the basis of its own national interest. India continues to rely on Russia for major defence supplies. The S-400 deal with Russia remains in the pipeline and is expected to boost India's security on its northern borders.

India has attached importance to the principle of sovereignty and territorial integrity and called for dialogue and diplomacy for settling disputes. India's abstention was not tantamount to endorsement of Russian military action against Ukraine. Nor did it imply recognition of the independence of Donetsk and Luhansk. In the past too, India did not recognize the Kosovo declaration of independence in 2008 from Serbia. Earlier, former prime minister Atal Bihari Vajpayee withdrew recognition of the so-called Sahrawi Arab Republic in 2000, undoing a folly committed in 1985.

India as anchor in the Indo-Pacific

India believes in humanity—'manavta'—and the Modi government has done the right thing by offering humanitarian assistance to the people of Ukraine in accordance with its ancient ethos.

India will have to find its own unique place in the emerging global order. It is a rising power. It has a demographic dividend and an open, transparent and democratic system. India has demonstrated a capacity to play a bigger role in the region and on the global stage for the common good, based on the principle of *vasudhaiva kutumbakam* (the world is one family). India's strategic autonomy, Neighbourhood First policy and Vaccine Maitri programme have enabled it to expand its circle of friends and emerge as a credible power. The world seems prepared to take a long term bet on India's economic rise. With a moral compass guiding its foreign policy, India stands for peace, prosperity and well-being for all. At the same time, India regards the principles of sovereignty and territorial integrity as sacrosanct. In recent years, it has demonstrated great capacity for resolute action against aggression, unilateralism and terrorism. India is bound to emerge as one of the foremost powers in the world by the middle of this century.

(The article was first published by the Parliament Library of India in July 2022).

REORDERING THE STRATEGIC LANDSCAPE

India and the pandemic world

Covid-19-induced disruption

Over the last few years, the global situation has witnessed rapid flux, with geopolitical and economic contestations creating profound uncertainty. Key drivers of globalization have experienced stress. International relations are increasingly marked by a proclivity to 'weaponize' trade and technology. An inward-looking United States, the world's flagbearer of democratic ideals, is trying to retain its position at the top of the international order while rejecting multilateralism. This has weakened the United Nations and its agencies such as the United Nations Educational, Scientific and Cultural Organization, the World Trade Organization, the Paris Agreement on Climate Change, and trans-Atlantic and trans-Pacific partnerships. China, on the other hand, is determined to preserve the gains of a liberal trading order and canvas for a global endorsement of its systems of political governance and economic development, ironically, without being liberal or democratic. Eroding US primacy in global political, economic and military affairs is an abiding Chinese objective, beginning with China's periphery. For instance, China is determined to thwart US intelligence surveillance missions off its territorial waters and in the South China Sea. Today, the fragile international compact has been rendered a huge blow by Covid-19—a fast-spreading and silent killer—which has quickly spread from China to the rest of the world. The pandemic has exposed flaws in multilateral structures and highlighted the lacunae in national capacities, particularly in healthcare. The great irony is that democracies appear to be lagging behind authoritarian countries like China.

Multilateralism has suffered retrenchment. The United Nations Security Council must be faulted for its egregious lack of action with regard to the Covid-19 pandemic in March of 2020 when China held the rotating post of president. It will remain one of the great ironies of history that China, which has increasingly sought to play a global leadership role, actively suppressed discussions in the UNSC at a time when the pandemic posed a threat to the lives and livelihood of millions of people around the world. The withdrawal of nearly $500 million worth of annual voluntary funding by the US to the World Health Organization (WHO) is clearly linked to WHO's questionable conduct and China-bias regarding calls for investigating the origins of the pandemic.

The global economy is beginning to reel under the unexpected effects of Covid-19, with the International Monetary Fund (IMF) predicting an impeding recession. The hardest hit, globally, are the service sectors and interdependent supply chains in the manufacturing sector. Global manufacturing has taken an unprecedented hit. One wonders if the current situation will strengthen the trend towards protectionism and emphasis on domestic manufacturing even if it is against the principles of market forces. A febrile and debilitated globalization featuring closed borders and disrupted trade and supply chains, ironically, coincides with a pressing need to evolve a fresh outlook on global interdependence and cooperation in dealing with pandemics and a host of other issues.

The daily information overload about the pandemic has created a surreal atmosphere within homes under worldwide lockdowns. Quotidian routines of work, leisure and human contact have been disrupted in myriad unrecognizable ways. 'Work from home' had led to a surge in users and data flow in the digital space. This has put huge stress on existing bandwidth capacities, which are not easily mutable. The very notion of critical infrastructure in the cyber domain is changing with the growing dependence on webinars and online tasks, including for hospitals, banks and providers of essential services.

These circumstances no doubt place a fresh premium on getting ahead in the race to develop a vaccine and to move from 'lockdown' to 'open' in a graded manner with the least possible risk. Simultaneously, the race is on to develop artificial intelligence (AI) and 5G capabilities to mitigate existing limitations in healthcare and the telecom sector respectively. The next generation of telecom infrastructure will have to cater, in terms of cost and scope, to the requirements of mass healthcare schemes.

The notion of national security, or global security, is also being reshaped by Covid-19. Armed forces everywhere, often deployed in confined spaces ranging from bunkers to tanks and armoured personnel carriers to naval ships and submarines, are facing tough choices in stemming the spread of the coronavirus without compromising national security.

The pandemic could have broader implications for military postures in the Indo-Pacific, as seen in the outbreak of the Covid-19 virus on board the US Navy's Theodore Roosevelt, a nuclear-powered aircraft carrier that heads the eponymous Theodore Roosevelt Carrier Strike Group (TRCSG), which had sailed from San Diego in January 2020 for a scheduled Indo-Pacific deployment. It is at the centre of a controversy involving the sacking of its captain and the vessel's ill-advised port visit to Da Nang in Vietnam earlier in March 2020 despite the high risk of contagion. Of course, China's PLA Navy could well be grappling with similar problems out at sea, but unlike in the democratic world, these facts will be treated as 'state secrets' and the world will never be wiser.

Beyond hard power and the threats of hybrid warfare, nations will have to rethink possible future scenarios and create numerically adequate forces of well-equipped pandemic experts, doctors and healthcare workers to be the new foot soldiers in this battle. Healthcare has emerged at the top of the critical infrastructure list in redefining the concept of national security.

Covid-19: India can lead

Yet, the rapid spread of coronavirus around the world has created fresh opportunities for dialogue. There is hope, and scope, for creating a new global compact. Contributions will be measured not in dollars and cents alone, but in the leadership that countries exhibit and their willingness to share ideas, best practices and available resources to develop an international mechanism for monitoring, verification, early warning and cooperation among nation states.

India's civilizational ethos

India's ancient civilization has given much to the world, among which Buddha's teachings of peace and non-violence stand out. Mahatma Gandhi's advocacy of a non-violent struggle for India's independence still resonates around the world. Gandhi also spoke of moderation in the use of the earth's limited resources. He famously said that the earth has enough to meet the needs of each one of us, but not our greed. Prime Minister Narendra Modi is a staunch believer in the natural harmony that should exist between humans and Mother Nature. This is particularly true as we endeavour to create a new cohort for cooperation in dealing with not just the Covid-19 pandemic but also the uncertainties surrounding economic growth, healthcare and food security in a post-Covid-19 era.

Scrutiny of wet markets

In light of Covid-19, there definitely exists a case for greater scrutiny of 'wet markets' in China, Southeast Asia and in many other countries around the world. With culinary traditions being a function of culture as well as geographical and climatic conditions, animals, from tigers, monkeys, donkeys and pangolins to snakes, bats, geckos and monitor lizards, have all been subjected to illegal poaching and trafficking of their parts around the world. These activities increase the potential for zoonotic transmission of unknown and deadly viruses.

The need of the hour is to devise means that can deal more effectively with the illegal slaughter of exotic animals for bushmeat and the use of animal extracts for traditional medicine. Efforts must be made to strengthen the Convention on International Trade in Endangered Species of Wild Fauna and Flora (CITES), a multilateral treaty with more than 180 member countries. There should be a renewed focus not only on the illegal international trade that is already covered by CITES, but also on the hazardous exploitation of exotic wildlife species within national borders. All signatory states, including China, must pass and enforce legislation to control the domestic consumption of wild animals and shut down the dubious 'wet markets' and animal farms.

India's record of legislation in conservation and the enforcement of penalties for the killing and exploitation of protected wildlife is better than most. There is considerable scope for the Modi government to take the lead in proposing that CITES be given more teeth to conduct international scrutiny and inspections.

Reform of the Biological Weapons Convention

Today, at a strategic level, global opinion seems weighted against China, notwithstanding its efforts to salvage credibility by shifting focus away from the origins of the coronavirus to the 'superiority' of its system in tackling the pandemic. There is talk of the coronavirus having originated in a laboratory in Wuhan, with theories abounding about biological warfare programmes and accidental release. This provides an opportune moment to turn the spotlight on the inherent weaknesses of the Biological Weapons Convention (BWC) of 1975. It is a disarmament treaty that does not prohibit the retention and use of biological agents, including coronaviruses, for prophylactic purposes, which encompass medical research for diagnosis and immunization. It has no verification protocol to deal with any suspected use of biological agents. Indeed, the UNSC can investigate complaints in this regard, but the veto power enjoyed by the permanent members, including China, renders this a chimera. In the run-up to the Ninth Review Conference of the BWC in 2021, India could engage in consultations with other middle powers to evolve a regime that can provide better oversight.

Promote holistic health

The Covid-19 pandemic, meanwhile, has brought across a home truth, that wealth is unable to protect even the most affluent people from a silent killer. Individuals with higher immunity levels have a better chance of survival if afflicted with Covid-19. In India, despite spikes in infection rates, the death toll has remained low proportionate to the country's population, possibly due to its youthful demographic profile and the naturally higher immunity levels of the less privileged sections of society who are routinely exposed to a higher risk of infections. The ancient Indian practice of yoga is known to boost immunity levels through the cultivation of a healthy mind and body. This is the time to further reinforce the worldwide practice of yoga under the banner of the International Day of Yoga, which was also an initiative of Prime Minister Modi. India should plan for special virtual events on 21 June this year to encourage people around the world to practice yoga as a means to promote holistic health.

India as 'vishwa vaidya'

As the world's largest producer and exporter of cost-effective generic drugs, India's readiness to ship the anti-malarial drug hydroxychloroquine to other nations to assist them in their fight against Covid-19 is a Good Samaritan act in consonance with the ethos of 'vasudhaiva kutumbakam'. India has sent rapid response teams to several countries. India is also in the race to produce a vaccine. If China is a 'factory to the world', India has the potential to be a 'pharmacy to the world'. It can take on a new and well-deserved moniker, that of 'vishwa vaidya' (global physician). This provides an opportunity to promote Ayurveda, which complements yoga.

Re-energize multilateral institutions

At a time when the UNSC, G20, G7 and the EU were inert, Prime Minister Modi stood out with his initiatives to develop a joint response to the Covid-19 pandemic. He convened a teleconference with the South Asian Association for Regional Cooperation (SAARC) nations, which led to the establishment of a SAARC Covid-19 Emergency Fund for rapid regional response. Since then, despite the great task of providing healthcare for its 1.3 billion people, India has despatched rapid response teams of specialists as well as medical equipment to several countries, including its neighbours. As Modi said, 'Our neighbourhood collaboration should be a model for the world'.

Similarly, Modi's proposal for cooperation among G20 countries led to an Extraordinary Virtual G20 Leaders' Summit on 26 March 2020 to discuss the challenges posed by the outbreak and to forge a coordinated global response. During this meeting, Modi underscored the need for 'reformed multilateralism'. He urged global leaders to usher in a new globalization for the collective well-being of humankind and have a multilateral focus on promoting the shared interests of humanity even when globalization had failed in many ways. Both Prime Minister Modi and Minister of External Affairs S. Jaishankar have been remarkably active in engaging counterparts from around the world to tackle the pandemic.

A 'Quad Plus' approach to the Indo-Pacific

On the geostrategic front, the Covid-19 crisis has nudged many countries to engage in new formats such as bilateral, tri-lateral and plurilateral in the face of debilitated multilateralism. Among these, the Quadrilateral Security Dialogue (Quad) is the most active grouping with a focus on ensuring a rules-based international order, freedom of navigation and overflight, unimpeded commerce, vaccine production and distribution and tackling supply chain disruptions. It is time for the Quad Plus—in which the US, India, Japan and Australia have recently engaged other countries such as the Republic of Korea, Vietnam, New Zealand, Israel and Brazil—to exchange views and propose cooperation with select African countries abutting the Indian Ocean. After all, the Indo-Pacific, which extends from the west coast of the US to the west coast of India, straddles the entire maritime space of the Indian Ocean. A Quad Plus makes the structure more inclusive and acceptable. There is scope to work together to promote connectivity and infrastructure projects for the entire region's benefit on the basis of key principles such as openness, transparency and the United Nations Convention on the Law of the Sea (UNCLOS), with development assistance being governed by international standards, fiscal responsibility and respect for the environment as well as for sovereignty and territorial integrity.

A new model of internet governance

In cybersecurity, India must redouble its efforts to push for a multistakeholder model of internet governance. This is especially relevant at a time when cybercrime and malicious attacks by state and non-state actors and threats to critical infrastructure are on the rise. Post Covid-19, there will be even greater reliance on AI, drone and other surveillance technologies, online platforms and big data.

Conclusion

A vaccine for Covid-19 will eventually emerge, but the world can avoid paying a heavy price by not treating pandemics as one-off events. Given the incidence of SARS, MERS and similar outbreaks in the past, Covid-19 is hardly an unexpected 'black swan' event. The human race may have to contend with many more of nature's calamitous challenges.

The outline of the post-Covid-19 era, particularly in relation to economic recovery, healthcare and food security, is far from clear. There appear to be no clear-cut winners at this stage. The pandemic has accentuated the rift between the US and China. However, given the centrality of the Chinese economy in global supply chains, it is a moot question if the economies of the US, EU or Japan can achieve a major decoupling. Covid-19 has shown how China's actions impact the entire world. Whatever the denouement in the matter of bringing China to book for its acts of commission or omission, its cooperation will be vital in reforming global institutions and practices.

Prime Minister Modi has done well to grasp the nettle and take the lead within SAARC and the G20 framework to forge a new global compact. India enjoys good relations with multiple powers and is well-regarded across the developing world. With excellent long-term economic prospects, a confident India appears fully capable of absorbing the shocks of the pandemic and striding forth to engage a world riven by trade wars and ideological contestation. There is no room for despair. Despite hardships, India can, and must, take the lead in bringing the world together to practice a new multilateralism that places the common interests of humanity above narrow national interests. Arguably, multilateralism in a post-Covid-19 world provides a strategic opportunity for India to emerge as an independent pole. To use Prime Minister Modi's mantra, in this task too, India will be guided by the values of 'samman' (respect), 'samvad' (dialogue), 'sahayog' (cooperation), 'shanti' (peace) and 'samriddhi' (prosperity).

(The article was first published in the *Naval War College Journal*,
Vol. 32, Annual Issue, 2020)

An Asian engine driven by India and China

The world today is undergoing a fundamental transformation, and there are several facets to the emerging uncertainty. Traditional and non-traditional security threats (economic and military competition, climate change piracy, radical ideology, cyber threats, drug and human trafficking and energy and food security) have grown in magnitude. Power whether economic, political or military, is fractured. Trade and technology are at the heart of a new round of competition and contestation. Nationalism and regionalism are on the rise. There is less multilateralism but greater multipolarity. Hedging and multi-alignment are the order of the day.

Obstacles ahead

All known paradigms are experiencing stress, which calls for readjustments. At the broadest level, the inadequacies of the post-

World War II international institutions are showing up because of the complexities and uncertainties characterizing global politics and the economy today. The old consensus is fraying, and a new consensus is yet to emerge.

The liberal trading order has encountered protectionism in the form of tariff and non-tariff barriers, which explains why India's service exports, that touch $29.6 billion in the US market, and pharma products, especially generic drugs that account for 20 per cent of global generic medicines, have barely been able to scratch the surface in the Chinese market. Cheaper imports from China, which practices 'state capitalism', threaten domestic manufacturing in India. Movement of talent and the service sector, important for India, have not received satisfactory attention. Many of these concerns are central to India's position on the Regional Comprehensive Economic Partnership (RCEP).

There is a looming danger for developing countries on account of 'zero-sum' mercantilism and rising protectionism in Western economies. There is no doubt that the US-China trade war has been disruptive.

Geopolitical considerations are increasingly driving trade and investment decisions; on the other hand, geo-economic forces unleashed by China's economic rise are redefining the geostrategic landscape of the Indo-Pacific region.

Worryingly, the global economy is likely to grow at its slowest pace in a decade, at 3 per cent in 2019.

Today, the momentum in manufacturing activity has weakened to levels unseen since the global financial crises of 2007-08. Investor and business confidence even in emerging markets are at a low ebb. Low productivity growth and ageing demographics in advanced economies have further compounded the problem. Most countries appear to be financially vulnerable. Key anchors in the global economy, including China, are experiencing a slowdown. Elsewhere, Europe is in the throes of a major readjustment in the context of Brexit. Yet, amidst the downturn, Asia is witnessing the simultaneous rise of several powers. Global engines of economic growth over the past three decades have shifted to Asia, first to the Asia-Pacific and now, more broadly, to the Indo-Pacific region that includes South Asia. The continent, home to over half the global population, has emerged as the new fulcrum for geo-economic and geostrategic realignments. High economic growth rates across the region are accompanied by some of the highest military expenditures in the world.

The external affairs minister of India presciently said recently that if the world is different, we need to think, talk and engage accordingly. The wheels of change appear to have been set in motion. In the face of automation, countries are undertaking structural reforms and emphasizing skills-training to raise productivity. Development and adoption of green technology is also a priority. Even Saudi Arabia, the quintessentially hydrocarbon-dependent economy, has endeavoured to diversify its economy through the Saudi Vision 2030 master plan.

Shaping trade and economy

Both India and China are expected to contribute to global economic growth in the future. India is also transforming into a knowledge-based, skill-supported and technology-driven society. A liberal foreign direct investment (FDI) regime combined with a youthful demographic profile make India an attractive destination. India attaches great importance to its relations with China, a large trade partner in goods. Since 2015, there has been a spurt in Chinese FDI in India (at around $8 billion). There is great scope for China to participate in flagship initiatives such as the Smart Cities Mission and Skill India programmes. As the world's second-largest economy, China can and must play a constructive role globally and within Asia to help the world return to higher growth rates. Bilateral trade today is approximately $95 billion. India faces a huge and rising trade imbalance. The decision at the Mamallapuram Summit, in October 2019, to set up a new mechanism to discuss the trade imbalance is aimed at addressing this issue.

As members of several multilateral institutions, India and China are in a unique position to give shape to their economic destinies. There are suggestions that the era of the World Trade Organization-anchored, Most-Favoured-Nation-based regime is drawing to a close and that the future lies in a web of free trade agreements. However, there is still scope for India and China to work together to strengthen the WTO.

The RCEP should have a wider ambit, including trade in services. Many countries (especially Japan, which still boasts the world's second-largest developed economy) have openly favoured a more accommodating position that addresses India's concerns and facilitates its joining the RCEP. China too should proactively work to ensure India's membership.

Beyond jointly training Afghan diplomats under the 'India-China Plus One' framework, China and India could explore the potential to work together on Asian infrastructure and connectivity development on the basis of equality and an open and transparent model under the Asian Infrastructure Investment Bank (AIIB).

As China's presence in South Asia grows, greater transparency in its actions and closer consultations with India are also necessary to help allay concerns. China should also be mindful of its forays into the exclusive economic zones of others.

Today, the global energy market is more favourable to consumers in the face of a supply-side glut. The Organization of the Petroleum Exporting Countries (OPEC) and non-OPEC oil and gas producers have come together to prevent a fall in energy prices. This should be a common concern for China and India. As two of the world's biggest importers of oil and gas, the two nations should have a joint consultative mechanism to protect the interests of consumers.

It must be remembered that Asia's rise is predicated on peace and stability. It is a sad fact that a stable regional security architecture has yet to emerge organically in Asia. It is worth recalling what Prime Minister Narendra Modi had stated at the Raisina Dialogue (an annual multilateral international conference on geopolitics and geo-economics held in New Delhi) in 2017: That there is enough room for all Asian countries to prosper together, and that the Asia of rivalry will hold us all back. It is the Asia of cooperation that will shape this century.

(The article first appeared in *The Hindu*, 9 December 2019)

Covid-19 will bring lasting changes in healthcare, security and governance

The global economy is beginning to reel under the unexpected effects of Covid-19, the coronavirus that has left scarcely any part of the world unscathed. The steep cut announced in the US federal interest rate, down a full percentage point to a range of 0-0.25 per cent, is a desperate bid to shore up liquidity in the world's largest economy at a time when stocks have tanked and the bond market is in disarray. Goldman Sachs has predicted that the US economy's growth rate will be flat for the first three months of 2020 and over the next three months, it will contract by 5 per cent. With unemployment rates set to double even faster than they did during the financial and economic crisis of 2008, the stage appears set for a recession that will not be limited to the US. It will compound the economic slowdown in the world's second-largest economy, China, which is the largest trading nation, and possibly set off a chain reaction.

The hardest hit, globally, are the service sectors and interdependent supply chains in the manufacturing sector. Business in travel, tourism, hospitality and public entertainment including restaurants, malls and theatres is at a complete standstill, destroying the means of livelihood of millions. Global manufacturing took a hit with the appearance of the coronavirus in Wuhan and China's lockdown. Now, with the pandemic spreading its tentacles around the world, it resembles a knockout punch. One wonders if the current situation will strengthen the trend towards protectionism and emphasis on domestic manufacturing even if it is against the principles of market forces. A febrile and debilitated globalization featuring closed borders and disrupted trade and supply chains, ironically, coincides with a pressing need to evolve a fresh outlook on global interdependence and cooperation in dealing with pandemics and a host of other issues.

The unprecedented challenge from Covid-19 is also creating new inflection points for the global economy. E-commerce, including online start-ups and delivery apps for groceries and merchandise, are likely to see a spurt in business, provided supply chains hold out. Online entertainment platforms, TV serials and home entertainment will see a surge in scope and stock value, but new productions will be difficult to create on account of restrictions, unavailability of locations and a depleted workforce.

The shutting of schools and universities means a huge boost for online education, distance learning and self-employment opportunities. Home learning with one-on-one lessons could spawn a new industry for those with adequate access to computers, broadband and Wi-Fi connectivity, with the advantage going to nations that enjoy greater internet penetration. This will also mean huge stress on existing bandwidth capacities for network and telecom service providers. Network capacities and related infrastructure, whether national or international, are not easily mutable, being capital intensive and time-consuming to develop. Throttling back on high definition (HD) services to free up bandwidth congestion in Europe is already being mulled by big operators such as YouTube, Netflix, Amazon Prime and Apple TV.

These circumstances no doubt place a fresh premium on getting ahead in the race to develop 5G capabilities to mitigate existing limitations, and this is true of the healthcare sector in particular. Global resilience in dealing with pandemics would be greatly enhanced by 5G technology, especially in large and populous countries like India.

The next generation of telecom infrastructure will have to be dovetailed, in terms of cost and spread, with the needs of mass healthcare schemes such as the Ayushman Bharat Pradhan Mantri Jan Aarogya Yojana, especially to cater to the most vulnerable segments in far-flung rural societies. It is these segments that are the mainstay of the labour force for food production, agro-based industries and manufacturing activity in smaller towns and villages. On their health and vitality will depend the lifeline of an entire nation. Arguably, there is a compelling need to look beyond urban-centric approaches in devising the response to pandemics.

In densely populated slums and even overcrowded prisons, social distancing is not an easy option. The challenges faced by India notwithstanding, there is widespread praise and popular support for the strong personal appeal by Prime Minister Modi to the people of India for their cooperation. The success of the 'Janata Curfew' on 22 March 2020 and the tribute paid by the masses from their doorsteps and balconies to the silent workers who provide essential services have raised the nation's morale.

The pandemic can be expected to goad overwhelmed healthcare systems around the world to do better, point them in new directions and provide investment opportunities in preventive and palliative care. Robotics and unmanned ground vehicles will play as much a role in patient access and care during contagions as they will in an era of informatized warfare.

Budgets around the world are likely to see a spike in allocations to the healthcare sector, and it can only be hoped that the higher standards of hygiene being implemented everywhere will create a new normal for the future. Above all, it is in the interest of all nations, rich or poor, to ensure that testing kits, drugs and vaccines are available at affordable prices, given that security against pandemics is indivisible.

If one were to go by the experience of China and others such as Singapore, there is a big role that artificial intelligence (AI), facial recognition and similar other technologies can play in contact-tracing. Singapore's Government Technology Agency (GovTech) and its health ministry have developed a smartphone app called TraceTogether, which works by exchanging short-distance Bluetooth signals between phones to detect other participating users within close proximity of two metres.

Clearly, the notion of national security, or global security, is being reshaped by Covid-19. Armed forces everywhere, often deployed in confined spaces ranging from bunkers to tanks and armoured personnel carriers to naval ships and submarines, will also face tough choices in stemming the spread of the coronavirus without compromising national security.

Beyond hard power and the threats of hybrid warfare, nations will have to rethink possible future scenarios and create numerically adequate forces of well-equipped pandemic experts, doctors and healthcare workers to be the new foot soldiers in this battle.

A vaccine for Covid-19 will eventually emerge, but the world can avoid paying a heavy price by not treating pandemics as one-off events. Given the incidence of SARS, MERS and similar outbreaks in the past, Covid-19 is hardly a black swan event. The human race may have to contend with many more of nature's calamitous challenges. Prime Minister Modi has done well to grasp the nettle and take the lead within the South Asian Association for Regional Cooperation (SAARC) and the G20 framework to forge a new global compact.

(The article was first published in The Indian Express,
25 March 2020)

India can absorb shocks of the pandemic, take the lead in reshaping global order

The Covid-19 pandemic has effectively exposed flaws in multilateral structures and highlighted the lacunae in national capacities, particularly in healthcare. Multilateralism has suffered retrenchment. The United Nations Security Council (UNSC) must be faulted for its egregious lack of action in March 2020 at the start of the Covid-19 pandemic when China held the rotating post of the president. It will remain one of the great ironies of history that China, which has increasingly sought to play a global leadership role, actively suppressed discussions in multilateral fora on the origins of the pandemic. The withdrawal of nearly $500 million worth of annual voluntary funding by the US to the World Health Organization (WHO) is a debatable move, notwithstanding the global consensus on the WHO's China-bias.

At a time when the UNSC, G20, G7 and the EU were inert, Prime Minister Narendra Modi stood out with his initiatives to develop a joint response. In bringing the South Asian Association for Regional Cooperation (SAARC) together to fight the pandemic, Modi said, 'Our neighbourhood collaboration should be a model for the world'.

The rapid spread of coronavirus around the world has created fresh opportunities for dialogue. There is hope, and scope, for creating a new global compact. Contributions will be measured not in dollars alone, but in the leadership that countries exhibit—and their willingness to share ideas and resources to develop an international mechanism for monitoring, verification, early warning and cooperation among nation-states, including in vaccine development. Such a framework will have to look beyond the limitations of the WHO.

In light of Covid-19, there definitely exists a case for the greater scrutiny of 'wet markets' in China, Southeast Asia, and many other countries around the world. Roadside quacks across South Asia, too, are seen extolling the spurious curative powers of lizard oils and other extracts of protected species. Even the US, which enacted the Endangered Species Act in 1973, has not been able to eradicate animal farms that breed and trade exotic species. China operates commercial tiger farms for traditional medicine and several countries in Southeast Asia do likewise with bears for bile extraction. All these activities increase the potential for zoonotic transmission of unknown, deadly viruses.

The need of the hour is to devise means that can deal more effectively with the illegal slaughter of exotic animals. Efforts must be made to strengthen the Convention on International Trade in Endangered Species of Wild Fauna and Flora (CITES), a multilateral treaty with more than 180 member countries. There should be renewed focus not only on the illegal international trade that is already covered by CITES, but also on the hazardous exploitation of exotic wildlife species within national borders. All signatory states, including China, must pass and enforce legislation to control the domestic consumption of wild animals. Dubious 'wet markets' and animal farms must be shut down.

India's record of legislation in conservation and enforcement of penalties for the killing and exploitation of protected wildlife is better than most. There is considerable scope for the Modi government to take the lead in proposing that CITES be given more teeth to conduct international scrutiny and inspections.

The Covid-19 pandemic has brought across a home truth: wealth is unable to protect even the most affluent people from a silent killer.

Individuals with higher immunity levels have a better chance of survival if afflicted with Covid-19. The ancient Indian practice of yoga is known to boost immunity levels through the cultivation of a healthy mind and body. This is the time to further reinforce the worldwide practice of yoga under the banner of the International Day of Yoga, also an initiative of Modi. India should plan for special virtual events on 21 June this year to encourage people around the world to practice yoga to promote holistic health.

As the world's largest producer and exporter of cost-effective generic drugs, India's readiness to ship the anti-malarial drug hydroxychloroquine to other nations to assist them in their fight against Covid-19 is a Good Samaritan act in consonance with the ethos of 'vasudhaiva kutumbakam'. India is also in the race to produce a vaccine. If China is a 'factory to the world', India has the potential to be a 'pharmacy to the world'. It can even take on a new and well-deserved moniker, that of vishwa vaidya. This provides an opportunity to promote Ayurveda, which complements yoga.

At a strategic level, global opinion seems weighted against China, notwithstanding its efforts to salvage credibility by shifting the focus away from the origins of the coronavirus to the 'superiority' of its system in tackling the pandemic. There is talk of the coronavirus having originated in a laboratory in Wuhan, with many theories about biological warfare programmes and accidental release. This provides an opportune moment to turn the spotlight on the inherent weaknesses of the Biological Weapons Convention (BWC) of 1975. It is a disarmament treaty that does not prohibit the retention and use of biological agents, including coronaviruses, for prophylactic purposes, which encompass medical research for diagnosis and immunization. It has no verification protocol to deal with any suspected use of biological agents. Indeed, the UNSC can investigate complaints in this regard, but the veto power enjoyed by the permanent members, including China, renders this a chimera. In the run-up to the Ninth Review Conference of the BWC in 2021, India could engage in consultations with other middle powers to evolve a regime that can provide better oversight.

The notion of national security is multi-faceted and includes information security as a key element. The very notion of critical infrastructure in the cyber domain is changing in myriad ways with a sudden surge in users and data flow in the digital space. This has created vast new attack surfaces in personal computers for hackers and cybercriminals, both state and non-state. Post Covid-19, there will be even greater reliance on artificial intelligence (AI), surveillance technologies, online platforms and big data. India must redouble its efforts, along with partners such as the US, to push for a multistakeholder model of internet governance.

The outline of the post-Covid-19 era, particularly in relation to economic recovery, healthcare and food security, is far from clear. The pandemic may serve to accentuate the rift between the US and China. However, given the centrality of the Chinese economy in global supply chains, it is a moot question if the economies of the US, EU or Japan can achieve a major decoupling. Covid-19 has shown how China's actions impact the entire world. Whatever the denouement in the matter of bringing China to book for its acts of commission or omission, its cooperation will be vital in reforming global institutions and practices.

India enjoys good relations with multiple powers and is well-regarded across the developing world. With excellent long-term economic prospects, a confident India appears fully capable of absorbing the shocks of the pandemic and striding forth to engage a world riven by trade wars and ideological contestation. Despite hardships, India can, and must, take the lead in bringing the world together to practice a new multilateralism that places the common interests of humanity above narrow national interests.

(The article was first published in The Indian Express,
4 May 2020)

Covid-19 pandemic may create opportunities to deepen India's engagement with Africa

Africa Day is observed every year on 25 May to commemorate the founding of the Organisation of African Unity (now known as the African Union). India has been closely associated with it on account of its shared colonial past and rich contemporary ties. The Manohar Parrikar Institute for Defence Studies and Analyses has hosted an Africa Day Round Table annually for the last four years to commemorate this epochal event. This year, however, the Covid-19 pandemic has marred the celebrations in India. Africa, too, has come to a standstill due to the coronavirus.

The World Bank's *Africa's Pulse*, a biannual analysis of the near-term macroeconomic outlook for the region, in its 9 April 2020 report, assessed that the Covid-19 outbreak has sparked the Sub-Saharan Africa (SSA) region's first recession in twenty-five years. Growth is expected to plummet to between -2.1 and -5.1 per cent in 2020, from a modest 2.4 per cent in 2019. With high rates of HIV, malaria, diabetes, hypertension and malnourishment prevalent, a large number of Africans were already facing a health and economic crisis. The steep decline in commodity prices has spelt disaster for the economies of Nigeria, Zambia and Angola.

Precarious fiscal positions have ruled out any major governmental stimulus. Public debt has mounted. According to the World Bank, the SSA region paid $35.8 billion in total debt service in 2018, 2.1 per cent of regional gross domestic product (GDP). Together, African countries have sought a $100 billion rescue package, including a $44 billion waiver of interest payment by the world's twenty largest economies. The International Monetary Fund's debt service relief of $500 million is meant for twenty-five countries, of which nineteen are in Africa, but that is a drop in the bucket. It is clear that without outside support, Africa will find it very difficult to meet the challenge of debt distress.

Africa's rich natural resources, long-term economic potential, youthful demography and influence as a bloc of fifty-four countries in multilateral organizations is apparent. In recent years, several extra-regional economies have strengthened their engagement with African states, with an eye to rising economic opportunities, including in energy, mining, infrastructure and connectivity. China's engagement in Africa, as elsewhere, is huge but increasingly regarded as predatory and exploitative. Its annual trade with Africa in 2019 stood at $208 billion, in addition to investments and loans worth $200 billion. Traditionally, China's participation in infrastructure projects has been astonishing. Having famously built the 1,860-km Tanzania-Zambia railway line in 1975, and the Addis Ababa-Djibouti and Mombasa-Nairobi lines more recently, China now has its eye on developing the vast East Africa Master Railway Plan.

It is also developing the Trans-Maghreb Highway, the Mambilla hydropower plant in Nigeria, the Walvis Bay container terminal in Windhoek and the Caculo Cabaça hydropower project in Angola. At the Forum for China-Africa Cooperation (FOCAC) in 2018, China set aside $60 billion in developmental assistance, followed by a whopping $1 billion Belt and Road (BRI) Infrastructure Fund for Africa. China has followed up with robust health sector diplomacy in the wake of the pandemic, but its image has been tarnished by defective supplies of personal protective equipment (PPE) gear and discriminatory behaviour against Africans in Guangzhou, leading to an embarrassing diplomatic row.

Japan hosted the Seventh Tokyo International Conference for African Development (TICAD) in August 2019. Russia hosted the first-ever Russia-Africa Summit last year. Brazil, home to the largest population of people of African descent outside of Africa, has also sought to develop closer ties. Cuba has sent medical teams to help Africa.

In the last few years, Prime Minister Narendra Modi has redefined India's relations with Africa. India-Africa trade reached $62 billion in 2018 compared to $39 billion during 2009-10. After South Asia, Africa is the second largest recipient of Indian overseas assistance with lines of credit (LOC) worth nearly $10 billion (42 per cent of the total) spread over 100 projects in forty-one countries. Ties were boosted at the India Africa Forum Summit (IAFS) in 2015. Forty per cent of all training and capacity-building slots under the Indian Technical and Economic Cooperation (ITEC) programme have traditionally been reserved for Africa. Approximately 6,000 Indian soldiers are deployed in UN peacekeeping missions in five conflict zones in Africa. Bilateral cooperation includes solar energy development, information technology, cybersecurity, maritime security, disaster relief, counterterrorism and military training. India has also launched several initiatives to develop closer relations, including the first-ever India Africa Defence Ministers conclave in February 2020 on the margins of the Defence Expo 2020. India provides about 50,000 scholarships to African students each year. The huge Indian diaspora is a major asset.

India had planned to host the Fourth India-Africa Forum Summit in September 2020. However, the Covid-19 pandemic may cause it to be delayed. India has already despatched medical assistance to twenty-five African countries and Prime Minister Modi has had a telephonic talk with President Cyril Ramaphosa of South Africa who is the current chairperson of the African Union, and separately with others such as the presidents of Uganda and Ethiopia. Minister of External Affairs S. Jaishankar has also reached out to counterparts in Africa to reiterate India's support in the fight against Covid-19. India could consider structuring a series of virtual summits in zonal groups with African leaders across the continent over the next few months that could both provide a platform for a cooperative response to the pandemic and serve as a precursor to the actual summit in the future.

There are several other ideas that could be pushed to deepen India's engagement with Africa. The Ministry of External Affairs has already extended the e-ITEC course on 'Covid-19 Pandemic: Prevention and Management Guidelines for Healthcare Professionals' to healthcare workers in Africa. The Aarogya Setu app and the eGramSwaraj app for rural areas for mapping Covid-19 are technological achievements that could be shared with Africa. Since the movement of African students to India for higher education has been disrupted, India may expand the e-VidyaBharati (tele-education) project to establish an India-Africa virtual university. Agriculture and food security can also be a fulcrum for deepening ties. With the locust scourge devastating the Horn of Africa and the pandemic worsening the food crisis, India could ramp up its collaboration in this sector.

India could also create a new fund for Africa and adapt its grant-in-aid assistance to reflect current priorities. This could include support for new investment projects by Indian entrepreneurs, especially in the pharmaceutical and healthcare sectors in Africa.

Both India and Japan share a common interest in forging a partnership for Africa's development. The Covid-19 crisis has nudged many countries to engage in new formats. It is time for the Quad Plus—in which the US, India, Japan and Australia have recently engaged other countries such as the Republic of Korea, Vietnam, New Zealand, Israel and Brazil—to exchange views and propose cooperation with select African countries abutting the Indian Ocean. After all, the Indo-Pacific straddles the entire maritime space of the Indian Ocean. The pandemic is a colossal challenge, but it may create fresh opportunities to bring India and Africa closer together.

(The article first appeared in *The Indian Express*, 29 May 2020)

Resilient supply chains as a pandemic lesson

A key lesson learnt by the world during the Covid-19 pandemic has been the importance of creating resilient supply chains that can withstand disruptions and ensure reliability for the global economy.

Disruptions in supply chains can be natural or man-made. In Japan's case, the great Tōhoku earthquake of 2011, followed by the tsunami, led to a nuclear disaster (Fukushima Daiichi), causing a sharp drop in Japanese automobile exports to the United States.

Examples that hit home

Man-made interruptions in supply chains are equally disruptive. Terrorist drone attacks on Aramco's oil refineries at Abqaiq and Khurais in Saudi Arabia in September 2019 resulted in a drop of 5.7 million barrels of oil per day, triggering a steep plunge in Saudi Arabia's stock market and a sharp spike in global oil prices.

China has long practised 'supply chain politics'. Japanese entrepreneurs learnt a hard lesson when the detention of a Chinese fishing trawler captain in 2010 near the disputed Senkaku Islands resulted in the Chinese government cutting off exports of rare earths to Japan.

When the novel coronavirus pandemic broke out, it had an immediate and telling effect on supply chains emanating from China. In India, several companies felt the disruption in the automotive, electronics and white goods sectors. India excels in the pharmaceuticals sector, but the over-reliance on active pharmaceutical ingredients (APIs) from China still creates vulnerabilities in the value chain.

Tensions with China led the United States government to impose restrictions on the export of microchips to China's biggest semiconductor manufacturer, Semiconductor Manufacturing International Corporation (SMIC), following assessment that there was an 'unacceptable risk' that equipment supplied to it could be used for military purposes.

A new initiative

Greater weaponization of trade and technology is here to stay. It is in this context that India, Japan and Australia initiated the Supply Chain Resilience Initiative (SCRI) in September 2020, aimed at creating a virtuous cycle of supply chain resilience in order to achieve strong, sustainable, balanced and inclusive growth in the region. The SCRI focuses on the automobiles and parts, petroleum, steel, textiles, financial services and IT sectors. The SCRI may be bolstered by the future involvement of France, though this might depend on the European Union's position. The UK has also shown an interest in the SCRI.

Geopolitics and geo-economics can never be truly separated. This is what Henry Kissinger called the 'principle of linkage' in his analysis of

US relations with the Soviet Union. When the Nixon administration came to power in 1969, the Soviet Union wanted access to some key Western technologies in computing. Yet, it was unwilling to accommodate US concerns on strategic and military issues. Kissinger clearly pointed out that to 'separate issues into distinct compartments would encourage the Soviet leaders to believe that they could use cooperation in one area as a safety valve while striving for unilateral advantages elsewhere…'

China has resorted to similar tactics, of maintaining advantageous trade and economic engagement, without relenting on strategic issues. China's calls for 'normal relations' with India are unrealistic given the continuing face-off in Ladakh.

Moves by Australia, Japan

China has often used its economic leverage to weaken an opponent's resolve on contentious issues. Facing such a dilemma, Australia has demonstrated strong political will in countering arbitrary Chinese sanctions imposed on its key exports of grain, beef, wine, coal and much else. This is a price that a democracy such as Australia finds worth paying, for demanding an inquiry into the origins of the coronavirus and advocating a robust Indo-Pacific vision.

Since the normalization of diplomatic ties in the 1970s, Japan has invested hundreds of billions of dollars in the Chinese economy. For many Japanese companies, global performance and profits are linked to manufacturing facilities and supply chains in China. Yet, they have shown an early capacity for risk mitigation through the 'China Plus One' business strategy, aimed at diversification of investments to the Association of Southeast Asian Nations (ASEAN), India and Bangladesh.

In the first phase of Japan's $2.2 billion relocation package announced in 2020, eighty-nine Japanese companies availed subsidies to diversify out of China. Of these, fifty-seven companies relocated to Japan, thirty to Southeast Asia and two to India.

A sizeable number of small and medium enterprises (SMEs) chose to relocate to Southeast Asian countries such as Vietnam, Thailand and Malaysia. This is hardly surprising since Japanese entrepreneurs are far more familiar with the cultural and business environment in ASEAN countries as compared to South Asia.

However, companies in healthcare and medical devices, especially those manufacturing personal protective equipment (PPE), would have benefited more by shifting to India, which offers a much larger domestic market as well as lower manufacturing costs for global exports.

India's vulnerabilities

A large emerging economy such as India can ill-afford the shocks of disruption in supply chains. Nor can it allow itself to be held hostage due to an over-reliance on imports. For instance, the pandemic caused a breakdown in global supply chains in the automotive sector since most global manufacturers in China abruptly went offline. For India, which imports 27 per cent of its requirement of automotive parts from China, this quandary was a wake-up call, given the sudden shortage of braking components, electrical components, interiors and lighting fixtures.

What is noteworthy is that despite being the fourth largest market in Asia for medical devices, India has an import dependency of 80 per cent. Among the biggest exporters to India in this field are China, the US, Germany, Singapore and Japan. This is clearly not sustainable. Given the renewed thrust in the healthcare sector, this is the right time to fill gaps through local manufacturing.

India's electronics industry was worth $120 billion in 2018-19 and is forecast to grow to $400 billion by 2025. Today, India is seeking to enhance its presence substantially in global supply chains by attracting investments in the semiconductor components and packaging industry. The government is actively promoting domestic manufacture of printed circuit boards (PCBs), components and semiconductors, as the Indian electronics sector gradually shifts away from completely knocked down (CKD) assembly to high value addition.

Defence beckons

Defence is among the key pillars of the Atmanirbhar Bharat policy. The Atmanirbhar Bharat policy aims to make India a strong and competitive player on the global stage. It is not an autarkic vision. It prioritizes self-reliance, not self-sufficiency. As a result, there is considerable scope to work with international partners around the world.

The government is providing a big boost to defence manufacturing under the Make in India programme. It has identified a negative import list of 101 items. There is a tremendous opportunity for foreign companies to enter into tie-ups with reputed Indian defence manufacturers to tap into the growing defence market in India.

The push for self-reliance through Atmanirbhar Bharat is not an autarkic policy. It does not imply closure of the Indian economy to foreign trade and participation in the global economy. On the contrary, it is aimed at strengthening India's capacities to participate more vigorously without falling prey to supply chain disruptions.

India has the capacity and the potential to become one of the world's largest destinations for investments and one of the world's largest manufacturing hubs in the aftermath of the pandemic.

(The article was first published in *The Hindu*, 30 December 2020)

QUADRILATERAL
SPHERE

India and the changing dynamics of the Indo-Pacific

The world is undergoing a fundamental transformation. The Covid-19 pandemic has exposed flaws in multilateral structures and highlighted the lacunae in national capacities. Multilateralism, already on the brink in recent years, has been pushed into an abyss not just by the rivalry between the US and the China-Russia tandem but by the greatest power on earth retracting in favour of an 'America first' policy. The global economy is reeling under the unexpected effects of Covid-19, with the International Monetary Fund predicting an impending recession. The notion of national security, or global security, is being reshaped. Trade and technology are being weaponized. Hedging and multi-aligning are part of every country's strategic toolkit. There is growing uncertainty across the globe.

'Indo-Pacific' has been variously interpreted in the vision documents of several nations; however, a distinct convergence has emerged in recent years at both the ideational and policy levels. Credit must go to the Trump administration for making a concerted effort to regain the ground lost by his shilly-shallying predecessors in the Asia-Pacific region—as much due to a blithe underestimation of the Chinese Communist Party as on account of a diversion of focus and resources to the global war on terrorism. The 'rebalance to Asia' announced but never fully implemented during the Obama years has been given a vigorous thrust under the Trump administration's 'free and open Indo-Pacific' (FOIP) strategy. However, its impact on irreversible changes in the region is moot, a case in point being China's blatant occupation and militarization of islands and features in the South China Sea over the past decade.

Effectively, China stepped into the vacuum left by the US. Ironically, it is now championing the liberal trading order and multilateral institutions with the express purpose of moulding them to suit its own ends. It is also unabashedly practising coercion and 'wolf warrior' diplomacy to ensure the global endorsement of its political and economic systems.

China's rise has not been smooth. The West took 150 years to achieve an enduring balance of power through a long process of industrialization, war and treaty negotiation. In China's case, change has been so dazzlingly rapid that it is not just the outside world that has found it difficult to adjust to China's rise. China itself seems entirely unprepared at the leadership level to accurately comprehend the implications of the change and expects the entire world to adjust. However, it is unwilling to acknowledge the achievements and aspirations of other countries, especially democracies.

In the past, the Portuguese, the Dutch and the British were motivated to acquire extraterritorial privileges and consolidate their presence using mare liberum and mare clausum strategies in the Indian Ocean. These privileges enabled the colonial powers to secure trading rights and monopolies over raw materials for manufacturing centres back home. Today, China appears to be driven by similar considerations as evident in the Belt and Road Initiative (BRI), its growing presence in the Pacific Island nations, its island-grabbing spree in the South China Sea, and its quest for ports and basing rights along the Indian Ocean littoral. There is also no doubt that the US-China trade war has been disruptive. No two rival powers are as interlinked by trade and investment, nor have other countries been as intertwined in a web of relations with both China and the US as they are today. This makes for difficult choices for all others, especially in the Indo-Pacific.

This essay examines the changing dynamics of the Indo-Pacific and assesses India's role in promoting an alternative to China's vision for the region.

The evolving dynamics of the Indo-Pacific

The term 'Indo-Pacific' is an affirmation of the natural spread of economic growth and prosperity in recent years over a wide region extending well beyond East and Southeast Asia to include South Asia and the dynamic east coast of Africa. The term 'Asia-Pacific' has always lacked the capacity to fully express Asia's true continental identity or the significance of the region. Indo-Pacific is more inclusive and accommodating of the growing aspirations of a wider constituency. It captures the interdependence of the oceanic spaces and the interconnectedness of trade, technology and security throughout the region.

It is lamentable, however, that economic success in the Indo-Pacific has not been matched by a corresponding consensus on a stable security architecture. In recent decades, the region has witnessed some of the highest military expenditures and most intractable territorial disputes in the world. Although US trade, economic and military presence in the Indo-Pacific has been a stabilizing factor since World War II, today the region is a contested space where China is moving to redefine its standing in the world order by trying to expel US forces through economic inducements and military pressure. This has implications for the region's ability to create a secure, prosperous and multipolar Asia.

China's growing assertiveness

China aims to become a moderately developed country by 2021, the centenary of the Chinese Communist Party's establishment. Furthermore, it seeks to modernize its military forces by 2035 and to realize the 'China dream'—the emergence of a strong, modern and rejuvenated Chinese nation—by 2050. The party's mantra, 'community of a shared future for mankind', is an ill-concealed effort to reinvent the Middle Kingdom, with China at the centre of a new world order. Policies such as Made in China 2025 and the creation of vast physical and digital infrastructure networks linking China's manufacturing nodes with global markets through the BRI are part of the stratagem.

China's aggressive actions in the South China Sea have pitted its ill-founded maritime claims against the rights of several members of the Association of Southeast Asian Nations (ASEAN), including Vietnam, the Philippines, Malaysia and Indonesia. For example, it has used illegal fishing to undermine Indonesia's sovereign rights in the Natuna Islands. Beijing summarily rejected the ruling of the Permanent Court of Arbitration (PCA) under the United Nations Convention on the Law of the Sea (UNCLOS) on China's so-called historical rights, nine-dash line and exaggerated exclusive economic zone claims. The PCA ruling had itself rejected China's claims to much of the South China Sea on grounds that they were ill-founded and not backed by any historical evidence.

China has used its People's Armed Forces Maritime Militia, popularly called the 'fishing militia', to enforce claims in both the South and East China Seas. In an unfriendly gesture, a Chinese submarine sailed without surfacing in the contiguous zone northeast of Amami Oshima in Japan's Kagoshima Prefecture. The Chinese defence ministry has also threatened Japan for hosting US intermediate-range missiles.

China harbours deep suspicions about the FOIP concept and the Quad grouping of Australia, the US, India and Japan, which it believes are driven primarily by the United States to contain China's rise. It also believes that trilateral and other dialogue structures involving the US, Japan and India or the US, Japan and Australia are aimed at containment. Recently, Chinese scholars and officials appear to have adopted a wait-and-see approach towards the Indo-Pacific instead of outright opposition. This is partly because 'ASEAN centrality' affords China an opportunity to dilute narratives in the Indo-Pacific that could prove inimical to its interests. China is a stakeholder, for example, in the code of conduct negotiations with the ASEAN countries, the outcome of which will decide the fate of the South China Sea and have implications for the broader region. Beyond ASEAN, China uses bilateral economic engagement with Japan and Australia to mitigate the effects of a pushback, whether in regard to Tokyo's partial economic decoupling or Canberra's deep scrutiny of its influence peddling. With India, however, China has less space for manoeuvring in light of the public outcry against its aggressive policies along the Line of Actual Control in the India-China border area.

Regional responses to China and the rise of the free and open Indo-Pacific

China's unilateralism and aggressive irredentism in pursuit of the China dream and disregard of core global values have inevitably encountered opposition. The Quad countries and many others have advocated for the creation of a free, open and inclusive regional architecture that preserves a rules-based order, freedom of navigation and overflight, and ASEAN centrality as key to a peaceful and prosperous Indo-Pacific.

China's actions in recent years have served to soften the nuanced differences among the Quad countries on the Indo-Pacific concept and their role in securing a better future for the region. Far from being an 'attention-grabbing idea' that would soon 'dissipate like ocean foam', as China's foreign minister Wang Yi once put it, the FOIP concept and the Quad have gradually acquired form and substance. There is pragmatic appreciation that not all nations grappling with the rise of China are democracies. In this spirit, the term 'democratic', part of the grouping's early lexicon, has quietly been dropped to facilitate a broader dialogue in the Quad Plus format with nations that are not liberal democracies but that share many of the same concerns about China's rise.

ASEAN countries' dependence on China for their economic prosperity, and in some cases security, has grown in recent years, with Laos, Cambodia and Myanmar in particular heavily reliant on China. Nonetheless, at the 36th ASEAN Summit in June 2020, some Southeast Asian leaders boldly raised China's bullying tactics in the South China Sea as an issue. Vietnam, the current ASEAN chair, called for a rules-based order in the region, and even Philippine President Rodrigo Duterte, long under China's influence, emphasized the need for respect of UNCLOS. Collectively, the ASEAN states have the capacity to mount a spirited response, but their response so far has been desultory at best. More fundamentally, at the individual level, they are often inclined to seek Chinese accommodation. As a result, the group's joint statements have limited impact.

Traditional US partners in the region such as Singapore, Malaysia and Thailand are caught in the US-China geostrategic contest. Even South Korea, a US alliance partner, is wary of embracing a FOIP strategy that Beijing perceives as a US-led containment ploy. Furthermore, the traditional rivalry between South Korea and Japan ensures that a trilateral alliance with the US in Northeast Asia remains a chimera. While Washington D.C. considers Seoul as a key anchor of the FOIP strategy, some Koreans view the strategy as a Japanese initiative, making the Japan-South Korea axis one of the weakest links.

Elsewhere in the region, Australia's 2020 Defence Strategic Update and 2020 Force Structure Plan, both released in July 2020, outline a new defence strategy and the investments necessary to develop relevant capabilities. Realizing the threat to its longer-term security, Australia is reorienting its defence strategy to mitigate the risk of exclusive reliance on its coalition partnership. Over the next ten years, the Australian government will bolster its defence spending and allocate A$575 billion to develop robust capacities of its own.

As the world's largest economic and military power, the US has long been accustomed to a degree of exceptionalism. This perhaps slows the pace at which opposition to China can coalesce. For example, the US concept of freedom of navigation is hard on friend and foe alike. The US routinely conducts freedom of navigation operations around several countries, including friendly nations such as India, Indonesia, Vietnam and the Philippines. In the case of the South China Sea, these operations are an optical symbol of US naval potency. Although they deny China the satisfaction of a complete takeover of the oceanic space, they do not reverse China's occupation and militarization of features in the South China Sea. Another debilitating factor is the US penchant for levelling criticism at potential partners on account of human rights and democracy. Not only are China and Myanmar cited in this context, but the Philippines (an alliance partner) is also a target. It could be argued that such an approach weakens consensus-building.

The emerging contestation in the Pacific pits US developmental programmes such as the Better Utilization of Investments Leading to Development Act of 2018 (BUILD Act), Asia Reassurance Initiative Act (ARIA) and Enhancing Development and Growth through Energy (Asia EDGE) against the blandishments offered by China to small island nations. Beyond revitalizing the Quad, Japan and Australia have joined the US in the Blue Dot Network and Indo-Pacific Business Forum to promote infrastructure and connectivity. In addition, during President Donald Trump's visit to India in February 2020, the US and India released a joint statement that clearly points to greater consultation between the two partners.

India's role in the Indo-Pacific

India is committed to an inclusive security architecture for the Indo-Pacific (including the South China Sea) on the basis of respect for the rule of law, freedom of navigation and overflight, equal access to the commons and its natural resources, and resolution of disputes through dialogue. India believes in a multipolar Asia in which there is no room for unilateralism or coercive behaviour that threatens peace and development.

This position has evolved over the years. If India had earlier opposed the presence of foreign powers in the Indian Ocean, it now welcomes the presence of the US, Japan, Australia and other partner countries in the region, and even carries out joint exercises with a number of them to promote interoperability. In fact, India's relations with the US, Japan and Australia, in particular, have been qualitatively strengthened in recent years with a new thrust on economic and defence cooperation. Prime Minister Narendra Modi has said that India considers the United States an indispensable partner in every sector of India's transformation and progress. The same could also be said of India's ties with Japan. Between these countries, there exists a growing convergence of views on the Indo-Pacific's emerging geostrategic and geo-economic changes.

Today, the US is arguably India's most important strategic partner—India conducts more bilateral military exercises with the US than it does with any other country; the US exercises more with India than with any other non-NATO partner. Agreements such as the General Security of Military Information Agreement, Logistics Exchange Memorandum of Agreement, Communications Compatibility and

Security Agreement, and Industrial Security Annex have opened up new prospects for defence cooperation. India and Japan have likewise deepened their 'special strategic and global partnership' to include closer defence relations. India and Australia upgraded their ties to a comprehensive strategic partnership in a June 2020 virtual summit, where important pacts were concluded such as the Mutual Logistics Support Arrangement and the Joint Declaration on a Shared Vision for Maritime Cooperation in the Indo-Pacific. With India and Australia moving closer through India's participation in Kakadu, Pitch Black and other exercises, the prospects for strengthening the Quad appear much brighter. Even though India is unlikely to enter into a formal alliance with any country, in recent years it has concluded logistics-sharing agreements with the US, Australia, France, Singapore, Japan and South Korea. The progress on these cooperative agreements indicates that there is a growing appreciation of the geostrategic disruption caused by the rise of China. A logistics-sharing agreement with Russia is in an advanced stage of negotiation. India also conducted a bilateral maritime exercise with Russia in the Bay of Bengal in September 2020. For India, Russia remains a Pacific power with a legacy footprint in the Indian Ocean.

Since 2014, India has also transformed its Look East policy into the Act East policy, enhanced engagement with West Asia and Africa, and strengthened ties with Pacific Island and Indian Ocean littoral nations. Prime Minister Modi pointed out that '…with a 7,500-kilometre-long coastline, India has a natural and immediate interest in the developments in the Indo-Pacific region.' In fact, more than 90 per cent of the country's trade traverses maritime routes. India's Security and Growth for All in the Region (SAGAR) vision includes a five-pronged approach that focuses on deepening economic and security cooperation, strengthening maritime security capacities, advancing peace and security, responding to emergencies, and calling for respect for international maritime rules and norms by all countries. Similarly, India has used its considerable naval and airlift capabilities to conduct humanitarian assistance and disaster relief operations, particularly to help Maldives, Sri Lanka, Indonesia, Fiji, Mozambique and the Philippines. The country also conducts coordinated exclusive economic zone patrols with Maldives and Sri Lanka, has played an active role in conducting antipiracy operations in the Gulf of Aden, and has hosted the Information Fusion Centre for the Indian Ocean Region for white shipping.

In his address at the annually held international security forum— the Shangri-La Dialogue in 2018—Modi emphasized the following key elements of India's vision of the Indo-Pacific: free, open and inclusive; ASEAN centrality; rules-based order; settlement of disputes through dialogue; equal access to the global commons with freedom of navigation and unimpeded commerce; security of the maritime environment; disaster relief; a balanced and stable trade regime; and connectivity. This approach has enabled India to strengthen its defence and security cooperation with partner countries in the region. In addition to the ongoing programmes, new developments include year-round military patrols in the Indian Ocean, improved maritime domain awareness, increased military training and technical support, and a quantum increase in bilateral and multilateral military exercises and dialogues. Modi also proposed an Indo-Pacific Oceans Initiative at the 2019 East Asia Summit to conserve and sustainably use the maritime domain and make meaningful efforts to create a safe maritime space. This is an extension of his earlier proposal for a blue economy.

A downturn in India-China relations

Recently, distrust between India and China has deepened against the backdrop of escalating tensions in their ongoing border dispute. China has also failed to reassure India about its new presence in the Indian Ocean and rent-seeking projects in South Asian countries such as Nepal, Bangladesh, Sri Lanka and Maldives. In light of these developments, New Delhi might need to review its Indo-Pacific vision, with a discernible shift from making policy pronouncements to developing strategies that leverage India's geographic location and naval power to offset Chinese pressure.

China must have noted that India's decision to cooperate in strengthening the Quad permitted it to meet at the ministerial level in 2019. China remains worried about the advantages that the Quad process might offer to India in the Indo-Pacific. China is also concerned about the presence and activities of the US, Japan, Australia, the UK and France, among others, in the waters surrounding India's Andaman and Nicobar Islands, just outside the Malacca Strait through which a great deal of China's vulnerable energy imports pass. The sharp downturn in India-China relations due to border tensions is creating new opportunities for the Quad on the maritime front. A recent example is the passing exercise between Indian naval vessels and the USS Nimitz-led task force near the Malacca Strait in July 2020.

The Andaman and Nicobar Islands could be further opened to friendly navies to promote greater cooperation. India's tri-service Andaman and Nicobar Command has progressively emerged as a linchpin of its regional maritime engagement in the Bay of Bengal and the Andaman Sea. Various multilateral and bilateral maritime engagements such as the Bay of Bengal Initiative for Multi-Sectoral Technical and Economic Cooperation, the Milan exercises, coordinated patrols and bilateral exercises with littoral states have contributed to India's engagement in this region.

As regional maritime forces have expanded their cooperation with the Indian Navy in recent years, there is a new appreciation in Southeast Asia for India's potential to offset China's dominance. There have been suggestions for coordinated surveillance of the Malacca, Sunda, Lombok and Ombai-Wetar straits through the collaborative use of the Andaman and Nicobar Islands and Australia's Cocos (Keeling) Islands. There have also been recommendations for collaborative anti-submarine warfare efforts in the Indian Ocean, in which the Andaman and Nicobar Islands could play a critical role.

Recent tensions and disputes between India and China have revealed two things: first, China is bent on defining its rise through unilateralism; and second, India remains resolute in defending its sovereignty and territorial integrity. As the next chapters of the Indo-Pacific saga unfold in the South and East China Seas, India will continue to play a critical role in opposing China's unilateralism and aggression.

The way ahead: Opportunities in a post-pandemic world

The Indo-Pacific region is destined for further change, especially since the outlines of the post-pandemic era are far from clear. The pandemic has shown how China's actions can affect the entire world. The decoupling of global value chains, trade and investment flows in the Indo-Pacific will remain a quandary for the US and many other countries. Over time, these have consolidated into well-entrenched regional networks, especially in East and Southeast Asia between China, Japan, Taiwan, South Korea and the ASEAN countries. Even as trade and technology are being weaponized, there is little doubt that the world is rapidly cleaving itself into mutually exclusive camps. A coalition against China is emerging in the Indo-Pacific through the proposed 'D-10 Club' summit (featuring G7 members plus India, Australia and South Korea), with the objective of preventing Chinese monopolies on 5G and other critical technologies.

However, the rapid spread of coronavirus has also created fresh opportunities for dialogue in the Indo-Pacific region and beyond. There is hope, and scope, for creating a new global compact. Contributions will be measured not in dollars and cents but in the leadership that countries exhibit and their willingness to share ideas, best practices and available resources to develop an international mechanism for monitoring, verification, early warning and cooperation among nation-states to deal with pandemics. Together, nations can address the real global challenges, such as climate change, clean energy, protection of the environment, terrorism and cybersecurity. This is true of the Indo-Pacific as well.

New partnerships and strong leadership will also be needed to address traditional security challenges in the region. A shift is visible in the US position on the South China Sea, for example. In 2016, when the UNCLOS tribunal gave its ruling rejecting Chinese claims in the South China Sea, the US spoke only of core principles and the binding nature of the award. At the time, it did not take a stand on the case's merits. In contrast, today the US has openly aligned its position with the substance of the decision, rejecting China's spurious claims, as evident in Secretary of State Mike Pompeo's July 2020 statement. This will strengthen the resolve of all ASEAN countries that are party to disputes in the South China Sea.

Joint exercises could be expanded in the future. The Malabar exercise between the US, India and Japan will most likely include Australia in its next iteration. The format could be further expanded to include Singapore, which was part of the one-off 2007 Quad maritime exercise. Indonesia is another potential invitee. Likewise, the Quad could be further strengthened if the US, Japan and Australia were to expressly support India, the only member with land borders with China, in the rejection of its northern neighbour's claims to Indian territory. The other members should make the necessary cartographic changes in their maps of India. In the absence of unequivocal support from Quad partners for its territorial integrity, India can hardly be expected to significantly step up its commitments and involve itself in maritime contestations beyond the Malacca Strait.

Developing dialogue structures beyond the Quad is crucial for the emergence of a stable security architecture in the Indo-Pacific. The Quad Plus format makes the structure more inclusive and acceptable, and Quad members have already carried out naval exercises with others in the region. India has exercised with the Philippines, Japan and the US, while Vietnam has exercised with Australia, Japan and the US. During the pandemic, Quad members have engaged in regular consultations, which have expanded to include Vietnam, South Korea, New Zealand, Israel and Brazil.

China is keen to ensure that the Quad does not evolve from a regional coordinating mechanism focused on capacity-building and developmental partnerships into an 'Asian NATO'. As far as the future of the format, however, much will depend on China's actions and their impact on the regional security environment.

For the foreseeable future, the Indian Ocean and the country's land borders will remain first order concerns in India's national security paradigm. New Delhi will continue to invest, though, in working with like-minded partners in the Quad and Quad Plus formats to ensure a free, open and rules-based order, with freedom of navigation and overflight, throughout the Indo-Pacific.

(The article first appeared in *Asia Policy*, Vol. 15(4), October 2020)

India must negotiate growing Chinese presence in Indo-Pacific

'Indo-Pacific' is today a buzzword that has been interpreted differently by various countries in their outlook or vision documents.

Back in 1971, when Sri Lanka proposed the notion of an Indian Ocean Zone of Peace (IOZOP), it was more about the presence of Western powers and establishment of foreign bases. Ironically, China then stood with countries like India in opposing bases in the Indian Ocean region. Its position was that it did not have, nor did it seek bases anywhere. That is a far cry from its strategy now of actively foraying into the Indian Ocean and seeking bases in Gwadar and Djibouti and special arrangements elsewhere. India's position has also evolved. If India earlier opposed the presence of foreign powers in the Indian Ocean, it now carries out joint exercises with a number of them to promote interoperability. It welcomes the presence of the US, Japan and other partner countries in the Indian Ocean as a counter to the growing Chinese presence.

In the Pacific Ocean, the debate was never about the presence per se of great powers. There, the US military presence on land and sea was taken for granted after World War II. The French and British too, as in the Indian Ocean, continued to have their colonies. The debate was about nuclear tests in places such as Bikini Atoll, French Polynesia and Christmas Island.

As a legacy state of the Soviet Union, Russia has never ceased to be an Indo-Pacific power. It avenged the humiliating destruction of its navy in the 1904-05 Russo-Japanese war by driving Japan out of the northern Korean Peninsula and taking South Sakhalin and the Kuril Islands in 1945. It enjoyed a key base in Cam Ranh Bay during the Cold War. Today, it holds joint exercises with China in the South China Sea and a trilateral exercise with China and South Africa in the Indian Ocean.

The situation in the South China Sea is more complex. Various claimants are pitted against one another, with China's irredentist nine-dash line engulfing the exclusive economic zones of several others. China has yet to produce a clear line with exact coordinates on a large-scale map in support of its claims. Earlier, in 1974, China took the Paracel Islands from South Vietnam, with a US in retreat turning a Nelson's eye. Later, China took Scarborough in 2012 and used swarming tactics involving fishing boats at Thitu Island against the Philippines in 2019, the defence treaty between the US and the Philippines notwithstanding. In general terms, the scramble in the South China Sea is more about fishing rights, natural resources and the domination of trade and energy sea lines of communication.

There are many contradictions in the context of the emerging construct of the Indo-Pacific. For example, the US, like India, Japan, Australia and many others, advocates freedom of navigation and overflight, and respect for the rule of law and international norms. It adheres to many tenets of the United Nations Convention on the

Law of the Sea (UNCLOS) without having ratified the treaty. China's adherence to UNCLOS is more honoured in breach than in observance.

Arguably, the US concept of 'freedom of navigation' is hard on friend and foe alike. The US conducted freedom of navigation operations in 2017 against a large number of countries, including friendly nations such as India, Indonesia, Vietnam and the Philippines. Similarly, the US Asia Reassurance Initiative Act (ARIA) of 2018, which embraces the Indo-Pacific as against Asia-Pacific, describes China as a strategic and economic competitor. Yet, it also has an entire section that seeks to 'promote US values in the Indo-Pacific region'. There is a reiteration of the US commitment to upholding rights and promoting democratic values. Not only is China cited in this context along with Myanmar, but an alliance partner such as the Philippines is also in the cross hairs.

On the other hand, China now justifies its increasing forays in the Indian Ocean region, including with nuclear submarines, by claiming that it has 'always' had a historical right to the Indian Ocean, citing the few voyages of Admiral Zheng He's fleet more than five centuries ago. In fact, there was no Chinese presence in the intervening period because after the brief maritime interludes during the Ming dynasty, China was not a maritime power until recently.

The Belt and Road Initiative (BRI) is supposed to endure for half a century. Yet, the absence of a key neighbouring country like India, for very valid reasons, has eroded its credibility. India has rejected the BRI since it was conceived and implemented without any consultations; moreover, it's flagship China-Pakistan Economic Corridor (CPEC) passes through disputed territory in Pakistan-occupied Kashmir (POK), which India regards as an integral part of its own territory. Now, many other countries are also questioning the BRI.

The world today is undergoing a fundamental transformation. There are several facets to the emerging uncertainty. Traditional and non-traditional security threats have grown in magnitude. The spectre of terrorism, especially cross-border terrorism, continues to challenge peace and prosperity. Geopolitical considerations are increasingly driving trade and investment decisions; on the other hand, the geo-economic forces unleashed by China's economic rise are redefining the geostrategic landscape of the Indo-Pacific.

There is no doubt that the US-China trade war has been disruptive. It has coincided with the waning of the global economy. No two rival powers are as interlinked by trade and investment as China and the US. Never before have all other countries been as intertwined in a web of relations with both China and the US as they are today. This makes for difficult choices. Power, whether economic, political or military, is fractured. No single country can dominate on all issues. Trade and technology are fiercely contested. Nationalism and regionalism are on the rise. There is less multilateralism but greater multipolarity. Hedging and multi-alignment are part of every country's strategic toolkit. The old consensus is fraying and a balance is yet to emerge. This calls for readjustments.

The 'Asian Century' appears inevitable, but the question remains as to whether it will be unipolar, bipolar or multipolar. Will it be a century of peace and development, or will it involve long-drawn contestations?

Asia is witnessing the simultaneous rise of several powers. Global engines of economic growth have shifted to Asia, first to the Asia-Pacific, and now, more widely, to the Indo-Pacific that includes South Asia. The continent, home to 60 per cent of the global population, has emerged as the new fulcrum for geo-economic and geostrategic realignment. One could argue that the natural evolution of trade, investment and energy flows favours the broader definition of the Indo-Pacific as against the narrower confines of Asia and the Asia-Pacific. The term Indo-Pacific is certainly more inclusive and better accommodates the growing aspirations of a wider constituency. However, the economic success in the Indo-Pacific region has not been matched by a stable security architecture. The region has some of the highest military expenditures in the world. Trade, territorial disputes and geostrategic contestations are rampant. This places limitations on the region's ability to engage in a process of give and take as seen in the Regional Comprehensive Economic Partnership (RCEP) negotiations. India withdrew from the RCEP negotiations keeping in mind the impact of cheap Chinese goods flooding its markets, as well as the sensitivities of its dairy and agriculture sectors.

There are fundamental disruptions to the existing equilibrium in the three sub-segments of the Indo-Pacific. The emergence of the US as a major energy exporter to Asia has eroded the importance of the Gulf oil producers in the western Indian Ocean. In the South China Sea, the dependence of the Association of Southeast Asian Nations (ASEAN) on China for its prosperity and security assurances is growing. In the Pacific, there is a new contestation, which pits US programmes such as the BUILD Act, ARIA and Asia EDGE against the inducements offered by China to small island nations. Japan and Australia have also joined hands with the US in the Blue Dot Network to promote infrastructure and connectivity.

The Chinese harbour suspicions about both the Indo-Pacific and the Quad as US devices to contain its rise. It regards trilateral compacts involving the US, Japan and India, and the US, Japan and Australia as adjuncts to strengthening the Quad. However, Chinese scholars and officials are beginning to resort to a wait-and-see approach, since ASEAN centrality is an opportunity to lean on them to shape favourable outcomes through the BRI project and the draft Code of Conduct.

India will have to manage its relations with China, no matter the challenges. Ties with Japan would remain a key component of India's vision for a stable Indo-Pacific and a cornerstone of its Act East policy. The Special Strategic and Global Partnership between India and Japan will be further strengthened during Prime Minister Shinzo Abe's visit, expected to take place in 2020. However, India at this juncture does not have to make a binary choice in the Indo-Pacific between a development-centric agenda with ASEAN centrality and a security-centric outlook revolving around the Quad. Both are likely to remain parallel tracks with some overlap for the foreseeable future.

(The article was first published in *The Indian Express*,
17 December 2019)

Time to leverage the strategic potential of the Andaman and Nicobar Islands

In recent years, the Government of India has adopted a proactive policy aimed at transforming the Andaman and Nicobar Islands, a tri-services command, as an economic hub and one of the key centres of India's defence and security strategy.

Until now, the balance between environmental preservation, tribal welfare, national security and economic development was skewed in favour of isolating the islands due to strategic considerations. The economic potential of the Andaman and Nicobar Islands had largely remained untapped. As the islands provide India a commanding geostrategic presence in the Bay of Bengal and access to South and Southeast Asia, a focused development plan for the islands is expected to greatly enhance the country's geopolitical leverage in the Indian Ocean region.

The Government of India constituted the Island Development Agency on 1 June 2017 for the development of islands. For the first time, under the guidance of the agency, an initiative has been taken for sustainable development in identified Andaman and Nicobar Islands. Four islands have been covered in the first phase. The focus is on creation of jobs through the promotion of tourism, seafood, coconut industry, etc. In the second phase, suitable sites in twelve more islands of Andaman and Nicobar have been covered.

The Andaman and Nicobar Islands have played a key role in enhancing India's regional engagement with the Bay of Bengal littorals.

This policy brief recommends the opening up of the Andaman and Nicobar Islands to other navies such as the United States, Japan, Australia and France, among others, to promote greater naval cooperation.

Strategic context

A combination of economic and strategic factors has significantly enhanced the strategic salience of the Bay of Bengal and its littorals. Strategically located, the Andaman and Nicobar Islands, larger than several island countries in themselves, are an asset in India's defence and strategic calculus. The islands straddle Duncan's Passage and the Ten Degree Channel. The Preparis Channel and Six Degree Channel are located to the north and south of the island chain, respectively. All these passages are important trade routes for any shipping destined for Southeast and East Asia. The 572 islands, out of which only 38 are inhabited, comprise 30 per cent of India's exclusive economic zone (EEZ). The Six Degree and Ten Degree channels in the Andaman Sea, which lead to the Malacca Strait, are vital to the sea lanes of communication along which flow global commerce, including energy trade, between Asia, Africa and the Pacific. The Andaman and Nicobar Islands are at the intersection of the Indian Ocean and the South China

Sea, and further to the Pacific Ocean, an important fulcrum of the strategic concept of the Indo-Pacific.

China's forays in the Indian Ocean

As China's economic and strategic interests have grown in the Indian Ocean, so has its natural imperative to secure those interests. The fact is that the Chinese presence in the Indian Ocean is rather new and, therefore, quite logically seen as disruptive. Except for a brief period in the fifteenth century when Admiral Zheng He's flotillas voyaged into the Indian Ocean, visiting Sri Lanka and southern India, China has never had an enduring historical presence in the Indian Ocean. This is different from the other great powers such as the US, France and Britain in particular, who have long maintained territory, populations and a naval presence in the Indian Ocean, going back an extended period of time. However, over the last decade or so, China has steadily expanded its maritime presence in the Indian Ocean littoral through the continuous deployment of its naval forces, arms sales, creating bases and access facilities, ramping up military diplomacy, cultivating special political relations with littorals, and lavishly disbursing developmental finance for strategic ends.

It has used the alibi of anti-piracy operations in the Gulf of Aden to ramp up the scale and frequency of its presence, without consideration for the threat perceptions of India. An egregious example is the deployment of a submarine, which berthed in Colombo in Sri Lanka in 2014, ostensibly on its way for so-called anti-piracy operations. China has also steadily enhanced its operational turnaround in the Indian Ocean and developed new bases, including at Gwadar and Djibouti. This broad-based trend in the evolution of China's presence is also reflected in the Andaman Sea and the Bay of Bengal, where Chinese naval and survey vessels have been on the prowl and have occasionally entered India's EEZ without prior intimation. China's economic and strategic engagement with Bangladesh, Myanmar, Thailand and Malaysia in the Bay of Bengal/Eastern Indian Ocean has been noticeable in recent years.

Access to Andaman and Nicobar Command

The tri-services Andaman and Nicobar Command has progressively emerged as a linchpin of India's regional maritime engagement in the Bay of Bengal and the Andaman Sea. Various multilateral and bilateral maritime engagements, i.e., the Bay of Bengal Initiative for Multi-Sectoral Technical and Economic Cooperation (BIMSTEC), the MILAN series of exercises, coordinated patrols, and bilateral exercises with littoral states in the Bay of Bengal and the Andaman Sea have contributed to this purpose. As regional maritime forces have expanded their cooperation with the Indian Navy in recent years, there is a new appreciation in Southeast Asia for India's potential in offsetting China's dominance of littoral Asia.

While regional navies of Southeast Asian countries have been making regular port calls to Port Blair, other major navies, i.e., the US, Australian, Japanese and French, have shown an interest in visiting the Andaman Islands for port calls and exercises. There have been some suggestions for coordinated surveillance of the Malacca, Sunda, Lombok and Ombai-Wetar straits through the collaborative use of the Andaman and Nicobar Islands and Australia's Keeling (Cocos) Islands. Similarly, there have also been some recommendations about collaborative anti-submarine warfare efforts in the Indian Ocean in which the Andaman and Nicobar Islands could play a critical role.

A few visits by other navies to the islands have taken place in recent years. The Royal Australian Navy has been participating in the MILAN series of exercises from 2003 onwards, which take place in the Andaman and Nicobar Islands. Also, Royal Australian Navy warships have made a few visits to Port Blair. A Japanese flotilla of minesweepers visited

Port Blair in 2011. The French Naval Ship *Var*, a logistics support ship, visited the islands in 2006. Similarly, a Royal Navy flotilla of the United Kingdom visited the islands in 2003. It needs to be highlighted that these visits have not only been sporadic, but have also been kept low-key with limited publicity, if any.

However, when it comes to the US, none of its naval ships or aircraft have been given access to the Andaman and Nicobar Islands in the past. This is a matter that needs to be rectified in light of the fact that India and the US have a Comprehensive Global Strategic Partnership and the US is India's biggest defence partner today.

Institutional reluctance

Notwithstanding episodic visits by other navies, there exists some traditional institutional reluctance towards allowing port visits to the Andaman and Nicobar Islands by foreign navies in general and the US Navy in particular. The origins of such a stand may lie in the past when the geopolitical situation was completely different.

The broader arguments against opening the Andaman and Nicobar Islands to other major navies could have been based on considerations such as:

(a) If naval vessels and military aircraft of other major navies become regular visitors to the Andaman and Nicobar Islands it could accentuate China's 'Malacca Dilemma', which refers to China's dependence on this key waterway, a lifeline for its energy needs in particular. Given the complexity of India-China bilateral relations, these strategic interactions at the islands may rile China and lead to further antagonism between the two countries.

(b) Enhancing interaction through visits by warships and military aircraft could be a slippery slope, which could progressively lead to more complex demands for strategic collaboration through the joint deployment of naval and military assets for other contingencies beyond the scope of India's direct strategic interests.

(c)   India may be seen as part of a collaborative framework against China in which other countries are already in a declared military alliance, for example, US-Australia, US-Japan, etc.

(d)   In case India takes a liberal approach towards visits by other major powers, there should be a substantive quid pro quo, particularly in relation to the US and Australia.

Analysis of considerations

The approach to the question of allowing the naval assets of other major powers—including friendly powers and partners—appears to be predicated on its conjectured impact on India-China dynamics. This appears to be the central reservation.

The China-centric approach to India's decision-making appears flawed for the following reasons:

(a)   India has complete sovereignty, territorial control and rights over its own territory. It is entirely for India to decide whether and which foreign navies can visit the Andaman and Nicobar Islands. The Malacca Strait is an international waterway. Hundreds of nations ply their naval and merchant ships through those waters, including Japan, the Republic of Korea and others. It is not used exclusively by China, nor does China have a lien on defining its strategic importance. Simply because it is a potential choke point does not mean that there is any intention on the part of India or any foreign naval vessel that India permits to visit the Andaman and Nicobar Islands, to threaten China's trade and energy flows through that waterway. In any case, foreign navies are regularly traversing the Malacca Strait and the international waters off the islands.

(b) On its part, China does not show any concern for India's sensitivities in its deployments in the Indian Ocean, not even when visiting its immediate vicinity. This is not analogous to foreign navies being permitted by India, on a case-by-case basis, to access the Andaman and Nicobar Islands. Such action is not taking place in China's immediate vicinity. India needs to delink visits by friendly navies to the islands from the so-called China factor (China's 'Malacca Dilemma').

(c) Allowing foreign naval vessels to visit the Andaman and Nicobar Islands on a case-by-case basis is not tantamount to a 'slippery slope'. It is entirely up to India to assess any future requests by foreign navies and decide whether to accede to requests for a strategic collaboration— including proposals for joint exercises— on a case-by-case basis. India retains the right to decline any activity that goes beyond its strategic interests or areas of operation.

(d) Ship visits are a normal and natural part of naval cooperation between friendly nations. This has no bearing on whether the visiting naval power has a defence partnership or alliance with third countries. China has held joint exercises with Pakistan in the Indian Ocean, and recently with Iran and Russia in the Persian Gulf and also with South Africa and Russia in the western Indian Ocean. India's concerns have not been a factor for China.

(e) If India allows the US Navy or any other navy to visit the Andaman and Nicobar Islands, indeed, there should be a well-considered quid pro quo.

Imperatives for review

An evaluation of the current policy must factor in China's unilateral approach and growing strategic objectives in the Indian Ocean. India's strategic autonomy should help it take a decision that is independent of any speculative assessments of Chinese perceptions of India's cooperation with other navies around the Andaman and Nicobar Islands.

Notwithstanding the self-imposed restraint by India in regard to granting access to the islands, China has shown scant regard for India's sensitivity in regional geopolitics. China's naval presence and strategic engagements in the Indian Ocean region have constantly seen accretion. Along with the permanent presence of a naval flotilla in the Gulf of Aden, Chinese submarines and research vessels are making regular forays in the Indian Ocean region. Of particular note is China's growing presence in the Bay of Bengal, and its strategic engagement with Myanmar, Bangladesh and Thailand, which has been significantly enhanced in recent years. The violation of India's EEZ around the Andaman and Nicobar Islands by a Chinese research vessel in December 2019 illustrated China's growing strategic presence and intentions in the Bay of Bengal.

India's strategic engagement of its partners through visits by their navies to the Andaman and Nicobar Islands cannot be construed as an alliance framework. In recent years, India has concluded logistics-sharing agreements with the US and Australia, as well as with France, Singapore and South Korea. A similar logistics-sharing agreement with Japan is in an advanced stage of negotiations. The progress on these foundational cooperative agreements, especially with the countries involved in the Quadrilateral Security Dialogue (Quad) or the Quad Plus, like South Korea, indicates that these apprehensions have been overcome.

Need for collaborative strategic anti-submarine warfare

The access to the Indian Ocean from the Pacific Ocean and vice versa is limited through defined choke points, which include the Malacca, Sunda, Lombok and Ombai-Wetar straits. Surveillance around these choke points is necessary for monitoring the movement of foreign naval vessels, particularly Chinese warships and submarines. In so far as submarines are concerned, submerged transit through the Malacca Strait is prohibited by regulations and is nearly impossible given the traffic density. The Lombok and Ombai-Wetar straits, however, do provide scope for submerged transit.

Given China's growing economic and strategic interests, Chinese naval presence in the Indian Ocean region is expected to increase, including regular forays by Chinese nuclear submarines. While monitoring warships is relatively simpler, keeping track of Chinese submarines through a wide strategic anti-submarine warfare network is an asset-intensive and complex task. A comprehensive maritime domain awareness would require granular and accurate knowledge of both surface and sub-surface actors.

The US and Japan have a robust collaboration in strategic anti-submarine warfare in the Pacific through a combination of a sound surveillance sensor chain and long-range maritime patrol aircraft. A similar approach for strategic anti-submarine warfare surveillance has been suggested in the Indian Ocean through collaboration between India, Japan, Australia and the US. In addition, there are suggestions that India and Australia could consider a collaborative deployment of their long-range maritime patrol aircraft from India's Andaman Island and Australia's Keeling (Cocos) Islands.

Recommendations

The Andaman and Nicobar Islands are a strategic asset for India to assert its dominance on the major east-west maritime trade route that passes through the Malacca Strait. It has often been referred to as India's 'unsinkable aircraft carrier' to the east. As close to 80 per cent of China's seaborne trade passes through this region, the possibility of it being throttled raises the spectre of the 'Malacca Dilemma' for China. Yet, there is no reason to deny the US, Japan, Australia, France or the

UK access to the Andaman and Nicobar Islands. Port visits can lead to further graded cooperation in all its dimensions in the islands between India and its key strategic partners.

Geographically, India does not stand to gain in any substantial way by seeking a quid pro quo to operate from Diego Garcia, the US/UK base in the Indian Ocean region. It can complicate India's relations with Mauritius, which has a historical claim over Diego Garcia/Chagos Archipelago (a claim supported by India in the International Court of Justice and the United Nations General Assembly). However, India can consider seeking in return advanced military technological transfer and transfer of sophisticated weapons, which the US may now, under the current geostrategic situation in the Indo-Pacific, be willing to provide to India.

Access to US assets to carry out operational turnaround at the Andaman and Nicobar Islands is in accordance with the Logistics Exchange Memorandum of Agreement, which is a bilateral matter that brooks no third-party interference or consideration.

In so far as Australia is concerned, the two sides upgraded their ties to a Comprehensive Strategic Partnership at the virtual summit on 4 June 2020 between Prime Minister Narendra Modi and Prime Minister Scott Morrison. Among the key pacts concluded were Mutual Logistics Support Arrangement and a Joint Declaration on a Shared Vision for Maritime Cooperation in the Indo-Pacific. In its 2017 Foreign Policy White Paper, Australia recognized India as a 'pre-eminent maritime power among Indian Ocean countries' and a 'front-rank partner of Australia'.

The strategic relevance of reciprocal access to the Andaman and Nicobar Islands and the Keeling (Cocos) Islands needs to be mutually appreciated along with the significance of Darwin, on the northern seaboard of Australia overlooking the Lombok and Sunda straits. While there exists a robust Maritime Domain Awareness (MDA) information-sharing agreement between India and Australia, the two sides should consider expanding the scope of cooperation by formalizing a protocol for ensuring an effective underwater surveillance system. This may include technical collaboration for a sound surveillance sensor chain around the Sunda and Ombai-Wetar straits. For this, both India and Australia should engage Indonesia as a key participant.

(The article first appeared as a Policy Brief on the website of the Manohar Parrikar Institute for Defence Studies and Analyses, 25 June 2020)

Quad needs a definitive blueprint to have meaningful impact

The second ministerial meeting of the four-nation Quadrilateral Security Dialogue (Quad) in Tokyo on 6 October 2020 was followed by a decision to include Australia in the Malabar 2020 naval exercise after a gap of thirteen years. The threat posed by China to the geostrategic and geo-economic landscape of the Indo-Pacific region ranks alongside the challenge of the pandemic in terms of disruption. The pandemic has stoked Chinese aggression, from the East and South China Seas to eastern Ladakh, but it has also provided others with opportunities to cooperate in maritime security, cybersecurity, data flows, quality infrastructure and healthcare.

That the 'Indo-Pacific' concept has gained fresh currency should not come as a surprise. It is an inclusive and representative term that reflects the contemporary interconnectedness of trade, technology and supply chains in a wider region. By comparison, the 'Asia-Pacific' represented the trans-Pacific strategic and economic impulses after

World War II, and was confined to East and Southeast Asia. Moreover, the Indo-Pacific is being redefined, ironically, by China's Belt and Road Initiative (BRI), debt-trap diplomacy, fictional territorial claims and a divide-and-rule strategy. The historical experience of Indo-Pacific strategies of the colonial age can help provide deeper insight into the malefic impact of China's neo-colonialism.

Beijing views the 'Indo-Pacific' as a direct threat to the BRI, and in classical 'wei qi' calculus, as an 'encirclement' strategy as part of its regional powerplay.

During his visit to Malaysia in 2020, Chinese foreign minister Wang Yi criticized the Quad, stating that Washington D.C. was aiming to build an 'Indo-Pacific NATO' through it. The very fact that China no longer describes it as 'headline grabbing' and 'foam on the sea' that would 'soon dissipate' is proof that the Quad is acquiring traction.

One can expect China to use wei qi principles and guanxi (networks and connections) to weaken the Quad, especially in Japan and Australia. The economies of these two key Quad members remain heavily dependent on China. Japan's efforts at economic decoupling and Australia's endeavours to subject Chinese investments and influence-peddling to greater scrutiny should be lauded. In all likelihood, the new Yoshihide Suga government in Japan will hold Prime Minister Abe's tough line on China, at least until the Liberal Democratic Party election in September 2021 and the lower house elections later that year. Japan's recent enabling agreements with Vietnam and Philippines for defence exports could lead to similar arrangements with Indonesia and Thailand. Hopefully, the Scott Morrison government in Australia will continue to receive full domestic support for its increasingly robust China policy.

Once a solitary voice, India's concerns about the BRI are now echoed by several countries. India took the lead in banning Chinese apps. Notably, it was India's changed assessment of the regional geopolitical situation that led to the elevation of the Quad dialogue to the ministerial level in 2019. Yet again, it is India that has shed its reticence and decided to welcome Australia to the Malabar 2020 exercise.

India's pull out from the Regional Comprehensive Economic Partnership (RCEP) negotiations last year may have appeared self-injurious then, but subsequent developments have put into sharper relief the deleterious role of China-centric supply chains.

China's actions have since led to the Resilient Supply Chain Initiative (RSCI) involving India, Japan and Australia, focused on key sectors such as semiconductors, pharmaceuticals, automobiles and telecommunications.

An ambitious China has consistently sought the expulsion of the US from its periphery. The US and others such as France and Britain are historically part of the region. The US has played a key role in the region's stability and prosperity following the Second World War. The US military presence prevented Japan from re-arming itself. It cautioned China against risking military adventurism across the Taiwan Strait that would have otherwise derailed its economic ascendance, and kept the peace on the Korean Peninsula for over six decades. Ironically, China, the biggest beneficiary of the trans-Pacific trade and investment flows, does not quite see it that way.

In the South China Sea, China's preposterous claims, island-building spree and militarization of oceanic space continue to grab headlines. China is a member of the United Nations Convention on the Law of the Sea (UNCLOS) yet disregards its precepts. Vastly adept at concocting 'historical evidence' to buttress claims, China has regularly used the classical 'wei qi' strategy of regional powerplay and playing off one against the other to fracture consensus among Association of Southeast Asian Nations (ASEAN) members. As the only major power involved in the Code of Conduct negotiations that seek to reduce the risk of conflict in the disputed waters of the South China Sea, China will probe chinks in the armour of 'ASEAN centrality' to exploit and shape outcomes.

The US position on the South China Sea is now fully in alignment with the Permanent Court of Arbitration's tribunal award of 2016. While it cannot restore status quo ante in the South China Sea, it does boost the morale of disputants such as the Philippines, who are routinely bullied by China.

In the Indian Ocean, China uses the cloak of anti-piracy deployments to maintain a quasi-permanent presence, with bases in Gwadar and Djibouti as beachheads for penetrating South Asia, the Gulf region and littoral Africa.

As was once the case in dealing with the Xiongnu—barbarians—on its northern borderlands, China continues to employ ancient stratagems to pit one nation against another on its periphery to weaken and subjugate contending forces through guile and inducements.

The Quad, having ensconced itself as the core of the free and open Indo-Pacific (FOIP) vision which revolves around ensuring a rules-based international order and securing the freedoms of navigation, overflight and unimpeded commerce on the high seas, now needs a definitive blueprint to have a meaningful impact. It should have a tough security-oriented core with a softer and inclusive exoskeleton that prioritizes the developmental agenda. The Quad Plus format should cater to the region's economic needs, including infrastructure, connectivity and capacity-building. Without generous alternatives, many countries will continue to be drawn to China, as moths to a flame.

Looking ahead, there is scope to convene a future Quad meeting in the two plus two format, with diplomats and civilian defence officials participating at the level of director general. Such an expanded format could gradually be elevated to the level of vice minister and minister. A joint statement by the four countries at the next meeting of the Quad in 2021, as against independent country statements, would also help consolidate the gains made so far.

(The article was first published in *The Indian Express*, 22 October 2020)

Yes, the Quad will endure!

The Quadrilateral Security Dialogue (Quad) Leaders' Summit held on 12 March 2021, the first of its kind, demonstrated just how quickly the four-nation dialogue involving the US, Japan, Australia and India moved from a reincarnated officials' level dialogue in 2017 to ministerial engagement in 2019 to an apex summit last month.

The Quad was born out of necessity during the coordination of relief operations after the Boxing Day tsunami in 2004. Yet, it was subject to prevarication and uncertainly on strategic challenges. The once inchoate group has now coalesced in response to the ominous clouds formed by China's economic and military ascendancy. Its form and substance are beginning to see greater alignment. Japan, for instance, was inducted as a regular partner in the Malabar naval exercise in 2015, followed by Australia last year.

Today, the Quad is complemented by a joint maritime exercise and a willingness to work together to meet the challenges of healthcare, new technologies and climate change. Here, as in the avowed goal of adhering to international law and bedrock principles such as freedom of navigation and peaceful resolution of disputes, the binding glue is provided by the antithetical alternatives posed by China. This is reflected in the emphasis on building resilient supply chains in critical and emerging technologies and in healthcare.

China's suspicions about both the Indo-Pacific and the Quad run deep. It views the Indo-Pacific concept as a direct threat to the Belt and Road Initiative (BRI), which is a gargantuan scheme aimed at creating new markets, standards and fresh growth opportunities for the Chinese economy.

Goaded into action, the US offers alternatives to Chinese 'debt trap' financing for regional infrastructure and connectivity projects through the Millennium Challenge Corporation (MCC), the Better Utilization of Investments Leading to Development (BUILD) Act, the Asia Reassurance Initiative Act (ARIA) and the energy initiative, Asia EDGE (Enhancing Development and Growth through Energy).

Japan and Australia, which have their own development assistance programmes, have joined hands with the US in the Blue Dot Network and the Indo-Pacific Business Forum. India too is promoting its own brand in the region. Over time, these have the potential to ease the BRI's vice-like grip, thus posing a long-term economic challenge to China as well.

China believes that the trilateral and quadrilateral dialogue structures, cross-servicing arrangements and naval exercises involving the US, Japan, India and Australia and others are aimed at strengthening the Quad. It naturally views the Quad through the lens of its 'wei qi' or 'encirclement' strategy, of which it has remained an avid practitioner.

In China's view, the Indo-Pacific and the Quad represent a 'Cold War mentality' and are attempts to form 'cliques' riding the back of a hyped-up 'China threat'. China suspects that the 'Indo-Pacific' reduces its salience whereas the 'Asia-Pacific' frame of reference acknowledges its centrality.

China's hopes of a better relationship with the Biden administration appeared to have been quickly dashed, going by the testy exchanges and mutual recriminations concerning US-China ties between Secretary of State Anthony Blinken, National Security Advisor Jake Sullivan and their Chinese counterparts Wang Yi and Yang Jiechi, at Anchorage in Alaska on 18 March 2021. The bilateral talks at Anchorage involved a series of meetings over a two-day period, coming in the wake of differences over trade, cyber espionage and human rights issues.

Quad statement: Pointers

The Quad leaders' joint statement, titled 'The Spirit of the Quad', not only speaks of 'ASEAN centrality' but also of ASEAN's 'unity', perhaps in recognition of the grouping's fragility on the question of China. ASEAN centrality is a mirage that no one seems to want to question. The vulnerability of Cambodia, Laos and Myanmar (the CLM trio) to Beijing's blandishments is well-recorded. Myanmar, too, is greatly dependent on China's support especially under military rule, which is a rather frequent and unfortunate phenomenon in that country.

As such, 'ASEAN centrality' is a double-edged sword. China itself would surely see advantage in the use of the term not only because of China's growing economic sway over the group, but also because the ASEAN countries are gradually becoming more dependent on China for their security. After all, China is the only external power involved in negotiating the elusive Code of Conduct on maintaining peace and stability in the disputed waters of the South China Sea with several of the ASEAN countries, and can use its clout over them to diffuse any emerging coalition against its interests.

Even though the individual statements of the US, Japan and Australia following officials' level meetings of the Quad had eschewed references to 'democracy' over the last two years to build a broader consensus with non-democracies in the region, the reference to 'democratic values', 'democratic resilience' and 'universal values' has resurfaced in the leaders' statement and is a significant pointer to the looming threat posed by China's counter-narratives in the Indo-Pacific region. The counter narrative creates doubts in several ASEAN countries that do not have Western style liberal democratic systems.

Is the Quad an alliance?

Many sceptics denigrate the Quad and warn India against getting dragged into a quagmire in areas remote to its interests such as the Pacific or the South China Sea. Others draw attention to its inability to meet China's economic or military challenge.

India's much-vaunted 'strategic autonomy' is also cited as an impediment. However, in their haste to prematurely write the Quad's obituary, they are missing some key points.

Indeed, the Quad is far from being an alliance and should not be judged by such a yardstick. At the same time, one must keep in mind that all the enabling arrangements for deeper military cooperation among the four nations are slowly and steadily coming into place. The US already has treaty alliances with Japan and Australia.

The US now has all the foundational agreements in place with India such as the Industrial Security Annex (ISA) to the General Security of Military Information Agreement (GSOMIA), the Communications Compatibility and Security Agreement (COMCASA), the Logistics Exchange Memorandum of Agreement (LEMOA) and the Basic Exchange and Cooperation Agreement (BECA).

Yet, many on the US side believe that India's reticence is a factor that holds up progress in furthering military cooperation. India now also has cross-servicing agreements with Japan and Australia, as do Japan and Australia with one another since 2017.

One can concede that the focus of each member is nuanced. India's main concerns are challenges to its land boundaries and to maritime frontiers in the Indian Ocean. The other three nations have a Pacific/South China Sea-centric approach. The Quad may have started out as the proverbial blind men feeling an elephant, but there is much greater congruence among them today on the nature, shape and size of the elephant in the room that is China.

China's rise and expansionism

The fundamental issue today is the rise of China. As its economic power aggregates over the decades into military muscle, it is increasingly pursuing unilateral policies and projecting its power in the broader region. The management of China's rise, let alone containment, is a huge challenge. This can only be done in two ways: on the basis of an existing 'open rules-based order rooted in international law' as the Quad leaders aver, or on the basis of a new one.

China bristles at suggestions that it abide by the existing rules-based order on the grounds that others have no right to unilaterally define it. It is an anti-status quo power that seeks to forge a new international order keeping intact the elements of the old order that suit it, yet redefining aspects that limit its choices on interpretation of its 'core issues' and sphere of influence.

Like some of the old colonial powers, China increasingly pursues a 'mare clausum' (closed seas) strategy, especially across the South and East China Seas. It has also adopted the 'island development' strategies of the colonials, stringing together several basing arrangements to facilitate further expansion.

The maritime challenge

Accretion in naval power has permitted China to significantly ramp up its presence in the Indian Ocean, where it has rotated about three dozen task forces over the last decade, including submarines, ostensibly for anti-piracy operations.

History reveals that attempts by major powers to upend the existing international order are met with determined resistance. Both Wilhelmine Germany and Imperial Japan suffered the consequences of a major backlash during World War I and World War II, respectively. Wilhelmine Germany's naval build-up was so rapid that it threatened to upset the equilibrium. It led to an arms race and contributed to the defeat of Germany/Central Powers by the Entente Powers. What is more interesting is that the alliance was not a pre-existing one. Japan joined in 1914, Italy in 1915 and the US as late as 1917.

Even the military alliances of World War II were arrangements of convenience, with different major powers coming on board at different times. The US entered World War II in 1941, two years after France and Britain declared war on Germany following its invasion of Poland. The Soviet Union entered the fray only after the German Wehrmacht launched an invasion of the Soviet Union in June 1941, their Non-aggression Pact of 1939 notwithstanding.

Despite the lessons of the rapid rise and fall of Kaiser Wilhelm II's navy, the Washington Naval Treaty of 1922 unravelled rapidly and could not control the naval arms race that contributed to the second Great War. Ominous from the contemporary viewpoint is the fact that no such treaty has evolved in a century since then to try and cap the disruptive build-up of the Chinese navy currently in progress. As in the case of its nuclear arsenal, there appears no compelling reason for China to agree to any restrictions on the expansion of its naval power.

Today, China's surface combatants outnumber those of the US navy, but that is not entirely a fair comparison. The Chinese navy's growth in numbers has come largely from smaller vessels such as cruisers, frigates, fast attack craft and some destroyers, with one operational carrier (Liaoning), which is half the size of any one of the US' eleven carriers (three of which—USS Theodore Roosevelt, USS Nimitz and

USS Ronald Reagan—operate in the region) and far less potent. The Japanese navy still remains ahead of the Chinese navy in sophistication.

China may not yet be a peer of the US in naval power, but it has certainly sought to bridge the gap through asymmetrical means, by developing anti-access area-denial strategies, anti-ship and carrier-killer missiles and by developing capacities to target space-based intelligence, surveillance and reconnaissance assets of the adversary.

Despite regular Chinese muscle-flexing off Taiwan, the US has not sent a carrier strike group through the Taiwan Strait since the USS Kitty Hawk last steamed through in 2007. Earlier, President Clinton had ordered two carrier strike groups to sail through in 1996. Recently, the US despatched the *USS Theodore Roosevelt*-led carrier strike group to the South China Sea through the Bashi Strait between Taiwan and the Philippines in January 2021. Neither that, nor the occasional transit of a guided-missile destroyer through the Taiwan Strait, as was the case of the *USS Barry* in April 2020, is the same as sending a carrier strike group through the Taiwan Strait where the balance of power has shifted perceptibly since the third Taiwan Strait crisis of 1995-96. At that time, the Chinese could do little other than watch two consecutive US carrier battle groups sail by through the waterway.

Some would suggest that this has given China extra confidence, perhaps even misplaced, in its own capacities. Chinese warplanes have increasingly entered Taiwan's self-declared Air Defence Identification Zone in recent days and the Chinese aircraft carrier Liaoning and its escorts have also staged exercises in the vicinity of Taiwan.

China has ramped up its submarine programme, comprising nuclear attack submarines (SSN), including the futuristic guided missile version (SSGN), along with its fleet of nuclear ballistic missile submarines (SSBNs) and conventional diesel submarines (including the rapidly growing AIP attack submarines—SSKs). These assets can enter the Indian Ocean through the Malacca and Sunda straits (where they would be spotted due to shallow depths) or sneak in undetected through the deeper Lombok and very deep Ombai-Wetar straits.

That should be a cause of worry for India. Our response has been rather good, focused on improving our intelligence, surveillance and reconnaissance assets through the P8i Sea Guardian drones and the Coastal Surveillance Radar System (CSRS), which now also covers Seychelles, Mauritius, Maldives and Sri Lanka. India has enhanced its cooperation with others through anti-submarine warfare and cross-servicing logistics pacts.

The Information Fusion Centre for the Indian Ocean Region (IFC-IOR) in Gurugram, and participation in the Regional Maritime Information Fusion Centre (RMIFC) in Madagascar, the European Maritime Awareness in the Straits of Hormuz (EMASOH) in Abu Dhabi and the IFC in Singapore, will add to India's maritime domain awareness.

The Malabar exercises are growing in sophistication with each iteration, but are nowhere near what can be described as joint operational activity as yet. As a so-called net security provider, India is working on closer cooperation with island and littoral nations of the western Indian Ocean.

While Chinese belligerence has certainly goaded the Quad into greater activity, it is not the only factor driving alignments in the Indo-Pacific. However, it represents a dominant geopolitical impulse across the region.

'An idea whose time has come'?

Unlike the archaic 'Asia-Pacific', the Indo-Pacific more closely reflects the contemporary reality of the spread of commercial and economic progress beyond East and Southeast Asia to encompass South Asia and the east coast of Africa as well.

The East Asia Summit (EAS) process, which acknowledges ASEAN centrality and includes the US as well as China and Russia, offers a good platform to explore a more inclusive architecture for the Indo-Pacific.

Prime Minister Modi's advocacy of the Indo-Pacific Oceans Initiative (IOPO) at the EAS Summit in Bangkok in 2019 complements his Shangri-La Dialogue address delivered in Singapore the previous year. The main thrust of PM Modi's address at the Shangri-La conference was on building an inclusive architecture for cooperation in the Indo-Pacific. The IOPO initiative further emphasized a global 'open to all' framework for securing maritime boundaries, trade and resources in seven key areas: Capacity-Building and Resource Sharing; Disaster Risk Reduction and Management; Maritime Ecology; Maritime Resources; Maritime Security; Science, Technology and Academic Cooperation; and Trade Connectivity and Maritime Transport.

India has been advocating the use of the EAS forum to promote its vision of an inclusive Indo-Pacific through the seven pillars for cooperation, itself taking the lead in two areas—maritime security and disaster resilient infrastructure. It is understandable, though, that China and Russia, the outliers, are loath to countenance the term 'Indo-Pacific' in the context of the EAS.

Contemporary contradictions

The Indo-Pacific, on the other hand, is more of an organic regional process that seeks the broadest possible common denominators on evolving geostrategic and geo-economic issues. Yet, it is not bereft of contradictions. The US proposes a free and open Indo-Pacific without having acceded to the United Nations Convention on the Law of the Sea treaty although it helped shape the convention. The US is a torchbearer of freedom of navigation, innocent passage, free trade and much else. Yet, US positions are not based on UNCLOS but on customary international law.

In a sense, the US is like the modern-day Hugo Grotius, the famous sixteenth-century Dutch lawyer who was commissioned by the Dutch East India Company to write a legal brief, justifying why Holland rejected the Portuguese definition of mare clausum in the Strait of Malacca. Grotius had claimed that the seas, like the air one breathes, could not be appropriated and that the seas were international territory that all nations were free to use. Grotius' legacy of mare liberum (open seas) is reflected in the concept of the free and open Indo-Pacific against the challenge of China's arbitrary Air Defence Identification Zone and its unilateral definitions of territory in the South China Sea.

But, as part of its exceptionalism, the US regularly conducts freedom of navigation operations (FONOPs) against friend and foe alike. On 7 April 2021, an Arleigh Burke-class guided missile destroyer of the Seventh Fleet, the *USS John Paul Jones*, carried out a FONOP near India's Lakshadweep Islands. The official statement of the Seventh Fleet stated that it '…asserted navigational rights and freedoms approximately 130 nautical miles west of the Lakshadweep Islands, inside India's exclusive economic zone, without requesting India's prior consent, consistent with international law'.

The US also rejects Part XI of UNCLOS, which defines areas beyond national jurisdiction (including their seabed resources) as the common heritage of the global community to be regulated through the International Seabed Authority. The US rejects what it regards as excessive claims of others in relation to their exclusive economic zones (EEZs). In this context, it treats the Chinese injunction against foreign military exercises in its EEZ and the Indian requirement of advance notification with equal disdain.

As a great power, the US is capable of the duality of engagement, with trade friction, human rights preaching and deeper military engagement proceeding parallelly. China, too, increasingly pursues 'exceptionalism with Chinese characteristics', seeking to rewrite the rules of existing and prospective global structures to accommodate its rising economic and military power. However, China also focuses on strategies to woo individual countries and constituencies in order to shape outcomes. Its actions may run contrary to the 'rules-based order' but are not without a degree of success.

One of the weaknesses of the Indo-Pacific is the absence of an overarching trading bloc in which all like-minded countries can harmonize their fundamental economic interests. India is absent from both the Comprehensive and Progressive Trans-Pacific Partnership (CPTPP) and the Regional Comprehensive Economic Partnership (RCEP). The US, too, is absent, but may reconsider joining the CPTPP. China rules the roost in the RCEP, ironically, in tandem with a key Quad member, Japan.

Meanwhile, China also cut a deal with the EU in the dying days of the Trump administration—the Comprehensive Agreement on Investment, pushed through by an over-zealous Germany. Of course, the European Council and the European Parliament have yet to approve it and ratification may take years.

The other tough reality is that economic disengagement from China is not much of an option for any country. However, 'less of China' in one's economy is achievable and that is precisely what the Quad countries are trying to achieve, especially in critical technologies such as 5G and artificial intelligence (AI), key supply chains, connectivity and infrastructure financing.

Another stress point is the colonial legacy or territorial possessions of the US, Britain and France, which are all resident powers of the Indo-Pacific. Britain, the erstwhile colonial power, is embroiled in a dispute with Mauritius over the return of Diego Garcia in the Chagos Archipelago, with India fully supporting Mauritius. Two years before Mauritius achieved independence from Britain in 1968, the latter had leased Diego Garcia to the US for fifty years for use as a military base and thereafter unilaterally extended the lease for another twenty years in 2016 despite Mauritius' protests.

The International Court of Justice has since ruled in favour of Mauritius, and the United Nations General Assembly has also passed a resolution endorsing Mauritius' stand, again with India's support. Some argue that there is a moral deficit in the US demand that China should respect the ruling of the Permanent Court of Arbitration in favour of the Philippines in 2016 in the South China Sea when it is not prepared to follow the same example.

France, too, is not without its own legacy issues. The people of Comoros have been protesting to reclaim Mayotte from France in the Indian Ocean. All this can potentially weaken support for the presence of the US, Britain and France in the Indian Ocean to offset the growing Chinese footprint.

The return of the prodigals

The Biden administration appears as determined as its predecessor to make up for the lost decade of this century, when the global war on terror and the global economic and financial crises absorbed the US to such an extent that China opportunistically sprang into action to occupy the vacuum. The return of the US is increasingly predicated on the notion of the Indo-Pacific, with multiple partnerships throughout the region, including with India.

France, Britain, Germany, the Netherlands, all ex-colonial powers in the Indo-Pacific, as well as the EU as a whole, have developed their own Indo-Pacific vision statements. France is a potent power, but tends to plough an independent furrow. It sits uneasily with the US. It is best for India to engage France bilaterally to shore up its own position in the western Indian Ocean on maritime security, counterterrorism, etc.

Germany, the Netherlands and the EU have all pegged their Indo-Pacific vision statements on mercantilist goals. Their primary objective is to sustain their economic and commercial interests in the region, especially with China.

A post-Brexit Britain is keen to return to greater engagement with Asia, a region with which it has great familiarity. Under the rubric of 'Global Britain', it is now also demonstrating willingness to recommit its naval power to the Indo-Pacific as evident in the despatch of the Queen Elizabeth aircraft carrier to Japan in 2021. On its part, Japan is perhaps the only one among the former colonial powers to have successfully recast its image as a pacifist power committed to economic growth and development.

The Quad's uniqueness

In contrast to the, as yet, more diffuse concept of the Indo-Pacific, the Quad is already a well-defined grouping. Its focus is on developing a habit of cooperation as a response to common concerns and challenges.

While there is every reason to strive for an inclusive Indo-Pacific, the Quad cannot, and should not, be hastily expanded. A premature expansion could dilute its focus. This should not rule out engagement with diverse countries such as Brazil, Israel, New Zealand, South Korea and Vietnam in the 'Quad Plus' format.

An ontological approach will not provide an accurate understanding of the Quad. Just because it exists does not mean that it is against China. At the same time, it is definitely for an open, rules-based order rooted in international law to advance security and prosperity, and is committed to countering threats in the Indo-Pacific and beyond, just as the Quad leaders have stated in their joint statement.

It is not an alliance as yet. As the Latin phrase goes, '*A posse ad esse non valet consequentia*'. One cannot conjecture from the mere possibility of an alliance that it does exist, or even that it must exist.

Nor should the lack of a full-fledged alliance in the Quad lead one to summarily disparage its potential role in influencing the processes of peace and security in the twenty-first century. After all, the two great wars of the last century reveal that alliances can emerge quite easily in particular situations.

The fact is that, all said, the Quad is definitely here to stay. It is no longer 'ocean foam that will soon dissipate', as Chinese foreign minister Wang Yi once put it.

The Quad's future will depend on the choices that China makes. The greater China's belligerence, the faster will the Quad's military-security agenda gather steam, perhaps even moving up into a two plus two dialogue format.

The future of the Indo-Pacific concept, on the other hand, will depend on whether others can offer attractive alternatives to China's economic and financial loans and assistance for developmental purposes.

(The article first appeared as a policy brief on the website of the Manohar Parrikar Institute for Defence Studies and Analyses, 9 April 2021)

An Indian sail to navigate the maritime environment

Prime Minister Narendra Modi's address on 9 August 2021 at the United Nations Security Council high-level open debate on 'Enhancing Maritime Security: A Case For International Cooperation', convened by India, was both timely and apt. He described the oceans as a common heritage for humankind and a lifeline for the future of the planet. In urging the global community to develop a common framework to deal with contemporary challenges, including maritime disputes and natural disasters, he outlined a far-sighted vision rooted in India's culture, history and geography.

Maritime traditions

With a long coastline and large island chains spreadeagled across the Indian Ocean, India has a natural seaward orientation, with key sea lanes of communication coursing through its surrounding seas.

India has ancient maritime traditions. In the fifteenth century, Vasco de Gama was piloted to the west coast of India from Zanzibar by a Gujarati seaman. Long before that, India's ancient mariners were trading with the old world. According to some, the very word navigation is derived from the Sanskrit word 'navgath'.

PM Modi enunciated five key principles in his address: removing barriers to legitimate maritime trade; peaceful settlement of maritime disputes on the basis of international law; cooperation in facing natural disasters and maritime threats created by non-state actors; preserving the maritime environment and resources; and, encouraging responsible maritime connectivity. Mr Modi also linked free and open trade to India's civilizational ethos. His words were a reminder of India's maritime trade with Mesopotamia 4,500 years ago. Lothal was a key maritime centre of the Indus Valley civilization.

The Prime Minister's home state, Gujarat, has one of India's oldest maritime histories. Kutch and Kathiawar as well as the Malabar coast enjoyed ancient links to Africa. A ship built indigenously and manned by a local crew voyaged to England and back in the time of Rao Godji II (1760-78) of Kutch. Buddhism and Hinduism spread to Southeast Asia by the maritime route. Even Islam took the maritime route from India to Southeast Asia.

Mr Modi reiterated the relevance of Security and Growth for All in the Region (SAGAR). He urged the international community to develop a cooperative and inclusive framework for maritime security, so essential for unimpeded trade and commerce. Ninety per cent of global trade is conducted on the high seas, for the simple reason that it continues to be the most cost effective mode of transport.

Disruption of sea lanes of communication has global repercussions. The blockage in the Suez Canal in early 2021 interrupted the flow of trade worth billions of dollars. In 1956, great powers intervened militarily when Egypt nationalized this key waterway. Today, a naval blockade at any choke point in the Indo-Pacific could prove catastrophic.

Freedom of navigation and unimpeded commerce are key to the spread of prosperity. Critical supply chains depend on the concept of mare liberum (open seas). The neo-colonial concept of mare clausum (closed seas) in the South China Sea is anathema to the future of the global economy.

Dispute settlement

Prime Minister Modi advocated peaceful settlement of maritime disputes on the basis of international law. This idea is rooted in India's values of peace and non-violence. India's acceptance of the award by the Permanent Court of Arbitration in 2014 paved the way for India and Bangladesh to put aside their maritime dispute and forge even closer ties. The award favoured Bangladesh, giving it 19,467 sq. km (76 per cent) of the total 25,602 sq. km maritime area, with India getting only 6,135 sq. km (24 per cent). The judgment also awarded to Bangladesh a 200-mile exclusive economic zone, the continental shelf beyond the 200-mile economic zone and access to the open sea. India's graceful acceptance of the award should be an example to others in the region. In 2016, China summarily rejected the Permanent Court of Arbitration ruling in favour of the Philippines and rejecting China's expansive claims to the South China Sea as devoid of historical evidence

Today, natural disasters and maritime threats posed by non-state actors have grown exponentially. Mr Modi called upon the global community to rally together to deal effectively with the ravages of cyclones, tsunami and maritime pollution. India's role as first responder in the Indian Ocean, whether in thwarting piracy or providing relief after the Boxing Day tsunami in 2004, is well-documented. The Indian

Air Force airlifted 30 tonnes of relief material to Mauritius in August 2020 to contain an oil spill that threatened to engulf the island nation's pristine coast.

The Indian Coast Guard's operational reach and capability has vastly improved in dealing with environmental hazards and piracy. The election, on 5 August 2021, of the Director General of the Indian Coast Guard as the executive director of the Regional Cooperation Agreement on Combating Piracy and Armed Robbery against Ships in Asia (ReCAAP) Information Sharing Centre, Singapore, is an endorsement of India's contributions. India now has white shipping agreements with several countries. The Indian navy's state-of-the-art Information Fusion Centre-Indian Ocean Region (IFC-IOR) based in Gurugram hosts officers from the United States, Japan, France, Australia and the United Kingdom. The Indian Navy regularly offers a large number of training slots to friendly countries.

Environmental concerns

Mr Modi's remarks underscored the importance of preserving the maritime environment and its resources. The oceans remain our lifeline. Yet, they have been overwhelmed by plastic waste, which chokes all forms of marine life. This, in turn, poisons the entire food chain and imperils the lives of millions.

Development of connectivity and infrastructure were also outlined as a major priority. There are heightened concerns today over China's Belt and Road Initiative. India stands for openness and transparency in the execution of projects, based on local priorities, with in-built fiscal viability and environmental sustainability. The US, Japan and Australia are also promoting better standards for global infrastructure through the Blue Dot Network.

Primacy of UNCLOS

As president of the United Nations Security Council for the month of August, India's leadership in the debate on maritime security, that too at the level of the prime minister, has strengthened its credentials as a key stakeholder in the maritime commons. The presidential statement issued on the occasion highlights the commitment of the United Nations Security Council to international law. More relevantly, it emphasizes the importance of the United Nations Convention on the Law of the Sea (UNCLOS) as the legal framework governing all maritime activity.

India's natural interests stretch across both the Indian and Pacific oceans as reflected in its inclusive Indo-Pacific vision. No doubt, India's initiative will further the prospects for a stable and enduring maritime environment.

(The article first appeared in *The Hindu*, 14 August 2021)

Japan as a strategic partner

India and Japan have undergone a major transformation at the strategic and economic levels since 2014, with Prime Minister Narendra Modi and Prime Minister Shinzo Abe investing personal capital in deepening bilateral ties. The partnership has received a big boost due to the personal attention given to the relationship by Prime Minister Modi. In fact, he has nurtured these ties from the time he was the chief minister of Gujarat. Japan is one of the few countries with which India has an annual summit at the level of the two heads of government.

In the words of Prime Minister Modi, 'India and Japan will play a major role in Asia's emergence. The growing convergence between India and Japan on strategic and economic issues has the capacity to stimulate the global economy'. Prime Minister Abe and his successors have considered robust relations between Japan and India to be a public good.

The Special Strategic and Global Partnership with Japan is now a cornerstone of India's Act East policy, which dovetails (in terms of intent and purpose) with Japan's Enhanced Partnership for Quality Infrastructure. The bilateral Act East Forum seeks to provide connecting tissue by developing India's Northeast.

As two of Asia's largest democracies, India and Japan have shared values that emphasize openness and transparency, rule of law and freedom of navigation and commerce in the Indo-Pacific region. Both nations are committed to an international rules-based order.

The interface between India and Japan at the strategic level has also broadened due to dialogue and cooperation in the context of the Quadrilateral Security Dialogue and the desire to work together to realize the goal of a free and open Indo-Pacific region.

Together with the others in the Quad, that is, the US and Australia, India and Japan are working on themes such as developmental finance, infrastructure development and critical supply chains in order to provide better alternatives to China's Belt and Road projects to countries in the Indo-Pacific. Japan plays a key role in anchoring the connectivity vertical in the Indo-Pacific Oceans Initiative (IPOI).

Prime Minister Kishida's visit to India in March 2022, which took place against the backdrop of the seventieth anniversary of diplomatic ties, provided an invaluable opportunity to work in tandem for sustainable growth in a post-Covid world with a focus on the Quad Vaccine Partnership, critical technologies, resilient supply chains, infrastructure and clean energy.

It has been argued by some that India's absence from the Comprehensive and Progressive Agreement for Trans Pacific Partnership (CPTPP) and the Regional Comprehensive Economic Partnership (RCEP) places limits on bilateral economic cooperation between India and Japan. The CPTPP is an agreement between eleven countries of the Asia-Pacific aimed at reducing or eliminating tariffs, and includes Japan. The RCEP is a trade agreement between fifteen Asia-Pacific countries, including China and Japan.

The Indo-Pacific Economic Framework (IPEF) proposed by the US is likely to help overcome these gaps and create new opportunities for cooperation on desired verticals. The IPEF also signals a fundamental shift in the US outlook towards the region, which so far had been highly security oriented. This had enabled China to gain the lead since its view on the region was multi-pronged in which economic objectives served to advance its strategic and security interests.

Despite reservations expressed in some quarters, there is little doubt that the Quad will strengthen in years to come. It is here to stay. It is developing a habit of cooperation on several geo-economic and geostrategic issues. Its future will also be determined by the actions of other states such as China.

Given the flux in international relations and the disruptions to stability in Asia as well as Europe, there are some who question the resilience of our bilateral ties. The fact is that the foundations of India-Japan relations are very strong. They run deep, based on our cultural and economic ties.

The India-Japan partnership cannot arbitrarily be benchmarked to geopolitical issues rocking the world, whether in Ukraine or elsewhere. Naturally, both India and Japan have their own views on international issues and the two sides must respect one another for that.

Japan as anchor in India's economic transformation

Although the India-Japan economic partnership has always been important, it has begun to achieve its true potential only in recent years.

Today, Japan is an indispensable anchor in India's economic transformation.

Japan has now emerged as a very important player in the infrastructure sector in India. It is part of major projects, whether roads, metros or high-speed railways. In the decade between 2008 and

2018, approximately 64 per cent of Japan International Cooperation Agency's (JICA) soft loans have been in the transport sector.

High-speed railway

The Mumbai-Ahmedabad high-speed rail project is an iconic example of Japanese technology as well as a symbol of strategic partnership and mutual trust. As Prime Minister Modi said, the first bullet train project will act as a catalyst for rapid economic progress and technological growth and innovation in India. Japan's presence in this high-speed rail project is expected to revolutionize the vast Indian railway sector, just as Suzuki Motors' entry into India thirty-five years ago fundamentally altered the Indian automotive sector and led to the presence of Japanese vendors, small and medium enterprises (SMEs) and supply chains in India. It will also create new avenues for employment, economic advancement and entrepreneurial activity.

The bullet train can be the future answer to smart cities by linking the heart of an urban centre to that of another city, resulting in savings in terms of commute and land costs. Besides high-speed rail, Japanese technology under Japan International Cooperation Agency (JICA)'s technical Cooperation Projects helps India in 'capacity development on railway safety' focusing on track maintenance, rail welding, rolling stock maintenance and metro projects. The emergence of high-speed railways in India will complement the Delhi-Mumbai industrial corridor, the Chennai-Bengaluru industrial corridor, and the western dedicated freight corridor, all being built with Japanese assistance.

Overseas development assistance (ODA) and investments

India is Japan's largest ODA partner while Japan is the fifth largest investor in India with cumulative foreign direct investment (FDI) inflows of $36.2 billion since 2000, which make up 7.13 per cent of India's total FDI inflows during the same period. Bilateral trade in 2020-21 stood at $18.5 billion. Although the trade balance is in Japan's favour, it is Japanese FDI that is of greater relevance to India's economic ambitions.

Japanese investments in India are on the rise. Between 2014 and 2019, the target of JPY 3.5 trillion (equivalent to about US$31.5 billion at the average exchange rate of one US$=JPY 110) worth of ODA and investment flows into India was achieved. The shared intention to realize JPY5 trillion (approximately $42 billion at average prevailing rates of exchange) of public and private investment and financing from Japan to India over the next five years between 2022 to 2027 is a measure of the confidence on both sides in the future of the partnership.

The outlining of the India-Japan Industrial Competitiveness Partnership (IJICP) roadmap during the summit should help improve manufacturing standards in India in the micro, small and medium enterprises (MSME) sector, which accounts for a large chunk (38 per cent) of India's exports. If we can get our MSMEs to become more competitive, we can really improve our standing in terms of exports to global markets.

The number of Japanese companies registered in India is rising. More than half of these are manufacturing firms. Every year, approximately 100 new Japanese companies are establishing their presence in India, including through joint ventures and acquisition of Indian companies. Of late, Japanese investments have made their presence felt in not only manufacturing but also in the logistics and service sectors. India's capital markets have also been attracting Japanese funds.

During Prime Minister Kishida's visit to India in March 2022, the two sides renewed the $75 billion currency swap agreement, which had been concluded during Prime Minister Modi's visit to Japan in October 2018.

This will deepen financial cooperation, strengthen financial safety nets and contribute to regional and global financial stability.

                         Sujan R. Chinoy

India's flagship projects

Japan has a significant presence in virtually every flagship initiative of the Government of India, including Digital India, Smart Cities, Startup India, Ayushman Bharat and others. Both sides have been working together to build stronger ties in new areas such as healthcare, disaster risk reduction, food processing, digital technology, waste-to-energy and waste management.

India and Japan have sought to deepen their cooperation in the agriculture and food sectors. In May 2018, the Japan India Food Business Council was established to facilitate investments and joint ventures, especially under the Make in India initiative in the food processing sector and in cold chains, distribution and mega food parks.

The Suzuki-Toshiba-Denso joint venture for automotive lithium-ion battery packs for the domestic and global markets as well as the export of made-in-India Baleno cars are seen as success stories of Japanese assistance in the Make in India programme.

A significant step forward during the author's term in Japan was the establishment of a series of Japan-India Institutes for Manufacturing (JIMs) and the Japanese Endowed Courses in regional colleges under which Japanese companies in India could participate in skills development programmes. Maruti Suzuki India Limited, for example, has trained students in Japanese manufacturing practices and processes at the JIM in Mehsana, Gujarat. Some JIMs offer special courses for female students, such as in the Uncha Majra JIM in Gurugram, launched by Maruti Suzuki in 2019. Similarly, Daikin Airconditioning India Pvt Ltd too established a JIM in Neemrana in 2017 to provide equal opportunities to female students. Today, about a dozen JIMs have been successfully launched around the country. More than 3,700 Indians were trained in JIMs and Japanese Endowed Courses in 2021 alone.

Similarly, Japan Industrial Townships provide investment incentives commensurate with the principal policy framework, for instance, in the operation of special economic zones and national investment and manufacturing zones. At present, there are 114 Japanese companies across the Japan Industrial Townships. Japan is the only country in the world to have twelve dedicated country-focused industrial townships in nine states across India. The India-Japan Industrial Competitiveness Partnership Roadmap that came out of the Modi-Kishida summit will further advance industrial and manufacturing standards in India in the MSME sector.

Healthcare

Japan has many strengths in the healthcare sector. There is a great deal that India and Japan can do together in this sector, especially in medical devices, trauma and geriatric care.

Our cooperation in healthcare is a new initiative launched in 2018, aimed at building synergies between Japan's Asia Health and Wellness Initiative and India's Ayushman Bharat healthcare scheme, which aims to provide quality and affordable healthcare to all citizens. The project envisages the creation of more than 1,50,000 primary healthcare centres dealing primarily with trauma and geriatric care. There is growing interest in Japan in Ayurveda, India's ancient traditional medicine system. In fact, the author succeeded in getting the first-ever memorandum of cooperation concluded between the Ministry of Ayush (Ayurveda, yoga and naturopathy, unani, siddha and homeopathy) and the Kanagawa Prefecture on Ayurveda and yoga during the visit of Prime Minister Modi to Japan in October 2018.

Resilient supply chains

Today, there is unprecedented emphasis on decoupling and creating alternative resilient supply chains, as seen at the Quad Summit Meeting in March 2021. Within the Quad, the India-Japan-Australia

Resilient Supply Chain Initiative launched in April 2021 is focused on diversification of supply chains.

Strategic supply chains, especially semiconductors, pharmaceuticals and telecommunications, must be restructured so as to reduce an undue dependence on China. Japan has earmarked $2.2 billion to enable its manufacturers to shift production from China to Japan or to relocate to other economies. Although only two companies relocated to India in the first round, namely, Sumida Corporation (auto components) and Toyota Tsusho Co. Ltd (rare earths), there is great scope to attract more Japanese companies as they seek to reduce the over-dependence on China-based supply chains. India will no doubt have to compete with Southeast Asian economies and provide equally good incentives to Japanese companies to succeed. Infrastructure, connectivity, logistical support, cost-effective warehousing, highly skilled yet cheap labour and a suitable legal framework are some of the core areas that need to be addressed. The production-linked incentive scheme of India gives incentives on incremental sales from products made in India across select sectors, is intended to boost the manufacturing sector and reduce imports. The PLI scheme is expected to attract Japanese investments as well.

Science and technology

Japan is at the cutting edge of technological advancement, including in artificial intelligence (AI), big data and internet of things (IoT). The memorandum of cooperation in cybersecurity and information and communication technology (ICT), signed during Prime Minister Kishida's visit, will advance information sharing and capacity-building in a digital era.

There is great scope in our bilateral partnership to find the right points of intersection between Society 5.0 of Japan and Digital India and Startup India in India. Society 5.0 is a new blueprint that aims to create a super-smart society, going beyond the Fourth Industrial Revolution. It seeks to transform the way of life by integrating cyberspace and the physical space. As a result, there is enormous potential for creating institutional mechanisms for cooperation in the areas of AI, big data and IoT. The India-Japan Digital Partnership (I-JDP) launched in October 2018 is aimed at propelling our cooperation in digital ICT. A memorandum of understanding (MoU) to enhance cooperation in ICT was signed in January 2021. It will promote cooperation in 5G technologies, telecom security and submarine optical fibre cable. Connecting Chennai and the Andaman and Nicobar Islands with submarine optical fibre cable is a successful example of India-Japan cooperation.

Japanese companies have invested billions of dollars in Indian start-ups. The Japan-India Startup Hub was launched in October 2018. It serves as an interface between respective start-ups and firms, facilitating collaboration with Japanese markets and Japanese investors. Startup India (under Invest India) and Japan Innovation Network have signed an MoU in June 2018 on innovation collaboration with a focus on Sustainable Development Goals (SDGs), connecting the start-up ecosystems in the two countries. The Japan-India IT corridor in Hiroshima has enormous potential in promoting B2B cooperation, attracting highly skilled labour and establishing collaboration between respective industries and institutions. While Hiroshima offers cutting-edge manufacturing technology, it lacks in IT and software industry, and this is where India can step in.

Movement of professionals

Another major area of progress is in regard to the movement of professionals. In January 2021, India and Japan signed a memorandum of cooperation on a basic partnership framework for the operation of the Specified Skilled Worker programme under which the Japanese government will accept Indian nationals who have a certain level of expertise and skill (professionals and IT talent) to work in Japan for limited periods of time. This will enable India and Japan to develop a robust digital partnership. Japanese companies, faced with the problem of an ageing society, have begun recruiting young IT professionals from India through job fairs in order to improve their own global competitiveness. Given the demographic landscape, Japan will also require skilled health workers such as caregivers and nurses.

The specified skilled worker programme is founded on an earlier path-breaking agreement concluded during the author's term as ambassador to Japan. It relates to the participation of Indian technical workers in the Japanese job market under the Technical Intern Training Programme for on-the-job training and working for a period of three to five years. This is an ideal platform through which the relative strengths of India and Japan can be leveraged for mutual benefit. Indian workers are trained in Japanese culture and shop-floor practices before being sent to Japan for productive periods of employment. When they return to India, they would become the nuclei for further change in the Indian economy by propagating Japanese best practices.

The launch of collaboration between Indian and Japanese universities as well as Japanese language teachers' training centres in India will promote avenues for cutting-edge research and collaboration and deepen people-to-people contact, respectively.

Given its history, Japan is a natural partner for India when it comes to the development of India's Northeast region. An India-Japan Coordination Forum on Development of Northeast was instituted in August 2017. In June 2019, Japan committed to investing JPY205.784 billion (approximately Rs 13,000 crore) in the Northeast region in projects ranging from sustainable agriculture to forestry, and biodiversity and environmental conservation. Japan initiated the IRIS programme in 2017 under which youth from Manipur and Nagaland are periodically selected to visit Japan for training and participation in capacity-building programmes.

Development of India's Northeast

The Act East Forum, established in 2017, seeks to build robust infrastructure within the states of Northeast India and then connect them to the emerging markets of Southeast Asia via the India–Myanmar–Thailand trilateral highway, the Kaladan multimodal transit transport project, the Asian highway network and the South Asia Sub-regional Economic Cooperation Road Connectivity Investment Programme. Japan has also provided considerable ODA loans for the Northeast Road Network Connectivity Improvement Project and for the improvement of NH-54, NH-51 and NH-40 in Mizoram and Meghalaya, and NH-208 (Kailashahar–Khowai).

Forest management projects in Sikkim, Nagaland and Tripura are in the pipeline. Oxygen generation plants are being set up in the Northeast with Japan's assistance through the United Nations Development Programme (UNDP). The Miyawaki forest technology of Japan has become hugely popular in India. The Miyawaki method of afforestation uses native plants to grow dense urban forests and expand the green cover in a very short span of time.

Tackling natural disasters

It is in the area of disaster risk reduction that Japan can truly play an important role. Japan is a country that has frequently faced natural disasters such as tsunamis, earthquakes and landslides in mountainous regions. Its best practices and the use of technologies to prevent disasters, including the building of disaster resilient infrastructure, is of great relevance to India. India also looks to Japan for partnerships in the development of smart islands. Fisheries and cold chains in the Andaman and Nicobar Islands, or elsewhere along India's long coastline, are an important element in the development of the blue economy and promoting livelihood for the coastal population. A Japanese grant is being used for a project to improve power supply in the Andaman and Nicobar Islands, including grid stabilization.

During the author's term as ambassador in Tokyo, the CEO of Sushi Zanmai chain of restaurants, Mr Kiyoshi Kimura, had expressed interest in collaborating with India in view of the depleting tuna reserves around Japan. The advantages of Sushi Zanmai collaborating with the fisheries department in the state of Tamil Nadu in India to equip local fishermen with Japanese fishing equipment and preservation technologies to augment their tuna catch for consumption in Japan were also apparent. This is an example of creating resilient supply chains for Japanese consumers for sushi and sashimi.

Defence manufacturing

Cooperation in defence manufacturing can grow under the Government of India's Atmanirbhar Bharat and Make in India initiatives. There are many opportunities for Japanese companies to enter into joint ventures and tie-ups with reputable Indian defence manufacturers, provided Japanese companies think big. The key question is whether Japanese companies are ready to risk entering into joint ventures or 100 per cent investments in India in this sector without any guarantee of contracts beforehand. They also need to compete with other global manufacturers who are more familiar with the Indian market. They cannot be in this space if they always expect government-to-government contracts of the type they are used to in the protected Japanese environment. Most Indian majors in the defence sector would be open to the idea of collaborating with Japanese companies provided the costs of technology and production in India are competitive. Of particular interest to Japan is the drone market in India.

5G technology

The security risks inherent in Chinese 5G network equipment are compelling. India and Japan can work together in 5G and radio access network (RAN) technology. Japanese companies are gearing up for the 5G race, which is at present dominated by Huawei, Ericsson, Nokia and others. NTT and NEC of Japan have joined forces to expand their footprint in the global market. Rakuten of Japan is launching the 5G network based on open RAN technology in Tokyo, Nagoya and Osaka. It has enlisted the help of Indian tech companies. Rakuten is collaborating with Indian companies such as Sterlite Technologies for hardware, and with HCL, Wipro and Tech Mahindra for software. Meanwhile, India's Reliance Jio has designed and developed a 5G solution. It is likely to be ready for trials as soon as the 5G spectrum is available. It is reported that both Jio and Rakuten rely upon the open RAN technology.

Liberalized visa regime

Before the pandemic disrupted travel, India had extended visa-on-arrival, e-Tourist visas and ten-year business visas to eligible Japanese travellers to facilitate business and people-to-people exchanges. There are growing links between Japan's prefectures and states in India. An MoU between Gujarat state and Hyogo Prefecture and a partner city agreement between Kyoto and Varanasi are some of the notable ones.

Recently, the Indo-Japan Friendship Association of Gujarat, of which the author is the honorary advisory patron, worked with Hyogo Prefecture and the Ahmedabad Management Association to create the first-ever Zen-Kaizen garden in Ahmedabad, inaugurated virtually by Prime Minister Modi.

The list of stakeholders in our deepening engagement is growing. There is every reason to believe that the India-Japan economic partnership is set to grow. Rationalized taxation, amended labour laws and free flow of data by rescinding regulations on data localization are some of the areas of concern of Japanese companies in India. A focused attempt to resolve the concerns of Japanese investors on logistics, customs clearance, export procedures and quality issues will help.

Indian industry also needs to understand Japanese cultural nuances. Japan commands international repute for its management practices, production methods, quality control and management. The Japanese standards of kaizen or its just-in-time efficient inventory control and their punctuality define their national character. Kaizen is a Japanese concept that seeks to implement continuous improvement in manufacturing processes, often through small, practical and incremental changes. India on its part will have to adapt to Japanese standards and best practices to enhance mutual confidence with Japanese counterparts. This, in turn, will provide a fillip to bilateral trade and business ties in the twenty-first century, particularly in relation to small and medium enterprises that play an important role in Japan's economy.

Cultural ties

Our cultural ties with Japan are anchored in history. They provide a firm bedrock to our partnership. We have a shared legacy of Hindu-Buddhist thought and philosophy. It is a legacy witnessed in the association of Indian monk Bodhisena with the consecration of the Great Buddha statue at the Todaiji Temple in Nara more than twelve hundred years ago, and with Bodhidharma, the founder of Zen (Dhyan) Buddhism. We share some rituals and ceremonies, even some words. The Sanskrit Siddham (Beej Akshar) script is present in Japan due to our ancient contacts. There are many deities that we worship in common, such as Ganesh, Saraswati and Laxmi.

There is great interest in Japan in Indian dance, music, yoga and Ayurveda.

In fact, there is deep mutual respect for one another's culture. One of the most outstanding enactments of the Indian epic Mahabharata is by a famous Japanese Kabuki troupe, directed by renowned theatre director Satoshi Miyagi and featuring actor Kikunosuke Onoe who plays the role of Karna. There are others in Japan who have related easily to Indian culture and have explored it in their art and literature.

Among Mahatma Gandhi's cherished personal possessions were small statues of Mizaru, Kikazaru and Iwazaru, the three wise monkeys, gifted to him by Nichidatsu Fujii, a Japanese monk and founder of the Nipponzan-Myōhōji order of Buddhism (also known as Fuji Guruji) who had visited Gandhiji in Wardha in the 1930s. Justice Radha Binod Pal is a revered name in Japan for his lone dissenting position during the International Military Tribunal of the Far East, also known as the Tokyo Tribunal. Gurudev Rabindranath Tagore's admiration for Japan and interaction with Okakura Tenshin were instrumental in forging early connections between artists and intellectuals on both sides. Netaji Subhas Chandra Bose and other freedom fighters also had a long association with Japan.

Kazuki Ebine, a Japanese manga artist, has published a powerfully illustrated biography on Mahatma Gandhi and his teachings. Recently, *Ramayana: Legend of Prince Rama*, a famous anime film co-produced by Indians and the Japanese, was relaunched in Japan in its latest digital version. The original version was produced by Japanese director Yogo Sako, animator Ram Mohan and music composer Vanraj Bhatia from India. What a wonderful way to bring our two peoples together!

There exists immense potential for combining Japan's enormous capital, technology and innovation with India's own rich human resources and skills. India has emerged as the fastest growing economy in the post-pandemic recovery phase, and this is an especially opportune moment to ramp up our economic partnership.

There is much that India and Japan can do together to promote peace and prosperity in the Indo-Pacific region. Our values-based partnership covers our discourse and cooperation at the United Nations, especially with regard to reforms and the expansion of the United Nations Security Council to accommodate countries such as India and Japan, and other issues such as food and energy security, the environment and pandemics.

The Abe era: The golden age of India-Japan relations

The Abe era from 2012 to 2020 was particularly productive for strategic ties between India and Japan. It coincided with growing challenges across the Indo-Pacific, especially due to the rise of China's economic and military power and its coercive policies.

Prime Minister Narendra Modi's keen interest in deepening relations with Japan, especially his personal rapport with Prime Minister Shinzo Abe, provided extra momentum to bilateral cooperation in diverse fields. Prime Minister Modi's first bilateral visit outside of South Asia after assuming office in 2014 was to Japan. It resulted in the Tokyo Declaration and elevated the relationship to a Special Strategic and Global Partnership. The following year, in 2015, the summit in India resulted in the India and Japan Vision 2025 for Peace and Prosperity of the Indo-Pacific Region and the World. The year 2015 was a watershed year in bolstering our defence and security relations. Japan not only became a permanent member of the Malabar Exercise, but we also decided to explore potential cooperation in high technology.

Big-ticket items such as the Mumbai-Ahmedabad high-speed rail project is but one of the many outcomes of their discussions. The 2016 summit in Tokyo saw the conclusion of the civil-military cooperation agreement, the first-ever to be signed by Japan with any non-signatory to the Nuclear Non-proliferation Treaty. In 2017, new areas were identified such as the Act East Forum, cooperation in disaster risk management, language studies and the Japan-India Institutes for Manufacturing aimed at skill development. The last summit between prime ministers Modi and Abe resulted in advancing cooperation in healthcare and wellness, a digital partnership, environmental cooperation, food processing technologies and processes and deepening naval cooperation. Under Abe, Japan became a permanent participant in the Malabar naval exercise and commenced annual exercises between the ground forces as well. All in all, Shinzo Abe was a major stakeholder in India's modernization, and the Abe years will go down in history as the golden years that laid the foundation for the future of bilateral ties between India and Japan in the twenty-first century.

(This article was first published by the Parliament Library of India in July 2022).

CHINESE CHECKERS

India-China boundary issues: A primer

Conceptual aspects

The India-China boundary question has been festering for decades. China's aggression, unilateralism and irredentism have acquired a sharper focus today, against the backdrop of its economic and military rise and the growing contestation between its autocratic and authoritarian system and a liberal, democratic, rules-based international order. The bloody confrontation between trespassing People's Liberation Army (PLA) troops and the Indian Army in Galwan in eastern Ladakh in June 2020 raises questions about the nature of the boundary dispute and differences over the Line of Actual Control (LAC).

It is tempting to examine the extent to which there are discernible parallels in India-China relations in the run-up to the 1962 border conflict and the current situation in Ladakh. Both situations concerned the boundary question although one can state that the focus in the 1950s was on the fundamental question of the 'territorial dispute' involving the whole of Aksai Chin claimed by India and the whole of the North-East Frontier Agency (NEFA; now Arunachal Pradesh) claimed by China. Today, with the Chinese firmly in control of Aksai Chin and India equally in control of Arunachal Pradesh, the issue has moved on to differences over the LAC, especially in the Western Sector. Traditionally, China has had an advantage of terrain and logistics in this region and, hence, greater scope for territorial expansion. In legal terminology surrounding such matters, 'territorial disputes' are typically different from 'boundary disputes'.

A boundary is typically a line without width determining the extremity of the possessions of two sides, and a dispute over a boundary hinges on differences over the alignment of such a line, which can generally be settled through 'rectifications'. A territorial dispute, on the other hand, is different, since it involves a fundamental divergence of claims over entire chunks of frontier territory that may have a distinct personality, on which the disputing parties have neither any agreement on a notional delimitation (conceptual identification/definition of the extent of territory involved/allocation), nor any agreement on its delineation on maps or demarcation on the ground of a mutually acceptable boundary through joint surveys and boundary markers. A 'border' by contrast is a more loosely defined term, similar to 'frontier' and could be a band with some width, with the precise alignment undetermined by two contending sides.

Putting aside this definitional aspect, the parallel is that China and India are contending today on the alignment of the LAC over which they have major differences involving substantial chunks of territory. This is in addition to the even larger issue of the dispute, for instance, over the entire Aksai Chin. The substantive dispute over the LAC is evident in areas such as Daulat Beg Oldie (DBO)/Trig Heights, Depsang Bulge, Galwan Valley, Hot Springs, Pangong Lake and Demchok in the Western Sector (Ladakh), and similarly in various 'pockets' in the Middle and Eastern sectors. In the Western Sector, where China has some advantages, the difficulty is compounded by China projecting a flexible and expanding version of the LAC. China has never clarified its LAC on a large-scale map to avoid being held to a particular line. China is precise enough to claim certain areas, but deliberately imprecise so as to avoid being tied down to a particular interpretation of the line on the ground. After the initial exchange of maps two decades ago of the Middle Sector where the dispute is relatively small, China refused to exchange maps with India to clarify the LAC in the Western Sector.

India's view of the territorial dispute in the 1950s was defensive and legalistic whereas China's view of it was strategic and opportunistic, with a firm belief that 'possession is nine-tenths of the law'. Today, India's view of the LAC is similarly more legalistic and ethical, premised on both sides honouring agreements that have been concluded and refraining from provocative behaviour in overlapping areas. China's stance is the same as it was in the 1950s, and the opposite of India's.

India had a boundary claim along the Kunlun Range in Aksai Chin and did not subscribe to the concept of the LAC in Ladakh until the mid-1970s. It was only when the two sides decided to restore ambassadorial-level ties in 1976 that India carried out the exercise of defining India's LAC in anticipation of future negotiations. Apart from the LAC, the Indian side had established limits of patrolling (LoP) at several places, which were short of the LAC that was projected on the maps in some places. Over time, the lack of patrolling in the gaps between the LoP and the LAC led the Chinese to contend that India had no control or presence in those areas, and also tempted them to move in. There are also areas in Ladakh where Indian graziers (Rebos) have stopped going up to their traditional pasture lands over the decades due to perceived lack of security vis a vis rival graziers or PLA troops from the Chinese side. Both the policy of the LoP, which over time led to confusion about the sanctity of the Indian LAC, and the difficulties in patrolling or grazing up to our LAC in overlapping areas led to gaps, which the Chinese systematically exploited and sought to occupy over the years. Over time, the Indian LAC became a cautious and defensive concept and the Chinese LAC an offensive and ambitious one.

Cutting forward to the present, the government's bold decisions to build much-needed roads and other border infrastructure have resulted in better logistics and supply lines for the Indian Army. This has facilitated our presence and patrolling right up to India's perception of the LAC for the most part, including in areas where the Indian side did not have easy access in the past.

However, renewed presence and patrolling beyond the LoP up to our LAC after a gap of many years is selectively portrayed by China as 'provocative' action. China also objects to any Indian presence and patrolling in areas that it claims as its own. China continues to blame India, and its objections to Indian presence and patrols in many places in Ladakh today sound similar to the note they struck in the run-up to 1962 when China had objected to India's 'Forward Policy'. India continues to regard its activities as falling on its side of the LAC just as it had declared in the 1950s that it was operating in its own territory.

As it did in the 1950s, China continues to project a unilateral definition of its LAC, which in its gradually expanding form is, by and large, co-terminus with its so-called boundary claim line in Ladakh, except for some pockets where the Chinese LAC is well short of China's claim line, as is the case in Demchok (called Parigas by the Chinese). As in the past, whenever the Chinese speak of 'the LAC' they are only referring to their own version of it, without taking into account the Indian version of the LAC. The *Global Times* version of the meeting between the Indian and Chinese defence ministers on 4 September 2020 in Moscow on the sidelines of the Shanghai Cooperation Organization meeting calls for a return to 'the LAC of 7 November 1959', which remains a unilaterally defined yet sufficiently vague line that the Chinese have been advocating since the 1950s, one that permits dynamic and expedient interpretations by Beijing.

The current context

The face-off along the India-China border areas on 15 June 2020, beginning with an incident in the Western Sector (Ladakh) on 5 May and at Naku La (Sikkim Sector) on 9 May, and escalating to a bloody altercation that resulted in twenty Indian casualties, caught the attention of the global community.[1]

Notwithstanding the tremendous military build-up on both sides in the aftermath, subsequent statements from both sides indicated the existence of some common ground—that both India and China were committed to a dialogue to resolve the issue on the basis of existing agreements, that both diplomatic and military channels of communication were open and available, and that third party involvement was not welcome. Dialogue, meanwhile, continued at the political, diplomatic and military levels to try and defuse the situation, with limited success.

The border row between India and China could not have come at a worse time. The global community, including India, was grappling with the deleterious effects of a once-in-a-century pandemic, with containment of the negative fallout on health and economic well-being emerging as a top priority. The global response and economic recovery were constrained by schisms that predated the breakout of the pandemic. The health crisis acted as an accelerant for a dangerous widening of differences. The US, still the world's largest economic and military power, no longer plays the dominant role that it once did. A

---

1   'Statement on All Party Meeting of 19th June 2020', Ministry of External Affairs, Government of India, 20 June 2020; https://www.mea.gov.in/press-releases.htm?dtl/32775/statement+on+all+party+meeting+of+19th+june+2020

part of the problem was self-abnegation in international affairs during the Trump administration and the resultant weakening of the global institutions that it helped create, such as the United Nations Security Council, World Trade Organization, World Health Organization, United Nations Educational, Scientific and Cultural Organization, the Paris Agreement and the trans-Pacific and trans-Atlantic trade and strategic partnerships (CPTPP and TTIP). President Biden has since reclaimed some ground by committing the US afresh to global institutions, including the United Nations and WHO, and rejoining the Paris climate change agreement. The renewed emphasis on alliance partnerships has also proved reassuring in highlighting the US presence as a factor for stability in the Indo-Pacific region.

China's rise, particularly its unilateral and aggressive policies, has also played a role in aggravating tensions in the region. Long feted as a country that would transform itself to mirror Western liberalism and democracy if only it became more prosperous, China has belied all such expectations, thrown aside all pretensions. It scrambled to use its early recovery from the pandemic to emerge as the world's largest economy by the end of this decade. It used its considerable economic heft and the success of its model of 'state capitalism' to claim, ironically, the mantle of leadership of the liberal trading order and globalization. The denouement a year later as a result of its 'Zero Covid' policy suggests disruption of supply chains in China and an economic slowdown that has caused the growth rate to plummet to 2.5 per cent.

China remains deeply suspicious of the US presence and influence in Asia and is increasingly paranoid that the Indo-Pacific construct is a diabolic ruse to contain China, and that the US increasingly regards India, a fellow democracy with which it has shared interests and values, as a key partner for the success of an emerging security architecture underpinned by US primacy in the Indo-Pacific.

It would be instructive to examine the current India-China border row in this broad context. Why did the Chinese step up their deployments in the border areas? What explains the Chinese behaviour? There could be several reasons. At the local level, it is usually in the early months of summer that the weather thaws and permits patrolling by both sides. Although China has the first mover's advantage, better border infrastructure on the Indian side now permits the Indian military to also patrol points up to its LAC, increasing the chances of run-ins between the troops of the two sides. Activity by either side in the border areas usually sparks off mirror activity by the other. The Chinese may well have sought to test India's will, preparedness and defences at a time when the coronavirus has created an economic recession. The heightened Chinese activity coincided with meetings of the National People's Congress and the Chinese People's Political Consultative Conference in 2020 when nationalism and hubris generally take centre stage for the consumption of the domestic audience. Or, it could well have been part of an overall combative and uncompromising Chinese posture in the face of external calls for accountability for the spread of the coronavirus and sensitivities with regard to the global scrutiny of its harsh policies in Xinjiang, Tibet and Hong Kong as well as aggressive tactics against Taiwan.

There is a view that the Chinese aggression in Galwan in eastern Ladakh had several underlying messages. To India, it was perhaps a message that a strategic partnership with the US was insufficient to deter China's military might. To the US, it could well have been a demonstration that China was capable of putting pressure on any of the former's close regional partners. To India's neighbours, it was an indication that it was China that mattered the most in this part of the world. China often indulges in operatic posturing. It is capable of creating issues and incidents, accompanied by shrill propaganda, with the sole purpose of raking up uncertainty and anxiety in the mind of the adversary and to then use calibrated reduction of pressure to extract concessions and favourable outcomes on the wider canvas of bilateral relations.

The India-China boundary question

There are three main sectors: Western (Ladakh), Middle (Himachal Pradesh and Uttarakhand) and Eastern (Arunachal Pradesh). India claims the whole of Aksai Chin in the Western Sector/Ladakh (approximately 38,000 sq. km), which is under Chinese control; China claims the whole of the Indian state of Arunachal Pradesh (approximately 90,000 sq. km) in the Eastern Sector; the two sides also have a relatively smaller dispute in the Middle Sector along the border with Himachal Pradesh and Uttarakhand (approximately 2,000 sq. km under dispute). According to India, the India-China LAC is approximately 3,488 km long. China is not ready to discuss the boundary west of the Karakoram Pass in Ladakh in the Western Sector with India since that is part of Pakistan-occupied Kashmir (PoK); in addition, India claims 5,180 sq. km of territory in the trans-Karakoram Shaksgam tract, which Pakistan illegally ceded to China as part of their so-called boundary agreement of 2 March 1963.[2]

India claims that the boundary between India and China is a historical, traditional and customary line backed by treaties (Treaty of Tingmosgang of 1684 and Treaty of Chushul of 1842 in the Western Sector and the Simla Convention of 1913-14/McMahon Line in the Eastern Sector). India's claim is based on the internationally accepted principle of the 'watershed' (parting of principal water systems), which generally runs along the highest crest line, whereas the Chinese have their own version of a so-called traditional and customary claim line, insisting that the boundary has never been delimited and cannot be based on any abstract geographical principle. China insists on looser principles, which include valleys, mountain passes, peaks, rivers/streams,

---

2　'Q No. 2282 Chinese Claim on Arunachal Pradesh and Aksai Chin', Ministry of External Affairs, Government of India, 18 December 2013; https://mea.gov.in/lok-sabha.htm?dtl/22677/q+no2282+chinese+claim+on+arunachal+pradesh+and+aksai+chin

and often, or no principles other than expediency, opportunistic and incremental claims.

In the 1950s, the differences over the boundary question, which had a history of their own during the colonial period, came to the fore as soon as China occupied Tibet in 1950-51. From the beginning, it was clear that the People's Republic of China was claiming in its maps large tracts of Indian territory in the Eastern and Western sectors and several smaller pockets in the Middle Sector. The boundary differences began with Barahoti, a disputed pocket in the Middle Sector, and moved on to the diplomatic exchanges over the illegal Aksai Chin highway G219, completed by China in 1957. The detention by China of the Indian patrol sent to verify facts on the ground in 1958, the attack and capture of our post at Longju in Upper Subansiri in the Eastern Sector and the ambush of an Indian patrol (in which nine of our police party were killed) at Konka La in the Western Sector in 1959 brought the boundary dispute into sharper focus.

Chinese Premier Zhou Enlai had given a vague indication of the existence of a Line of Actual Control during talks with Pandit Nehru in 1956, but without providing details. There were also hints that China, while not recognizing the McMahon Line of 1914, was willing to treat that as the basis for the Line of Actual Control in the Eastern Sector. When Nehru raised the matter of Chinese maps claiming Indian territory, Zhou said that these were old maps of the previous regime (the Republic of China) and that they had not had the time to study and revise them. Later, in a communication to Nehru dated 7 November 1959, Zhou gave details of China's so-called LAC for the first time, but this was years after China had already crept up and incrementally occupied Indian territory in the Western Sector. Even then, in reality the Chinese presence was nowhere near the LAC that they claimed. They came up to their LAC, and even beyond in some places, through further aggression after 1959, particularly in the course of the 1962 border war.

The situation spiralled downwards, but by the late 1950s India had taken a definitive position on what it regarded as its territory. Talks between Nehru and Zhou Enlai as well as the official-level talks of 1960 failed to make any breakthrough, leading to more friction in the border areas. To counter China's salami-slicing of territory, India's 'Forward Policy' involved setting up about sixty small 'penny-packet' posts deep inside Aksai Chin, often behind Chinese posts in a zig-zag fashion. By the summer of 1962, the Indian posts were outnumbered by a division-size force. These were eventually surrounded by the PLA, which cut off the rudimentary Indian supply lines. Many of the posts were maintained by helicopters, including for induction and de-induction of troops. They were overwhelmed and mostly wiped out by the massive Chinese aggression that began on 20 October 1962, though not without extraordinary acts of bravery and resistance put up by inadequately equipped Indian soldiers under exceptional leadership, as was the case at Rezang La in Ladakh in the Western Sector, where the Charlie Coy of 13 Kumaon regiment led by Major Shaitan Singh, Param Vir Chakra (posthumous), fought to the 'last man last round'.

India did not use the air force during the hostilities for various reasons, apparently on the grounds that it did not have night-capable interceptors and there was concern about population centres becoming targets. Lack of 'jointness' in terms of the ability to carry out air operations in tandem with the army is also considered a factor.

Bilateral agreements

The following bilateral agreements have been concluded between India and China to maintain peace and tranquillity in the border areas: (i) 1993 Agreement on Maintenance of Peace and Tranquillity along the Line of Actual Control (LAC) in the India-China border areas (also known as the BPTA); (ii) 1996 Agreement on Confidence-Building

Measures (CBMs) in the Military Field along the LAC in the India-China border areas (also known as the CBMs Agreement); (iii) 2005 Agreement on the Political Parameters and Guiding Principles for the Settlement of the India-China Boundary Question; (iv) 2005 Protocol on Modalities for the implementation of the CBMs in the Military Field along the LAC; (v) 2012 Agreement on the establishment of a Working Mechanism for Consultation and Coordination on India-China Border Affairs; and (vi) 2013 Border Defence Cooperation Agreement. Notably, all these were signed four decades after boundary disputes first arose and three decades after the two sides fought a war in 1962.

The focus of these agreements is broadly on eschewing the use of force, maintaining peace and tranquillity through confidence-building measures along the LAC, and to be better able to do that, clarifying differences over the alignment of the LAC. The 2005 Agreement on Political Parameters and Guiding Principles is more fundamental since it seeks to provide a framework for an early and peaceful settlement of the larger boundary question. This agreement emphasizes the importance of a package settlement, one that is final, covering all sectors of the India-China boundary. It is different from the 'package' proposal offered by Zhou Enlai to Jawaharlal Nehru in 1960 and by Deng Xiaoping in an interview to the Indian journal *Vikrant* in 1982, and subsequently repeated to G. Parthasarthy, the then chairman of the Policy Planning Committee of the Ministry of External Affairs of India, in Beijing later the same year.

The previous package proposal suggested that both sides would accept the de facto situation and formalize the status quo, with Aksai Chin remaining in China and NEFA in India. The package settlement of 2005 implied that boundary negotiations and territorial swaps would be necessary, but that it would be a holistic one, covering all sectors. More importantly, the 2005 agreement also includes some key principles that had evolved in the course of the official-level talks in the 1980s, such as the basis of a settlement and the importance of safeguarding the interests of the settled populations in border areas.

The Line of Actual Control

It is pertinent to point out that the LAC between India and China has never been mutually delimited, delineated on a map and demarcated on the ground. The boundary between Sikkim and Tibet, agreed to way back in 1890 as a result of the Anglo-Chinese Convention of 1890, was an exception.

For India, the word LAC did not exist until well after the dust had settled on the Chinese aggression in 1962. During the 1960s and even up to the mid-1970s, the very word 'LAC' was anathema to the official Indian lexicon and, when used, was either in parenthesis or prefaced with 'so-called'. It was only around the time of a thaw in relations leading to the re-establishment of ambassadorial-level ties in 1976 that India began to consider the notion of an LAC, anticipating negotiations in the future, even though it was clear that there were differences on both sides as to where the line might run.

The major difference in concept in the Western Sector is that for India, there was no such thing as 'Line of Actual Control'. India had an international boundary along the Kunlun, encompassing all of the Aksai Chin area that it had inherited historically from the British claim line (the expansive Ardagh-Johnson Line of the nineteenth century). It was only an occasional border patrol that ventured across the Karakoram Range as far as Haji Langar, at the upper extremity of the road connecting Xinjiang and Tibet constructed stealthily by China in the early 1950s. For China too, all along, there was a huge gap between its claimed international boundary, broadly along the Karakoram Range, and its physical presence on the ground, which fell hundreds of kilometres short.

Before China sent troops into Xinjiang in 1949 and occupied Tibet in 1950, it had scant presence or control over any of the border areas it claimed after the establishment of the People's Republic of China. With regard to the Western Sector, Chinese maps of the Qing era clearly showed the Kunlun Range as the farthest extremity of Chinese dominions. In regard to the Eastern Sector (Arunachal Pradesh), China was virtually absent from Tibet even before the collapse of the Qing dynasty in 1911, except for the short-lived probing by Qing troops in the first decade of the twentieth century, mostly along the Lohit frontier when the collapsing Qing regime was seeking, unsuccessfully, to establish a new administrative region called Zayul.

In many areas along the LAC, the Chinese have long enjoyed the advantage of flatter terrain and superior logistics and infrastructure. This has permitted them to patrol the LAC from bases and posts located deeper inside the territory long held by China. India's infrastructure was lagging behind, limiting its activity along the LAC, particularly in the Western Sector. In recent years, India's airlift capability and infrastructure in the area, including roads and advanced landing grounds, have all improved dramatically, permitting much better induction and improved scale and frequency of access to forward patrolling points. In a way, India has played catch up, although China has long had the first-mover's advantage. With Indian patrols more regular within what both India and China regard as their sides of the LAC, there is much greater chance of run-ins between border patrols all along the overlapping claims.

LAC in the three sectors

In the Western Sector, the so-called Chinese LAC of 7 November 1959 is for China essentially coterminous with its claimed boundary, though there are pockets of differences such as Depsang, Pangong Tso, Hot Springs and Demchok. In the area known as Aksai Chin, today under Chinese occupation, China was not physically present up to the boundary claimed by it until it mounted aggression against India through the 1962 border conflict.

In the Middle Sector, the Indian perception of the LAC runs along the international boundary as depicted on Indian maps. The so-called Chinese LAC is by and large coterminous with the international boundary except for the Barahoti or 'Hoti' pastureland (called Wu-je by China), just south of the Tunjun La Pass in Uttarakhand and a few other pockets in Spiti, Shipki, Nilang-Jadhang, Lapthal and Sangchamalla. The Agreement on Trade and Intercourse between the Tibet Region of China and India of 29 April 1954 clearly mentioned the passes to be used for trade and pilgrimage: (1) Shipki La (2) Mana (3) Niti (4) Kungri Bingri (5) Darma and (6) Lipu Lekh, but later in the case of some of them the Chinese claimed that these had never been recognized as 'border passes'.

The Indian perception of the boundary/LAC lay along the watershed, which itself, in principle, generally runs along the highest crest line, but with exceptions. Some issues cropped up because of differences over what comprises a watershed when a major river cuts through from north to south on a frontier running east to west, and which thereby creates multiple basins with multiple run-offs in terms of the water flow. China claims that the watershed principle is not the only yardstick for determining the boundary. Some of the disputed passes, both in the Middle or Eastern sectors, lie on the highest crest line, just south of the watershed, giving rise to the dispute.

In the Eastern Sector, the international boundary for India lies along the watershed in accordance with the guiding principle of the McMahon Line, which came about as a result of the convention between Great Britain, China and Tibet in 1913-14. The British had sought to demarcate a line based on the traditional and customary boundary read in tandem with the commonly accepted international watershed principle that generally runs along the highest crest line, but not always. This was true of the boundary between Sikkim and Tibet as indicated in the Anglo-Chinese Convention of 1890, or more broadly through the Simla Convention. If a literal interpretation of the thick pencil line rendition of the McMahon Line were transposed on the ground, there are gaps where the line, in contrast to its avowed logic, runs short of the watershed in a few places, and, in other spots, even falls across the watershed. The watershed principle does not match the highest crest line, which runs south of the watershed in the Eastern Sector in several places. Such were the limitations of cartography at the time.

In the Western Sector, to consolidate its then tenuous hold on two territories that had already been assimilated (Tibet and Xinjiang), China completed the strategic Highway 219 in 1957, cutting through Indian territory in Aksai Chin. After that, it executed a series of moves to claim an extended line of control to the highway's west, projecting its presence well westwards of the highway in the Soda Plains of Aksai China towards the Karakoram Range, and well westwards of the Lak Tsang Range in the southern part to engulf the Lingzithang Plains. It artificially advanced its traditional boundary and then began to consolidate and gradually advance its military patrols and posts towards it. In 1959, the Chinese were still far short of their boundary claims. Even as late as on 8 September 1962, on the eve of hostilities in the Eastern Sector, the Chinese in Ladakh were far short of their so-called LAC of 7 November 1959 and the expansive boundary claims put forth in the 1960 official talks.

In the Middle Sector, the differences as also armed conflict had been minimal, but one can say that Barahoti is the pocket where differences first erupted in 1953 even before the negotiations had begun on the 1954 Panchsheel Agreement. This was long before India discovered the illegal 'western highway' constructed by China in Aksai Chin, and well before altercations in several places resulted in the Chinese attack and capture of the Indian post at Longju in the Eastern Sector in August

1959 followed by the ambush of a police party led by Havildar Karam Singh at Kongka La in the Western Sector near Hot Springs, across the Chang Chenmo river basin. Differences also cropped up in Spanggur in the Western Sector, not far from the famous Rezang La where the pitched battle was fought in 1962 by gallant Indian soldiers against overwhelming odds.

The Chinese have never accepted the interpretation of the McMahon Line drawn up at the Simla Convention (1913-14) either as the boundary or as the LAC. The Chinese have consistently termed it in bilateral discussions as 'illegal' and as the 'so-called McMahon Line', but as Zhou Enlai had also stated to Jawaharlal Nehru, China was willing to accept it as some kind of a working boundary.

There is not much discrepancy between India's physical presence along its LAC and the boundary alignment in the Eastern Sector. It was never India's intention to go north beyond the customary watershed boundary, but that caution and moderation could not be said of China. The Chinese interpretation of the McMahon Line has resulted in several disputed pockets in the region, and that is how the border conflict flared up in the Eastern Sector starting with the altercations at Thag La along the Namka Chu stream in Tawang district in Arunachal Pradesh. The great irony though is that China, while rejecting the watershed principle of the McMahon Line with India, accepted it in its boundary settlement with Myanmar in 1960 (the McMahon Line on the map appended to the Simla Convention had also delineated the boundary between Myanmar and China).

In some places in the Eastern Sector in Arunachal Pradesh, the gap between the two interpretations is several kilometres wide. Chinese troops seek to intrude into these areas, which they consider to be on their side of the LAC. The relatively imperfect cartographic science available to the early explorers and officials of British India is also responsible for creating the differences that exist over the western tri-junction between India, Bhutan and China, which, according to the watershed principle of the 1890 Anglo-Chinese Convention concerning Sikkim's boundaries, ought to run along the Batang La-Merug La-Sinchela ridgeline. The highest crest/ridge line is the one that starts from the tri-junction between Nepal-India-China and terminates at Batang-La. This is also the true parting of the watershed between the river systems of the Teesta in Sikkim and the Mochu in Tibet, as per the principle in Article One of the Anglo-Chinese Convention of 1890.

Both Bhutan and India claim that the tri-junction lies at Batang-La, which is about 6.5 km north of Mt Gipmochi, a point that China rigidly insists on as the tri-junction in accordance with the Anglo-Chinese Convention of 1890 even though it is not located as per modern cartographic tools on the watershed/crest line. China's rigid interpretation, in disregard of internationally accepted principles such as the watershed principle, and its insistence on Mt Gipmochi near the Jampheri ridge as the tri-junction, explains the dispute with Bhutan over the Doklam plateau. The Chinese stand has serious implications for the security of the narrow 'chicken neck' Siliguri corridor that connects the Northeast region to the rest of India. China's claim to Doklam and insistence on the tri-junction at Mt Gipmochi in disregard of Article One of the Anglo-Chinese Convention of 1890 would permit it to have a deeper dagger-like wedge of territory directly overlooking the Siliguri corridor.

The Chinese have no qualms in accepting the Anglo-Chinese treaty of 1890 since it suits them but which, strangely, did not include as participants either Bhutan, Tibet or Sikkim, the three kingdoms of the time directly affected by the outcome. Thus the Chinese rejection of the Simla Convention on the specious grounds that the line was drawn behind China's back by British India and Tibet is unfounded. China was part of the trilateral convention and the Chinese representative

Ivan Chen even initialled the draft document though Beijing later repudiated it; moreover, Tibet was then independent and entitled under international law to take its own decisions. In any case, the focus of the Simla Convention, including the differences between the Chinese and the Tibetan representatives, was with regard to the line separating Inner and Outer Tibet. The discussions on the McMahon Line were between the British Indian representative, Sir Henry McMahon, and the Tibetan representative, Lonchen Shatra, who were dealing with one another as two sovereign participants. The representatives of British India, China and Tibet all participated in the Simla Convention on an equal footing.

The Chinese view of the LAC

China suspects that India is keen on clarification and confirmation of the LAC as a means of achieving a de facto permanent settlement, despite the fact that the bilateral agreements of 1993 and 1996 clearly state that this exercise would be without prejudice to either side's position on the boundary question.

China's version of the LAC is an active, expedient and aggressive concept aimed at claiming more territory. India's reluctant acceptance over time of the very idea of a LAC in the Western Sector was predicated on a conservative and defensive approach. Generally speaking, Indian patrols in the past used to slog it out on foot in the last mile areas and heights due to terrain disadvantage in the rear areas; the Chinese have always been prone to use vehicles and horses/mules due to their terrain advantage on the plateau. India is now closing this gap gradually with better roads and tracks on the Indian side as, for e.g., along the Darbok-Shyok-Daulat Beg Oldie axis in the Western Sector, as also along the road that originates at Ghatiabagarh and ends at Lipulekh Pass in the Middle Sector and other lateral roads along the LAC in the Eastern Sector.

For China, the LAC has always been a flexible concept, one related less to China's physical presence and more to its aspirational claims. China has never agreed to share with India its LAC on a large-scale map, except for the map exchanged for the Middle Sector in 2001. For years, India had to go by small-scale maps of the so-called Chinese LAC published by authoritative journals, read in tandem with the Chinese description of their claimed boundary in the Report of the Officials of 1960.

It is important to note that there is no clarity on the exact delineation of China's LAC. This fact should be borne in mind when analysts and media commentators talk about the 'Chinese LAC' or attempt to depict it on maps in an authoritative manner. The Indian side has a rough estimate of its alignment but on the ground, based on general Chinese explanation, their small-scale maps and a meticulous plotting of all the points up to which their patrols come. Even so, there are likely to be substantial differences and lack of clarity until the two sides exchange large-scale maps depicting their respective versions of the LAC. So far, this has been done only for the Middle Sector. Here too, the exercise has not progressed to delineate the LAC of each side on large-scale maps, let alone to conduct joint surveys and demarcation on the ground.

It is clear that China was never sincere about the LAC clarification exercise, which would have required it to commit to a line on a large-scale map. Such an option, without a joint survey and in the absence of a physical Chinese presence on the ground up to the claimed line would also have prevented them from continuing to use the flexible and incrementally expansive approach that they employ, often on the basis of a military appreciation and the desire to hold heights and secure local terrain advantages in the last-mile areas, with no basis in history or traditional and customary usage. The Chinese disregard for agreements and desire to nibble away at territory have resulted in the emergence of new areas of differences other than the well-known pockets.

Dialogue mechanisms: Joint Working Group, Expert Group and Special Representatives Dialogue

As during the 1960 officials talks, China was not ready to discuss the boundary west of the Karakoram Pass with India, having 'settled' its boundary along PoK with Pakistan as part of their so-called boundary agreement of 2 March 1963. This is also one of the difficulties encountered subsequently in carrying through the exercise of exchanging maps of the Western Sector.

The eight rounds of officials-level talks from 1981 to 1988 did not yield much except some inconclusive exchanges about principles governing a settlement, with China doing a volte face at the sixth round in 1985, stating that the greater dispute lay in the Eastern Sector and that India should make substantial concessions in that sector whereupon China would make corresponding adjustments in the Western Sector.

The Joint Working Group (JWG) on the Boundary Question was established during the late Prime Minister Rajiv Gandhi's visit to China in 1988, when the author was the desk officer for China in the Ministry of External Affairs and a young member of the Prime Minister's delegation. The JWG held its first round of discussions in 1989. The idea was to compartmentalize the boundary row from the rest of the relationship without allowing progress in other areas to be held back. The mandate of the JWG was to look for ways and means to resolve the boundary question and to maintain peace and tranquillity along the LAC. However, border issues generally got short shrift in the JWG meetings since the agenda tended to expand to include wider bilateral, regional and international issues.

By 1986, India and China were dealing with the serious issue of a major Chinese incursion and subsequently occupation of a seasonal post used by our Special Security Bureau on the bank of the Sumdorong Chu in the area of Tawang in the Eastern Sector. The Chinese refused to reverse their occupation of the post, which was used by India during the summer months and vacated in the winter, and both sides quickly mobilized troops to bolster positions, with India moving an entire brigade by newly acquired helicopter lift capabilities under Operation Falcon right on to the Hathong La–Lungro La ridgeline overlooking the Chinese and also placing troops eyeball to eyeball on the southern bank of the Sumdorong Chu where the Chinese had established a new presence. It took several years before the two sides agreed to mutually disengage, with India pulling back its posts Jaya and Negi from the southern bank of the stream to relocate them along the Hathong La–Lungro La ridgeline in 1994.

Such a complex situation highlighted the need for a working mechanism on border issues, which is the reason for the Expert Group of Diplomatic and Military Officials (EG) being set up by both sides as agreed to in the Agreement on the Maintenance of Peace and Tranquility along the Line of Actual Control in the India-China Border Areas, also known as the Border Peace and Tranquillity Agreement (BPTA) of 1993.

The EG functioned as a sub-group of the JWG. The JWG was headed by the foreign secretary on the Indian side and the vice minister for foreign affairs on the Chinese side. The EG was headed by the joint Secretary/director on the Indian side and the director general/deputy director general of the Asia Department on the Chinese side. The JWG and the EG stopped functioning after 2005, even as the focus shifted to the talks between the Special Representatives (SRs) appointed by the two sides.

Essentially, it was the EG that did all the nitty gritty work, even meeting regularly on the sidelines of the JWG meetings. It was the EG that was tasked by the JWG to implement the BPTA of 1993, and subsequently, the Agreement between the Government of the Republic of India and the Government of the People's Republic of China on Confidence-Building Measures in the Military Field Along the Line of Actual Control in the India-China Border Areas, also known as the Confidence-Building Measures Agreement of 1996. It dealt with discussions on intrusions, differences over the LAC, confidence-building measures such as border personnel meetings/flag meetings, hotlines for communications, etc. The clarification and confirmation of the LAC through a map exchange was also part of its mandate. This was not an easy matter since the Chinese were always cagey about giving India any satisfaction or making any progress. The hotline at Nathu La took years before it was set in 1997. It was damaged subsequently due to a landslide, and the Chinese dragged their feet on its repair and restitution in 1998 because India had by then conducted its nuclear tests and the Chinese had taken offence. Differences over the exact location of the LAC prevented the expansion of additional points for border personnel meetings in the Eastern Sector.

This author led the talks with the Chinese in the EG on the Indian side from the end of 1996 till the end of 2000. The JWG ran its course into the sand with fifteen rounds between 1989 and 2005, by when the SR mechanism set up during then Prime Minister Atal Bihari Vajpayee's visit to China in 2003 had already met for the fifth time. It was clear by then that the JWG, which had not met for years in between (the fourteenth round of the JWG met on 21 November 2002 and the last round, the fifteenth of that series, met only on 30-31 March 2005), was not going to deliver any results. The EG's fate was linked to the JWG and the format, which had proved very useful in addressing tensions in the aftermath of India's nuclear tests, petered out along with the JWG after 2005. The Working Mechanism for Consultation and Coordination on India-China Border Affairs (WMCC), established in 2012, is essentially a resuscitation of the EG, doing similar tasks, once again at the level of joint secretary on the Indian side and director general on the Chinese side.

With the end of the JWG/EG mechanisms, the focus shifted to the SRs' framework, which was led by senior personalities on both sides enjoying direct political access and the confidence of the leadership. The WMCC handles border management whereas the SRs endeavour to seek a resolution of the boundary question. The SRs have held twenty-two rounds of discussions so far, mostly on principles for a resolution of the boundary question. At the functional level, the WMCC and the relatively new format of core commanders' meetings have continued to focus on disengagement and other confidence-building measures.

Overlapping LAC claims

It should be of interest to note that key agreements such as the Border Peace and Tranquillity Agreement of 1993 and the Confidence-Building Measures Agreement of 1996 clearly conceded that there are differing perceptions of the LAC all along the India-China border areas. They recommended specific measures to ensure peace and tranquillity. After 1993, the EG was required to go into the nitty-gritty of issues relating to differences and to pursue the clarification and confirmation of the LAC. It was also required to work on confidence-building measures to maintain peace and tranquillity.

One key difficulty in the language of the 1996 Confidence-Building Measures Agreement was the term LAC itself. The intention of the agreement was to enjoin upon both sides to refrain from several types of military activity within the grey zone of the overlapping lines. Often, it was clear that the Chinese side was determined to go only by its own interpretation of the LAC without taking into account India's line.

Chinese activity in the border areas is not new. There are well-established special operating procedures (SOPs) on handling these, including banner drills, flag meetings etc. These have been flouted by the Chinese side, most egregiously at Galwan in 2020.

China has been improving its infrastructure for years in the border areas. This has facilitated both their extended presence, patrols and other activity. The British, prior to India's independence in 1947, followed a policy of deliberately maintaining under-developed frontiers. After the 1962 war, India was loath to build infrastructure on the logic that it might facilitate use by the adversary. This mind-set resulted in a huge gap between the availability of infrastructure on the two sides. This approach continued for many decades. On their part, the Chinese had always adopted a policy of building roads and tracks for foot and vehicle-mounted patrols right up to their claimed LAC.

It is only in recent years, particularly since 2014, that India has truly devoted resources to building better infrastructure and improving existing infrastructure such as the Darbuk-Shyok-Daulat Beg Oldie road in the Western Sector. Notably, India has confined its infrastructure building within its own perception of the LAC. In areas where there was not much activity in the past, both sides have often displayed a reactive policy. If one side conducts a new activity, including construction of new infrastructure, the other side usually responds with its own flurry of activity. In most places, however, China has the first-mover's advantage and inevitably responds to Indian activity with an even greater spurt in activity of its own.

There is no reason for India to desist from building infrastructure in areas it regards as its own. The way forward is for the Chinese to adhere to the existing agreements. Article X of the Confidence-Building Measures Agreement of 1996 enjoins upon the two sides 'to speed up the process of clarification and confirmation of the line of actual control' and this can only be done if the two sides were 'to exchange maps indicating their respective perceptions of the entire alignment of the line of actual control as soon as possible' as further agreed to in the same article. Twenty-seven years on, the Chinese are still loath to exchange maps because it suits them not to do so.

The difficulty with 'clarification and confirmation of the LAC' is self-apparent. Clarification means that both sides should clarify their position to the other through an exchange of large-scale maps depicting their respective perceptions of the LAC. This implies the potential existence of two overlapping lines at many places. The purpose of 'confirmation' of the LAC cannot simply be to accept the opponent's viewpoint. It also implies that wherever there are overlapping lines, the two sides should endeavour to reduce differences and arrive at an agreed-upon definition. This should be possible since the LAC has never been jointly demarcated on the ground.

Conclusion

After the border war in 1962, it took fourteen years to normalize relations at the ambassadorial level. In the wake of India's nuclear tests in 1998, it took only two years to normalize ties. After the stand-off at Doklam (2017), the two leaders met within days at the BRICS Summit in Xiamen. The cyclical disruptions are now shorter and sharper. The border stand-offs at Deepsang (2013) and Chumar (2014) in Ladakh in the Western Sector were of relatively shorter duration, whereas the current situation at multiple friction points in Ladakh is enduring in nature.

Both India and China are keen to deepen engagement and impart stability and predictability to their relations. The two sides should work on the basis of the 'Wuhan Consensus' and the 'Chennai Connect' and abide by the strategic guidance emanating from the informal summit meetings between Prime Minister Narendra Modi and President Xi Jinping held in the eponymous cities in 2018 and 2019 respectively. For ties to remain stable and to progress along other dimensions, including cultural and economic fields, China must respect the status quo to which it has committed itself in numerous bilateral agreements with India.

India-China relations have witnessed many peaks and troughs. The grave confrontation at Galwan in June 2020 shattered the consensus of 1988. Now, the question of peace and tranquillity in the border areas is at the forefront of the discourse. The idea that relations can progress normally in other fields while both sides continue to deal with the outstanding boundary question is no longer acceptable to India unless accompanied by peace and tranquillity in the border areas. Ties obviously cannot be considered normal if there is bloodshed in the border areas.

There is no gainsaying the fact that India and China must work together to forge stable relations in which competition does not lead to conflict nor differences to disputes. India and China will always have to coexist cheek by jowl, as they have done for millennia. It is in the larger interests of the two peoples that there be greater trust and cooperation and that there be deeper friendship at all levels. However, whether this is realizable or remains a pipe dream will depend on whether China is willing to introspect and reign in its aggressive tendencies, especially the irredentism and unilateralism that it exhibits with regard to territorial issues, whether in the South and East China Seas or in the India-China border areas.

A future beyond the past

Henry Alfred Kissinger is perhaps the only titan among all the strategic thinkers and practitioners of national security and foreign policy to have stridden like a colossus during the Cold War, shaped its direction, and to now have the burden of reflecting on his own role as chief architect of President Richard Nixon's outreach to China against the backdrop of a new Cold War in the twenty-first century. The contemporary shifts in Sino–US relations afford the nonagenarian a chance to review the underlying assumptions of the past. It also affords the international community an opportunity to challenge his thesis in his presence. The Cold War that followed World War II had involved the Soviet Union. The substantive stakes for the US had revolved around trans-Atlantic European security. The new Cold War of the twenty-first century involves an Asian power, the People's Republic of China, which threatens peace and security in the Indo-Pacific.

US-China historical engagement

The US, the world's oldest democracy, is also among its youngest nations. Historically, the US had demonstrated a streak for isolationism, perhaps drawn out of it only by the realism of its participation in the two great wars, its emphatic use of the enormous power of the atom bomb and the finality of the end of Pax Britannica after 1945. As a great power drawn into a global role, the US had no real experience of China, situated in Asia, far away from the continental US. This is unlike India, which has coexisted with China cheek by jowl for millennia, or even the European colonialists who had obtained trading rights and territorial concessions in enclaves along China's southern and eastern seaboard.

After US independence, over the next half century, American merchants were also lured by the prospects of trade with Canton, plying, among other things, quantities of lower quality Turkish opium. It was in 1844 that the US first entered into a official treaty, the Treaty of Peace, Amity and Commerce, with the Qing empire, which remained in effect till 1943, until it was replaced by the Sino-American Treaty for the Relinquishment of Extraterritorial Rights in China. However, the Old China Trade under the 'Canton system' as it was known, brought about many changes in China's engagement with the external world. The early commerce between the Qing Empire and the US operated under the Canton System, in which trade was largely confined to the southern port of Canton, with middlemen, or 'hongs', appointed by the central government, controlling the interface. The Old China Trade and the Canton system collapsed with the breakout of the first Opium War in 1839 when the British demanded access for their opium trade through new ports and lower tariffs in general. By then, the foundation laid by the commercial ties between China and the US had paved the way for the controversial influx of thousands of Chinese émigrés for the California Gold Rush, and later as a labour force for building railroads. It led eventually to legislation and bilateral treaties in the 1880s to prohibit immigration from China.

Yet, through all this, there was a certain fascination for the esoteric land of the Middle Kingdom, distant, mysterious, yet beckoning. Missionaries and Southern Baptists were drawn in sizeable numbers by the prospects of proselytization among the teeming millions in China.

The Boxer Uprising of 1900, in which foreigners and European missionaries were massacred, resulted in a punitive mission; what is noteworthy is that US Marines were part of the Eight Nation Forces that sacked Beijing in 1901 and forced China to pay huge indemnities. This was the first instance of US armed action against the Chinese people, bracketing the US alongside the European colonial powers that had long engaged in depredations in China against an enfeebled Qing regime.

Broadly speaking, there was also a fascination among Americans for all things Chinese, bordering on romantic notions of deciphering a forbiddingly remote agrarian Asian society. American author Pearl S. Buck epitomized such writing. Later, Edgar Snow romanticized the life of Mao Zedong and his band of survivors of the Long March in his book *Red Star Over China*. Spending some time in the hardscrabble mountains and barren loess plateaux of Yan'an in Shaanxi Province in China with Mao, he introduced Mao's thoughts to Americans flirting with Marxist ideology in the aftermath of the Great Depression.

The McCarthyism of the post-World War II period, which shaped US policy towards communism, most notably under Secretary of State Dulles in 1953–59, had its roots in the First and Second Red Scare; US apprehension about the implications for the US of the emerging world of communism had an even track record going back to the Bolshevik Revolution in Russia and the rise of leftist political thought in advanced liberal societies as the very antithesis of capitalism.

Kissinger's intellectual moorings

Professor Kissinger made his debut in a government position in a world in which he explored strategic thought, international relations and foreign policy with his books such as *Nuclear Weapons and Foreign Policy* (1957) and *The Necessity for Choice: Prospects of American Foreign Policy* (1961). He had no known training as a China specialist nor did he speak any Mandarin. In 1957, China had no nuclear weapons and could not have figured centrally in his book as it might today with long-range missiles that can threaten every part of continental US and even erode its superiority at sea and in space through asymmetrical means.

In many ways, Henry Kissinger's thoughts on China have displayed the lack of the familiarity and historical perspective that might come naturally to peoples and nations with a longer history. As a brilliant polemicist, his thoughts about China were bereft of the baggage of the past. They had a freshness of purpose, hope and excitement and even dispassionate objectivity in dealing with the contemporary. His own life experience, as a young German immigrant fleeing persecution for a better future in the US, no doubt honed a certain neuroplasticity to spot, interpret and seize strategic opportunities.

For a European immigrant, it would have come naturally to Kissinger to be steeped in the statecraft of Klemens von Metternich and Carl von Clausewitz and the Westphalian balance of power politics of three centuries. His doctoral dissertation, understandably, was on *Peace, Legitimacy and the Equilibrium (A Study of the Statesmanship of Castlereagh and Metternich)*, an early deep dive into the world of realpolitik that would define him as a pre-eminent national security advisor and secretary of state under two administrations and an informal advisor to several others.

Kissinger would undoubtedly have known, better than most while still at Harvard in the 1950s, how Wilhelmine Germany had picked up the mantle of a German empire united by Otto Von Bismarck to upset the balance of power through imperialism, ultra-nationalism, naval expansionism and competition with England, and a scramble to seek colonial privileges in Africa.

Many of these traits, Kissinger would not fail to notice now, are evident a hundred years on in China's unilateralism and aggressive policies. As the world rapidly cleaves itself into two camps led by the US and China, a new Cold War looms ahead. China under President Xi Jinping is actively seeking to replace the US as the world's largest economy and most powerful nation. It promises to be a titanic struggle between a wealthy single-party autocracy founded on extreme notions of ideology and nationalism, and an inclusive rules-based order favoured by liberal democracies.

Kissinger's understanding of Asia

Kissinger looked at the issue through the lens of classic European balance of power. It is one of the greatest shortcomings of US strategic thought, including Kissinger's own, that it could never quite clearly reticulate the various parts of the Asian power equation. The big pieces of the jigsaw puzzle in Asia, such as the question of Taiwan, peace on the Korean peninsula, Indo-China and the rise of communism, were apparent. However, Kissinger's appreciation lacked a proper understanding of other dynamics such as relations between China and neighbours such as Japan and India.

For a post-World War II US, flushed with victory, the priority in East Asia was to keep Japan from remilitarizing, and to leverage its considerable trade and investment ties, alliance partnerships and bases to maintain equilibrium in the Asia-Pacific. The US opened up its market across the Pacific to resurrect Japan's economy and extended similar access to other Asian economies such as the Republic of Korea, Taiwan, Singapore and Hong Kong. In incrementally providing China the same advantages after the great reset in relations following the Nixon visit in 1972, the US failed to fully foresee the longer-term implications of such a policy, including the flow of high-end technologies in the defence sector, leading to the economic and military rise of China.

From all that he has written about China, particularly in his seminal book *On China* (2011), it is clear that Kissinger was fascinated by the possibility of creating history. His record of meetings with Chinese leaders reveals the constant awe in which he held them, especially during one-on-one meetings with Mao Zedong and Zhou Enlai, both hardened veterans of the Long March and masters of guile. Even President Nixon, during his historic visit in 1972, was summoned by Mao for a meeting without any advance notice, as if that were the most natural thing to happen to a person occupying the world's most powerful public office, to be ushered into the presence of a 'philosopher-king' and subjected to his musings for an indeterminate period of time.

US opening to China

By the end of the 1960s, it had become apparent that Sino–Soviet relations had fundamentally deteriorated. The breakthrough in ties with China came within two years of Nixon's inauguration as President in 1969.

China dreaded the possibility of a full-fledged Soviet attack after the armed border clashes of 1969, the most serious of which was at Damansky/Zhenbao Island on the Ussuri River. The US spotted an opportunity to provide strategic reassurance to an erstwhile inveterate foe. A triangular relationship was established over the next few years. An implicit strategic partnership between two ideological adversaries was forged to overcome a common challenge they faced from the Soviet Union.

In opening up to China, diplomatically and through economic ties, the US set into motion a process over which it later lost control, leading to vested political and commercial interests driving US policy towards China. A China, which regarded any US presence on its periphery ever since the formation of the People's Republic of China in 1949 to be 'encirclement' that thwarted its rise, was unhesitatingly supported by the US. A policy, once implemented, has its own logic, and in this case, it rested on the premise that if the US opened up its markets, investments and technologies to access by the Chinese, it might lead one day to a more prosperous and democratic China. US entrepreneurs dreamt of big profits if the billion-plus Chinese people drank Coca-Cola, imbibed Starbucks coffee or ate McDonald's hamburgers. The naivety lay in the expectation that once the Chinese wore jeans and adopted some of the American lifestyle, an ineluctable process of political change would be set off in China. A 'peaceful evolution' implied, for a generation of policymakers that followed Kissinger, a possible change in the system of governance by the Communist Party of China.

Over the last seventy years, the US has repeatedly misread China's true intentions or chosen to sacrifice reality at the altar of political expediency and commercial interests. Numerous examples of the strategic misreading of China by the US, resulting in outcomes being diametrically opposite to those envisaged in the original calculus, can be gauged from James Mann's trenchant book *The China Fantasy: Why Capitalism Will Not Bring Democracy to China*, published in 2008. The book lays bare the weaknesses of all the premises of the Nixon–Kissinger duo that continued to guide US policy towards China well into the present times.

When one assesses US motivation in seeking a rapprochement with China, it is clear that the seeds of such policy reorientation were visible soon after Nixon took oath in 1969. The threat of an expansionist Soviet Union with conventional superiority in Europe, fast closing the gap with the US in strategic missiles, was a primary consideration. The US obviously had an eye to achieving an honourable retreat from the quagmire of an unending war in Vietnam. There was the unprecedented public reaction to the body bags coming in and the rampant drug abuse among the American soldiers, apart from the astronomical economic and political costs. Alongside a reset in triangular relations, things between the two superpowers began to look up somewhat in 1972, with progress on Strategic Arms Limitation Talks (SALT) and better economic and trade arrangements. Of course, this was only superficial progress as some might aver, perhaps a limited corollary of the forward movement in Sino-US relations. The decade of the 1970s no doubt continued to demonstrate that genuine détente was all but buried, Soviet interference in Angola and Ethiopia showed no sign of abeyance and the arms race reached its acme. The decade ended with the Soviet occupation of Afghanistan in 1979, further fuelling the rise of neoconservatism in the US.

The Nixon–Kissinger move at the start of the 1970s had the effect of ensuring that China would emerge, as surely as would a butterfly from a chrysalis, from the limitations of the self-imposed isolation of the Cultural Revolution. By the end of the decade, China under Deng Xiaoping had created the right framework in support of the open-door policy and the Four Modernizations to make the fullest use of propinquity in a new-found partnership with the US.

By the end of the decade, the Soviet threat was already receding, having reached its zenith. Unlike the brutal military interference during the Hungarian Revolution in 1956 and the Prague Spring in 1968, the Communist Party of the Soviet Union, under an ailing Leonid Brezhnev, did not intervene in the Solidarity Movement, which started at the Gdańsk Shipyard in Poland in 1980, leaving it to General Wojciech Jaruzelski to deal with local opposition through martial law.

In November 1983, the Reagan administration publicly announced new regulations for the transfer of technology to China. These were designed 'to reflect a more liberal export control policy' by raising dramatically the volume and sophistication of technologically advanced goods developed in the US available for licensing and export to China. To facilitate the policy, the administration even reassigned China to the country grouping under the Export Administration Regulations placing it alongside the NATO countries and other friendly non-aligned nations. The immediate effect of this re-categorization was that the export of most goods and technology to China began to be fast-tracked rather than be subjected to the old policy of case-by-case reviews.

Ironically, with the path paved by the Nixon–Kissinger opening to China in the course of the previous decade, it was under a neoconservative president, Ronald Reagan, that the US transferred several military technologies to the People's Republic of China in 1983–87, although the momentum in such cooperation was disrupted by the Tiananmen massacre, and never quite regained subsequently. Reagan's military cooperation had a precedent in the Carter administration's erroneous assessment, as Kissinger himself asserts, that an increase in China's technological and military capacities enhanced global equilibrium and American national security!

Looking beyond Tiananmen

In fact, after the Tiananmen events of June 1989, President George H.W. Bush almost competed with Nixon in sending secret outreach missions to China. Within weeks of the crackdown that led to global outrage, Bush sent his National Security Advisor Brent Scowcroft, accompanied by Deputy Secretary of State Lawrence Eagleburger, to Beijing on a secret trip in July, followed by another trip later. The Soviet Union disintegrated in 1991, and for reasons that were no longer related to the original motivations of the early 1970s, the US resumed full cooperation with China after only a short interregnum.

The dissolution of the Soviet Union in 1991, in a way, had removed the fundamental underpinning of the triangular logic of US policy towards China, in which it sought better ties with both China and the Soviet Union as compared to what the other two had with one another. The Chinese Communist Party's harsh crackdown on peaceful demonstrators at Tiananmen in 1989 and its reaction to the end of the Soviet Union should logically have alerted the US to the real nature of China's political system. The US failed to be mindful of the ominous implications of the rise of communist China as a global power. Following a brief interregnum, ties were normalized and China resumed its growth trajectory.

By the time President William Jefferson Clinton took office in 1992, levelling the charge that his predecessor George H.W. Bush had been 'coddling the butchers of Beijing', other interests had taken over. US entrepreneurs viewed China as an opportunity to lower manufacturing costs, access the growing Chinese domestic market and expand markets globally. After initial friction over trade and human rights, followed by tensions sparked by Chinese missile tests across the Taiwan Strait, Clinton ordered two US carrier battle groups to steam through the narrow waterway. After that, things moved quickly to reveal contradictions in the US's China policy. On the one hand, a US warplane 'mistakenly' bombed the Chinese embassy in Belgrade in 1999, leading to unprecedented mass demonstrations against US diplomatic compounds in China. On the other hand, Clinton moved from annual trade certifications for China to granting permanent normal trade relations, previously known as Most Favoured Nation (MFN) status, through the US-China Relations Act of 2000.

From then on, there was no looking back for China. Unimpeded and guaranteed access to the US market paved the way, under the subsequent Republican administration of President George Bush, for China's entry into the World Trade Organization. Since then, the entire world has been China's oyster. Its 'state capitalism', backed by hidden subsidies, has helped it notch up huge trade surpluses, especially with the US. In the two decades since, China has hollowed out many a manufacturing capability in the world's most advanced economy.

Today, after decades of unbridled growth, China can claim satisfaction from the fact that it outwitted the US, thanks to the fundamentally flawed premises of the US policy, the groundwork for which was laid by Henry Kissinger under Nixon. China's state-led economy emerged relatively unscathed from the Asian financial crisis of 1997 and succeeded in locking many Asian countries in its embrace through currency swap agreements under the Chiang Mai Initiative. Its endurance during the global economic and financial crises a decade later left it in an advantageous position vis-à-vis the US and other large liberal democratic capitalist economies. Both before and following the outbreak of the Covid-19 pandemic, China's 'socialism with Chinese characteristics' and 'state capitalism' have demonstrated greater capacity than others for economic growth and recovery, thoroughly disproving Kissinger's view of the 1970s that wherever market economies and communist economies have competed in roughly comparable circumstances, the communist economies have been left far behind.

Departure from policy reticence of the past

The US traditionally had no interest in challenging China's territorial integrity, with the proviso that force would not be used to resolve the question of Taiwan. When Japan occupied Manchuria in the 1930s and expanded its conquests across much of East China, it was ironically the colonialists and the US that sought to preserve China's independence. In fact, Secretary of State Dean Acheson had stated as early as in January 1950 that China's integrity was in American national interest regardless of communist China's ideology. Though the Taiwan Relations Act of 1979 kept Taiwan within the US security perimeter, it is only recently that the US passed the Taiwan Allies International

Protection and Enhancement Initiative (TAIPEI) to encourage countries to maintain ties with Taiwan and back its participation in international organizations such the World Health Organization.

The US had little interest in Tibet's independence or even autonomy in the years leading to the formation of China and its military takeover of Tibet in 1950. It took no heed of Tibet's pleas to the United Nations for assistance in 1950, or later, when the Dalai Lama fled to India in 1959. For a brief while during World War II, President Roosevelt had reached out to the Dalai Lama's administration in Lhasa for access to Tibet's territory to aid the war effort. Even the low intensity covert operations by the Central Intelligence Agency (CIA) ended with the Sino-US rapprochement in 1971. President Trump filled in the vacant post of special coordinator for Tibetan issues in the Department of State, building on the Tibet Policy Act of 2002, the Reciprocal Access to Tibet Act of 2018 and the Tibet Policy and Support Act of 2019.

Hong Kong's future has figured on the list of US interests only recently, sparked by the trampling of democracy and human rights. A subject long outsourced to the British, the US was happy to make use of the territory to monitor China and for rest and recreation by US vessels in the region. Growing Chinese sensitivity to US military activity on its periphery, including in the Taiwan Strait, has put an end to this. The US recognized Hong Kong's autonomy through the Hong Kong Policy Act of 1992 and adjusted policies to give the territory trade and other benefits even after its handover to China in 1997. Since then, China has systemically eroded the territory's special status guaranteed under the 'One Country Two Systems' formula. The brutal repression of pro-democracy protests followed by the passing of a new draconian National Security Law 2020 by Beijing led to the US President signing the Hong Kong Human Rights and Democracy Act of 2019.

Of the many examples of China's heavy-handed actions, none is perhaps as egregious as the treatment of the Muslim minority in the

Xinjiang Uygur Autonomous Region (XUAR). The US has boldly criticized China for its human rights violations, forced detentions, desecrations of mosques and restrictions on religious symbols and practices. The US has passed the Uyghur Human Rights Policy Act 2020 authorizing periodic reviews, freezing of assets and sanctioning of Chinese entities and officials involved in surveillance and human rights violations.

In the South China Sea, the US has not done enough to prevent China's territorial grab or restore status quo ante. Under President Obama, the pivot to Asia was little more than lip service. President Xi executed his own pivot after coming to power in 2012, defying the United Nations Convention on the Law of the Sea. Attempts to reticulate the region through the Belt and Road Initiative and predatory finance have further complicated the situation in Southeast Asia. The Trump administration finally realigned its official position with the 2016 tribunal ruling of the Permanent Court of Arbitration, which deemed Chinese claims over the South China Sea to be unlawful and devoid of historical evidence.

The more things change the more they remain the same

Some aspects, especially in China's character, transcend both its ancient civilization and modern ideology and have remained unmuted over the past half century. The concept of 'strategic encirclement' remains ingrained in Chinese strategic thought. As was once the case in dealing with the xiong nu—barbarians on its northern borders—China continues to employ ancient stratagems to pit one nation against another on its periphery to weaken and subjugate contending forces through guile and inducement.

There are both similarities and dissimilarities that can be observed through the lens of half a century. Mao, nearing his end when Nixon visited him, had no real successor. He had identified and banished several over time, and Hua Guofeng, the anointed one at the time of his death, was a nondescript provincial lightweight who was quickly removed by Deng Xiaoping. Today, Xi Jinping, like Mao, has arrogated extraordinary powers to himself. Xi too has no successor in place. Xi, like Mao, appears to have anointed himself leader in perpetuity. If Mao said in the 1970s to Kissinger that China would not foreclose its option to use force over Taiwan, and indeed expected to have to use it someday, Xi Jinping's China has taken the same line.

There are subtle differences too: Xi Jinping's resurrection of Confucius, who had been denigrated by Mao, to justify the imposition of his own version of harmony and order under the heavens. Having explored the limits of China's 'socialism with Chinese characteristics' in reconciling China's economic development and the growing aspirations of its people, Xi Jinping is now using China's ancient civilization, as embodied by Confucius, to demand complete order and loyalty of citizens to the authoritarian Chinese Communist Party. In his keynote speech on 24 September 2014, commemorating the 2,565th anniversary of Confucius' birth, Xi Jinping held up the Chinese Communist Party as the 'successor to and promoter of fine traditional Chinese culture'.

From the outset, as Kissinger writes, Mao had no intention of accepting an international system in the design of which China had no role. Today, under President Xi Jinping, China is following a subtler policy. It has greatly benefited from the post-World War II financial and political structures in the creation of which communist China had no role, such as the United Nations Security Council or the World Trade Organization. It has spearheaded new ones such as the Asian Infrastructure Investment Bank (AIIB) and the New Development Bank (NDB) of the BRICS (Brazil, Russia, India, China and South Africa) grouping. The US pull-out from the Paris climate change agreement and Trans-Pacific Partnership (TPP) negotiations under

President Trump, as well as withdrawal from the United Nations Educational, Scientific and Cultural Organization (UNESCO) and the United Nations Human Rights Council (UNHRC) in 2017 and 2018 respectively, created new opportunities for China. Trump imposed cuts in financial contributions to United Nations agencies such as the United Nations Population Fund (UNFPA) as early as in 2017, and later, in the midst of the Covid-19 pandemic, announced a decision to cut funding to WHO. In the meanwhile, China has championed free trade and emerged as the largest economy in the Regional Comprehensive Economic Partnership (RCEP), besides offering to ramp up its funding to United Nations agencies.

A common Chinese assessment that runs through the 1950s to the time of Kissinger's visit to China and up to now, is the belief in the superiority of China's systems and the conviction that the US is on the decline. More than the actual decline of the US, it is the perceived relative decline in US power that has often led China to believe that it is in a stronger position. Mao had labelled Hitler, the tsar of Russia, General Chiang Kai-shek, Imperial Japan and the US as 'paper tigers'. The others had met their end, and so would the US one day, he averred. This unrealistic assessment of US power did not prevent Mao from bringing China closer to the US to ward off the Soviet threat.

New Cold War

So much has changed in the last fifty years. Already the world's second-largest economy today, China hopes to overtake the US around 2027, the year in which the People's Liberation Army will celebrate its centenary.

Over the decades, the US has not only run up a colossal annual trade deficit of about $450 billion, but it has also allowed itself to walk into a blind alley of dependence on China in biotechnology, pharmaceuticals, rare earths and even micro-electronics such as integrated circuits and transistors, which are used in critical platforms such as satellites, cruise missiles and drones, not just cell phones.

More than in trade, it is in technology that the new Cold War is manifesting itself. The extreme dependence of Chinese tech giants such as Huawei, ZTE and SMIC on US exports of chips and semiconductors does not diminish the fact that its research and development budget was \$321.3 billion in 2019, dwarfing the US outlay of \$156.8 billion.

The new Cold War is playing out in myriad ways—competing lending mechanisms and programmes for regional economic development, capacity-building and connectivity. For many, Pax Sinica is emerging as an alternative to Pax Americana.

Today, slogans such as the 'China Dream', 'New Type of Great Power Relations', 'Community of Shared Future of Mankind', backed by 'wolf-warrior diplomacy' are a means of enforcing a China-centric unipolarity in Asia.

Conclusion

To borrow a phrase from Kissinger's own writings, he has remained the 'perennial counsellor' to presidents and secretaries of state. Recently, in an interview to Bloomberg, Kissinger warned the incoming Biden administration to move quickly to restore lines of communication with China frayed during the Trump presidency to avoid drifting towards a catastrophe comparable to World War I.

Communication at this stage should mean firmly conveying US rejection of China's unilateralism and assertive policies. Now firmly in place, the Biden administration can ill afford to be lulled into the same sense of complacency that afflicted previous administrations. It should not allow China to get away with egregious violations of international law and blatant disruption of the regional balance of power.

A softer conciliatory approach by Biden will embolden China to continue to question the existing rules-based order. It will not prevent China from working on an old objective, a priority since 1949, of seeking the complete eviction of the US from Asia. Kissinger would understand this better in light of the US's historical experience of the Monroe Doctrine in the nineteenth century, which sought to keep the Americas as a US preserve.

A Biden administration that eases pressure on China to conform to a rules-based order would sow the seeds of doubt in the capitals of all its alliance partners about the emergence of a potential US-China condominium, much like the 'Super-Yalta' feared by Europe in the 1960s. So far, all indications point to the Biden administration sharing its predecessor's misgivings about China.

Fifty years after Kissinger's trip to China, a new relationship similar to the one that he helped forge between the US and China is now taking shape between India and the US. As between the US and China at the time, the new partners today seek to coordinate their actions without creating a formal obligation to do so. China's avowed goal to enlist the US as a counterweight to the 'polar bear' (Soviet Union) is similar to the way the US and India view one another in an attempt to deal with the 'dragon' (China).

Kissinger suggests in his book, *On China*, that an aspect of strategic tension in the current world situation stems from the fact that China fears that the US is seeking to contain China, and that this is paralleled by the US concern that China is seeking to expel the US from a region to which it has long contributed through trade, investment and security. This is an assessment that was valid in the 1950s and the 1970s, and rings true even today.

The difficulty with superpowers, or perhaps great powers would be a more apt description today, is that they seek exceptionalism as a matter of right. Today, both the US and China seek exceptionalism in their own ways. The difference is that the systems created by a US-led world order have proven themselves over the past seventy-five years and have succeeded in keeping peace through the Cold War and beyond. But the alternative order that China seeks to shape and to lead into the twenty-first century through its slogans for 'community with a shared future for mankind' and 'wolf-warrior diplomacy', is unlikely to promote regional peace and stability. For that to happen, China will have to change. China's purposes withal will need to change.

(The article was first published in Sanjaya Baru and Rahul Sharma (eds), *A New Cold War: Henry Kissinger and the Rise of China*, HarperCollins India, 2021)

China must respect existing agreements and refrain from unilateral action

The death of twenty Indian military personnel, including the commanding officer of the 16 Bihar Battalion deployed in the Galwan Valley along the Line of Actual Control (LAC), in an altercation with the Chinese People's Liberation Army (PLA) troops on 15 June 2020 has sent shock waves throughout India. For weeks, the nation has been following the standoff in Ladakh in the Western Sector that started after an incident on 5 May. There were reports of a Chinese military build-up at multiple points, eliciting a robust mirror response by India. Desolate locations such as Daulat Beg Oldie, (DBO), Galwan, Hot Springs, Pangong Tso, Spanggur, Chushul and Demchok became household names. Few are aware of their evocative and emotive history as places where Indian troops of 5 Jat, 1 Jat, 1/8 Gurkha Rifles, 13 Kumaon and 7 JK Militia fought valiant battles in 1962.

The two sides had made statements in the first week of June indicating their commitment to resolving differences through diplomatic and military channels, in accordance with the institutionalized framework already in place. There were encouraging signs, especially after the productive meeting of senior commanders on 6 June. Just when it appeared that tensions were abating, something went terribly wrong.

The Indian Army has confirmed that the loss of lives took place during the disengagement process. It appears the commanding officer was leading a confirmatory patrol to monitor compliance when the retreating Chinese troops attacked them with rods and stones. In the melee, large numbers of troops from reserve echelons on both sides reportedly fell upon each other, leading to casualties on both sides. Matters were made worse by the darkness and the sheer cliffs from where a number of soldiers reportedly fell into the freezing waters of the Galwan River and died of grievous injuries and exposure. Reports indicate sizeable casualties on the Chinese side, but an opaque system that routinely camouflages facts can hardly be expected to inform the world of its own casualties.[3]

The border row between India and China could not have erupted at a worse moment. The world is grappling with a once-in-a-century coronavirus pandemic and a global recession that promises to leave none unscathed. China, which is increasingly censured for obfuscating the origins of the pandemic, appears to have chosen bellicosity, sacrificing all norms of responsible international conduct, as is evident in its aggressive stand on Taiwan, Hong Kong and the South China Sea.

For many years now, China has used a flexible, expedient and self-serving concept of the LAC to gradually inch further up to its

---

3   'Official Spokesperson's response to media queries seeking comments on the statement issued on 19 June by the Chinese Spokesperson on the events in Galwan valley area', Ministry of External Affairs, Government of India, 20 June 2020; https://mea.gov.in/response-to-queries.htm?dtl/32770/official+spokespersons+response+to+media+queries+seeking+comments+on+the+statement+issued+on+19+june+by+the+chinese+spokesperson+on+the+events+in+the+galwan+valley+area

specious boundary claim lines. Maintaining a duplicitous position on the agreements reached in 1993 and 1996 to clarify and confirm the LAC, it has dragged its feet on the exchange of maps to identify differences, which is the first step in the delineation and demarcation of the LAC. Meanwhile, China has built vast modern infrastructure all along the LAC to facilitate its patrols and forward presence. Despite China's first-mover advantage, India has also stepped up its game in recent years. It has considerably improved its infrastructure, such as the Darbok-Shyok-DBO road, advanced landing grounds and tracks up to its traditional patrolling points. Areas where Indian troops earlier were obliged to undertake long-range patrols on foot are now accessible much faster. Advanced surveillance technologies reduce the warning time and both sides often scramble to reach the same spot to stave off the other.

Standard operating procedures (SOPs) and drills for run-ins have been painstakingly worked out by the two sides over the years—banner drills and flag meetings—to maintain peace and tranquillity and disengage. The panoply of confidence-building measures includes regular border personnel meetings, ad hoc flag meetings and hotlines for communication. These have worked well until now, given that run-ins by the two sides are a common feature in all the sectors. Going by the number of stone-pelting incidents and physical scuffles between the two sides in recent years, it is obvious that many of the protocols are not fully adhered to by the Chinese troops. Unbridled nationalism and arrogance permeates the Chinese system, and the PLA is hardly immune to that contagion.

The last incident involving loss of life was in 1975 when an Assam Rifles patrol was ambushed by the PLA on the Indian side of the Tulung La Pass in Arunachal Pradesh. Since then, there have been occasions when things have threatened to escalate, as during the long-drawn eyeball-to-eyeball confrontation along the Sumdorong Chu in Tawang district in Arunachal Pradesh, sparked by China in 1986 and resolved only in 1994. Face-offs have also taken place at DBO, Deepsang, Pangong Tso and Chumar over the past decade, but both sides have stayed their hand, with no loss of life. It takes great discipline on the part of soldiers to observe restraint in the face of grave provocations. The Indian side has been scrupulous in the observance of protocols during face-offs, but that cannot be said of the Chinese troops.

India is committed to a dialogue for the peaceful resolution of differences. However, no self-respecting nation can be expected to cave into China's irredentism, least of all India. What is the way forward? The first step is for China to restore status quo ante in all the areas where it has created new de facto situations. Second, China must respect the existing agreements between the two sides and refrain from any unilateral action. Third, China must work together with India to clarify and confirm the LAC through the exchange of large-scale maps. Fourth, ineffective border management protocols and drills should be reviewed and improved upon through discussions. Fifth, both sides should rein in their media and encourage more responsible reporting. Sixth, China must particularly instruct its 'wolf warrior' nationalists to eschew arrogance and cooperate with India in maintaining peace and tranquillity. Lastly, the Chinese side should match India in adhering to the strategic guidance that Prime Minister Narendra Modi and President Xi Jinping have agreed to provide to their respective sides through informal summits to ensure that such incidents do not occur.

After all, China should follow its own dictum, 'he who tied the knot should untie it'.

(The article was first published in *The Indian Express*, 18 June 2020)

Modi's resolute China policy

In June 2020, a commentary in the *Japan Times* titled 'India's appeasement policy toward China unravels' questioned India's policy toward China. India and China have many outstanding issues including border disputes, the Line of Actual Control (LAC) and China's close security ties with Pakistan against India's interests.

That India and China have had an uneasy relationship since the 1950s is well documented. China's military takeover of Xinjiang and Tibet in 1949 and 1950 forever blurred the historical boundaries. The freshly minted People's Republic of China steadily encroached on large tracts of Indian territory in the Aksai Chin region of Ladakh, leading to the border conflict in 1962 in which China occupied more territory.

In the halcyon days of the 1950s, Indian pronouncements were blithely laced with calls for fraternal bonds between the world's two most populous countries. India supported China at the United Nations when the latter was pilloried as the aggressor on the Korean Peninsula. India even lobbied to have China represented on the United Nations Security Council. Preoccupied with global causes such as chairing the

Neutral Nations Repatriation Commission in the Korean War and co-founding the Five Principles of Peaceful Coexistence at Bandung, India was blindsided by a militaristic China.

Meanwhile, China was inching forward to usurp Indian territory. After China moved into Tibet, Sardar Vallabhbhai Patel, a nationalist politician, presciently warned Prime Minister Jawaharlal Nehru, in his letter of 7 November 1950, of China's vacuous 'professions of peaceful intention'. On 9 November 1962, the late Prime Minister Atal Bihari Vajpayee, then a young leader of the Bharatiya Jana Sangh, one of India's smallest opposition parties, lamented in a parliamentary debate that even fifteen years after independence, the nation's soldiers had not been equipped with automatic rifles or proper uniforms. During the 1950s, India had reduced its defence budget even though it was staring a belligerent China in the face. It had a telling effect during the hostilities in 1962.

Ironically, India was among the first to recognize Tibet as a part of China in 1954 through the short-lived Agreement on Trade and Intercourse between the Tibet region of China and India. India did not object in 1965 when China created a rump Tibet Autonomous Region (TAR) by lopping off historical Tibetan lands and published maps that claimed Indian territory in Arunachal Pradesh. Yet, China brazenly adopted double standards when India carried out internal constitutional changes in Jammu and Kashmir through the repeal of Article 370 in August 2019, itself a bold and unprecedented decision.

Successive Indian governments have countenanced an aggressive China. Emboldened by its heady economic rise in recent decades, China has sought to alter the status quo along its periphery, both terrestrial and maritime. Its unilateral attempts to redraw boundaries in the East and South China Seas are reminiscent of tactics long practiced along the border regions of India. The Chinese military presence, growing infrastructure and territorial advances are entrenched features of its policy that pre-date Modi's ascendance to power. What is different today is India's firm resolve to strengthen its armed forces and empower them to deliver a robust military response if provoked. This is exactly what happened in the Galwan Valley, where Indian soldiers sacrificed their lives to thwart Chinese designs. In recent years, Modi's thrust on developing infrastructure along the Indian side of the LAC appears to have rattled China.

As chief minister of Gujarat, Modi had endeavoured to expand trade and economic ties with China in keeping with the imperatives of globalization. Upon assuming office as prime minister in 2014, he opened the doors of the Indian economy to global trade and investment to boost economic growth and potential. Discounting the impact of the Covid-19 scourge, foreign direct investment flows into India rose 13 per cent to a record $49.97 billion in the financial year 2019-20, up from $44.36 billion in the previous year. Economic ties with China have also rapidly expanded, but a historically weak domestic manufacturing sector could not keep pace, setting the stage for a ballooning trade deficit with China. Other countries too face this dilemma. Both Japan and the US have strong economic ties with China with large trade deficits.

The implementation of an electronic visa facility for Chinese travellers to India, as well as for visitors from elsewhere, was aimed at enhancing business and people-to-people ties and building a developmental partnership. Issuing electronic visas is an international practice, subject to standard verification procedures. Moreover, it is the least likely to lead to a repeat of a situation that prevailed a decade ago when India's tourist visa was routinely exploited by Chinese companies to dispatch unskilled labour for infrastructure projects.

Modi has regularly engaged President Xi Jinping even though it is the Chinese Premier who is nominally his counterpart. This has raised India's leadership profile vis-à-vis China. The informal summits with Xi at Wuhan and Mamallapuram have facilitated one-on-one conversations without the straitjacket of choreographed meetings.

Modi did some plain-speaking with Xi on the border face-off with China in Chumar in 2014, which unfolded even as he was playing host to him in Ahmedabad. The stand-off at Doklam in 2017 clearly underscored a new resolve on India's part. It has succeeded in preventing any unilateral changes to the location of the sensitive tri-junction with Bhutan.

In 2014, India reminded Chinese foreign minister Wang Yi through its doughty foreign minister, the late Sushma Swaraj, that the new government supported the One China policy, but it expected China to reciprocate with a One India policy. Those words take on a new significance today. The global response to the constitutional change effected in Jammu and Kashmir in August 2019 suggests that the world has increasingly taken note of the One India policy.

As in the 1950s, China remains wary of India's position in its rapidly deteriorating ties with the US. Its mistrust of Japan runs deep, with historical schisms barely cloaked by the recent diplomatic thaw. But the reality is evident in the growing Chinese incursions in the Senkaku Islands where matters are bound to come to a head one day. Today, India and Japan are sailing in the same boat. Like India under Modi, Japan under Prime Minister Shinzo Abe has reviewed its vulnerabilities and strengthened its defence. India and Japan have a strategic partnership and both have a growing convergence of interests with the US and Australia in the Quadrilateral Security Dialogue. India's rising profile in the Indo-Pacific and defence logistics pacts with several countries have led to unease in Beijing.

It takes courage to wage war, but it takes even greater courage to wage peace while protecting national interests. Modi and Abe have demonstrated that they can pursue peace in earnest, but would never compromise on the defence and security interests of the nation.

(The article was first published in the *Japan Times*, 30 June 2020)

The cartographic route to deeper strategic partnerships

In recent years, India has developed close strategic partnerships with the US, Japan and Australia in the framework of the Quadrilateral Security Dialogue, or the Quad. It is instructive to review how the Quad partners stand on issues concerning India's sovereignty and territorial integrity. This is of particular significance at a time when India is facing an aggressive China on its borders where a bloody incident on 15 June 2020, triggered by Chinese troops, led to a military face-off.

United States

In 1962, the then Prime Minister Jawaharlal Nehru, according to publicly available information, wrote to the US President John F. Kennedy through the US Ambassador to India, John Kenneth Galbraith, requesting urgent military assistance in the face of the massive Chinese aggression along India's borders in 1962. The wish list included twelve squadrons of supersonic all-weather fighter aircraft and two squadrons of B-47 bombers, with supporting radar and personnel. Before a sympathetic US could provide substantial assistance, a ceasefire was announced.

During the 1965 India-Pakistan war, the US observed neutrality despite a close security partnership with Pakistan and placed an arms embargo on both countries. During the 1971 war, the then US President Richard Nixon and national security advisor Henry Kissinger sent the US Seventh Fleet's Task Force, led by the nuclear-powered aircraft carrier Enterprise, to the Bay of Bengal and failed to convince China to open a new front with India. India's nuclear weapons tests in May 1998 elicited sharp reactions from the US, as from Japan and Australia. But the US behind-the-scenes role was instrumental in getting Pakistan to back off finally in the face of resolute military action by India during the Kargil war in 1999. Ties with India could not be more different today, with the US having emerged as India's biggest defence partner in terms of joint exercises and sale of defence equipment.

A scan reveals that US maps depict Kashmir as a disputed region with a tripartite division under the administration of India, Pakistan and China. Around 1968, US government maps began to extend the Line of Control (LOC) between India and Pakistan beyond its terminus at Point NJ9842 all the way up to the Karakoram Pass. This was tantamount to reflecting the Pakistani position on the Siachen Glacier. From around 1987 onwards, the US has corrected its position, terminating the LOC at Point NJ9842. The US takes a neutral position on the sovereignty of the Siachen Glacier, which is depicted as a contested area though it is under Indian control and an integral part of its territory of Jammu and Kashmir.

It is noteworthy that maps of the Central Intelligence Agency (CIA) of the US depict the traditional boundary claimed by the former princely state of Jammu and Kashmir encompassing the trans-Karakoram Shaksgam tract ceded by Pakistan to China under their

Boundary Agreement of 2 March 1963. In depicting the Shaksgam tract, the US maps clearly state that this is 'territory ceded by Pakistan to China in 1963 and never recognized by India'. The US depicts Aksai Chin as disputed territory while unequivocally recognizing Arunachal Pradesh as an integral part of India.

Today, the US and India enjoy a comprehensive global strategic partnership with wide-ranging cooperation in every conceivable field. India-US defence ties are deep and expanding, with several key agreements for the exchange of military information, logistics support and communication. The Industrial Security Annex of December 2019 is expected to spur cooperation for Make in India in the defence sector. The US has been supportive of India's position in the ongoing border tensions with China in Ladakh. US Secretary of State Michael Pompeo conveyed condolences and supported the peaceful resolution of the border issue. Assistant Secretary of State for the Bureau of East Asian and Pacific Affairs David R. Stilwell went further by criticizing China's actions vis-à-vis India, the South China Sea and other issues.

Australia

India and Australia have also drawn increasingly closer in recent years. Economic and strategic ties have been strengthened as reflected in the outcome documents of the virtual summit between prime ministers Narendra Modi and Scott Morrison held on 4 June 2020. Defence and security ties are a cornerstone of the Comprehensive Strategic Partnership. Joint naval exercises such as AUSINDEX and Kakadu, the Indian Air Force's participation in Australia's Pitch Black exercise, and the conclusion of a Mutual Logistics Support Agreement in particular, will contribute to the strengthening of defence cooperation. The Joint Declaration on a Shared Vision for Maritime Cooperation in the Indo-Pacific will provide a fillip to maritime domain awareness activity involving submarines and P8 maritime patrol aircraft of the two countries. The 'two plus two' dialogue, upgraded to the ministerial level, augurs well for the future of ties. On the border tensions with China, the Australian government has conveyed its condolences to the families of Indian soldiers who lost their lives in the clash at Galwan on 15 June 2020.

The official tourist map produced by Geoscience Australia, available through the website of the Department of Foreign Relations and Trade, depicts Pakistan-occupied Kashmir as a part of Pakistan, Jammu and Kashmir and Arunachal Pradesh as part of India and Aksai Chin as a part of China. Australia's stand on Aksai Chin differs from that of the US government, which depicts it as a disputed territory. Also, in marked contrast to the US, the Australian map arbitrarily extends the LOC of 1972 beyond Point NJ9842 to the Karakoram Pass, thus mirroring Pakistan's spurious position on the Siachen Glacier.

Japan

Japan is today unquestionably one of India's closest friends with a robust Special Strategic and Global Partnership that encompasses economic and defence cooperation. One of India's biggest investors, Japan is present in virtually every large infrastructure and developmental project in India. It has been a permanent partner since 2015 in the trilateral Malabar naval exercise, along with India and the US. A military logistics agreement, known as the Acquisition and Cross-Servicing Agreement, is under discussion. Moreover, the personal friendship between prime ministers Narendra Modi and Shinzo Abe has truly deepened mutual trust.

Recent efforts to decouple Japan's economy from that of China are not going to substantially alter the reality that the Japanese and Chinese economies are strongly intermeshed and expected to remain so, especially when economic contraction occasioned by the Covid-19 pandemic is a common scourge.

Despite growing tensions with China over the Senkaku Islands, Japan's ties with China, in fact, have thawed in recent years. In the past, Japan had a close relationship with Pakistan, fostered through years of intimate cooperation during the Soviet occupation in Afghanistan. Even today, Pakistan frequently tries to tap into the lingering sympathy for Pakistan in the political, bureaucratic and media circles of Japan.

Like the Australian map, the official travel advisory map carried by the website of the Ministry of Foreign Affairs of Japan inaccurately shows the Karakoram Pass as the terminal point of the LOC, instead of terminating at NJ9842. It too depicts Aksai Chin as an integral part of China without indicating its disputed status, unlike the US depiction of Aksai Chin.

In a statement issued after the 15 June 2020 clash between Indian and Chinese troops in Galwan, the spokesperson of Japan's Ministry of Foreign Affairs expressed hope that the 'situation will be resolved peacefully through dialogue between the concerned parties'. Japan's Ambassador to India, H.E. Satoshi Suzuki, stated in a tweet on 3 July that Japan 'hopes for a peaceful resolution through dialogues'. More relevantly, he emphasized that 'Japan opposes any unilateral attempts to change the status quo'.

Conclusion

The US, Japan and Australia are today among India's closest friends and partners, with growing economic cooperation and deepening defence and security ties. Hence, projections by strategic partners of India's boundaries and territorial claim lines assume a deeper salience especially in light of a convergence of interests in the unfolding geostrategic landscape of the Indo-Pacific.

How far the relationship between India and Australia has been transformed can be judged from the period in which Australia had close security ties with Pakistan in the framework of the Southeast Asia

Treaty Organization (SEATO), a regional defence organization that existed from 1955 to 1977. During subsequent decades, Australia was seen as tilting towards Pakistan.

As China's economy began to envelop the world, Australia's commodities-based economy became heavily reliant on the Chinese market. In recent years, Australia has tried to shake off strategic Chinese investments and influence-peddling in Australia by undertaking a thorough review of the insidious impact of Chinese policies on its national security interests. In keeping with its true character, Australia has been remarkably bold in calling out China on the issue of the origin and spread of the coronavirus. Even so, the fact cannot be glossed over that with 30 per cent of its exports destined for China, Australia remains heavily dependent on it for economic prosperity.

There is no gainsaying that the US, Japan and Australia are close strategic partners of India and have generally adopted helpful positions with regard to core issues of concern for India such as terrorism and the constitutional changes in Jammu and Kashmir. Considering that the US, Japan and Australia have a growing convergence with India on the geostrategic changes underway in the Indo-Pacific, it is an appropriate moment for them to address legacy cartographic anomalies in their maps. In the case of Japan and Australia, a beginning could be made by them to depict the LOC accurately on their maps, terminating at NJ9842. It will bring their position in line with that of the US. After all, even the United Nations map depicts the terminal point of the LOC at NJ9842.

(The article was first published on the website of the Manohar Parrikar Institute for Defence Studies and Analyses, 3 July 2020.

India, China must shift focus to maintenance of status quo along each other's perception of LAC

India's defence minister, Rajnath Singh, made firm and thoughtful statements in the two Houses of Parliament on 15 and 17 September 2020 concerning the military stand-off between India and China in eastern Ladakh following China's aggression in Galwan earlier in June 2020. Apart from lauding the indomitable courage and readiness of India's armed forces to deal with any eventuality to protect the country's territorial integrity, he gave a broad overview of the boundary question and the Line of Actual Control (LAC).

One of his key points was that there is no commonly delineated LAC in the border areas and that after 2003, the LAC clarification exercise ground to a halt due to China's intransigence. China had agreed in the 1993 Agreement on the Maintenance of Peace and Tranquillity along the Line of Actual Control in the India-China Border Areas that, pending an ultimate resolution of the boundary question, the two sides shall strictly respect and observe the LAC. Further, there was agreement that, when necessary, the two sides shall jointly check and determine the segments of the LAC where they have different views regarding its alignment. Article X of the 1996 Agreement on Confidence-Building Measures in the Military Field along the Line of Actual Control in the India-China Border Areas also commits the two sides to speed up the process of clarification and confirmation of the LAC in order to arrive at a common understanding.

It is clear that without exchanging maps depicting each other's LAC, a common understanding will remain elusive. Even after reaching that goal, there will remain the challenge of ensuring that both sides refrain from activities in and along the overlapping areas that threaten peace and tranquillity. Confirmation of the LAC presupposes its delineation on a map and thereafter demarcation on the ground of a single, mutually accepted line. This is an altogether more difficult task since it may entail territorial adjustments. So far, the first step of clarifying each other's perception of the LAC has only been carried out in the Middle Sector, which refers to the boundary between India and China in Himachal Pradesh and Uttarakhand.

Why has China declined to continue the LAC clarification exercise? In the Western Sector, China's so-called LAC of 7 November 1959 is essentially coterminous with its boundary claim line, except in Demchok, where it falls short. In some places, the post-1962 variant of its LAC went beyond the line that China had claimed before the conflict. When India-China border talks recommenced in December 1981, the Chinese side had essentially reiterated the 'package proposal' first conveyed by Deng Xiaoping to then foreign minister Atal Bihari Vajpayee in 1979, and subsequently aired through Indian journalists, suggesting a settlement based on the de facto LAC in the Eastern and Western sectors. However, at the crucial Sixth Round of the Official Level Talks between India and China on the boundary question in 1985, the Chinese did a volte-face. They claimed that the largest dispute lay in the Eastern Sector and that India would have to make substantial concessions, to which China would reciprocate with corresponding adjustments in the Western Sector. China subsequently never clarified the details.

China's reluctance to clarify the LAC today stems from its specious position that India's LAC claims are exaggerated concerning its actual control and effective jurisdiction. Little does this argument take into account the fact that China itself had never physically controlled any part of Aksai Chin until the People's Liberation Army (PLA) rolled into Xinjiang and Tibet in 1949 and 1950, respectively. Thereafter, the story of the Chinese LAC is one of nebulous claims followed by an incremental acquisition of territory.

The separate meetings in Moscow in September 2020 between the defence ministers and foreign ministers of India and China on the side-lines of the Shanghai Cooperation Organisation (SCO) ministerial meetings, have provided an opportune moment for both sides to reduce tensions. The five-point consensus reached by the foreign ministers recognized the importance of dialogue, disengagement and bilateral confidence-building measures. The joint press release of the Sixth Round of the senior commanders' meeting is encouraging, since it speaks of strengthening communication, avoiding misunderstandings and refraining from any further action, including build-up of troops and unilateral attempts to alter the ground situation. In his statement at the 75th Session of the United Nations General Assembly on 22 September 2020, President Xi Jinping made two key points—that China has no intention of fighting a Cold War or a 'hot war' with any country, and that China will continue to narrow differences with others through dialogue and negotiations.

The bilateral consensus and subsequent pronouncements offer India and China an opportunity to break the impasse. The consensus reached so far can be further buttressed by both sides reiterating at their next meeting a key formulation contained in Article 1 of the 1993 agreement, that 'neither side shall use or threaten to use force against the other by any means'. This, of course, requires China to sincerely walk the talk by refraining from unilateral action and military means to address differences. It would also require China to stop insisting on a unilateral interpretation of the LAC and to disengage meaningfully its unilateral military deployments that triggered the escalation along the Line of Actual Control in eastern Ladakh in the first place.

Henceforth, the focus should shift to the maintenance of the status quo along each other's perception of the LAC and within the overlapping areas in many of which both sides have patrolled in the past. It is here, as India has made clear to China through both diplomatic and military channels, that any unilateral attempt to change the situation is unacceptable.

Despite the unrealistic claims made by the Chinese mouthpiece *Global Times*, the military balance in the border areas in eastern Ladakh is, in fact, fairly symmetrical. It is a tribute to India's armed forces that neither the difficult terrain nor inclement weather have prevented them from responding robustly to the Chinese build-up in Ladakh, leaving Beijing in no doubt that any adventurism would prove costly.

By adopting the path of peaceful negotiations that President Xi mentioned in his address at the United Nations, China stands to benefit from a much-needed image makeover at a time when it faces widespread opprobrium for its unilateralism, aggression and 'wolf-warrior diplomacy'.

The last fundamental jolt to bilateral relations was in May 1998, when China abruptly cancelled all engagements in the aftermath of India's nuclear tests. The exception then was a pre-scheduled meeting of the Experts Group of Diplomatic and Military Officials (EG), led by the author on the Indian side, which was used to gradually restart the process of engagement, leading to the visit of External Affairs Minister Jaswant Singh a year later and culminating in President K.R. Narayanan's state visit in May 2000.

What is encouraging about the situation today, as compared to May 1998, is that dialogue has remained intact at all levels. It is noteworthy that while expressing India's firm resolve to defend its territory, the defence minister also alluded in his speeches in Parliament to the desire to address the current situation through dialogue. Taken together, these recent developments provide an opening to China to grasp the nettle and to recognize its own interest in building enduring ties with a large and populous neighbour like India, whose friendship and goodwill will continue to play a crucial role in endorsing the 'peaceful rise of China'.

(The article was first published in *The Indian Express*, 24 September 2020)

The forgotten fact of China-occupied Kashmir

Following the abrogation of Article 370 in August 2019 and the reorganization of the Indian state of Jammu and Kashmir (J&K), a China-Pakistan tandem has emerged to internationalize the issue, including in the United Nations Security Council. Pakistan has feigned solidarity with the people of Kashmir and continues to train and fund separatists and terrorists. The Financial Action Task Force (FATF), the global watchdog that monitors terror financing, has retained Pakistan on its Grey List for a good reason. China's support for Pakistan is motivated by a desire to perpetuate its own territorial grab in the trans-Karakoram Shaksgam tract of Kashmir.

Legitimately India's

China treats the J&K issue as a 'bilateral dispute left over from history' to be resolved between India and Pakistan. It has turned a blind eye to the constitutional shenanigans by which Pakistan's so-called federal Ministry of Kashmir Affairs and Gilgit-Baltistan has acquired complete sway over Pakistan-occupied Kashmir (PoK). It ignores Pakistan's agenda of integrating Gilgit-Baltistan as its fifth province. Yet, China has the temerity to question the establishment of the Union Territory of Ladakh and to term it a 'unilateral' attempt to change 'the status quo in the Kashmir region'. China has no locus standi to comment on India's internal affairs since the erstwhile princely state of J&K acceded to India through the Instrument of Accession on 26 October 1947.

The Shaksgam Valley in the trans-Karakoram tract, part of PoK, was handed over on a platter by a supine Pakistan to China through an illegal border agreement on 2 March 1963. However, the continuing Chinese occupation of Kashmir's territory does not find adequate mention in the contemporary discourse surrounding this issue.

China occupies 5,180 sq. km in the Shaksgam Valley in addition to approximately 38,000 km in Aksai Chin. China and Pakistan have colluded to obfuscate these facts, even as they brazenly promote the China-Pakistan Economic Corridor (CPEC), which runs through parts of Indian territory under their respective occupation.[4]

History, underhand methods

Historically, China played an insidious role in changing the frontiers of Jammu and Kashmir through fictitious claims and unscrupulous alliances with local chieftains. China exploited the 'Great Game' between British India and Russia in the late nineteenth century.

---

4   'Question No. 648 Shaksgam Valley', Ministry of External Affairs, Government of India, 4 February 2022; https://mea.gov.in/lok-sabha. htm?dtl/34811/question+no648+shaksgam+valley

It pitched territorial claims far beyond the traditional frontiers of Xinjiang. It gradually crept into areas in the Taghdumbash Pamirs and the Karakorams, well south of its frontier along the Kunlun mountains.

While the British and the Russians were busy creating buffer zones along the frontiers of Xinjiang and Tibet, China was systematically stepping into the void. By the 1890s, China had started asserting its presence in the valleys between the Kunlun and the main Karakoram Range. The British eroded the traditional frontiers of the Maharaja of Kashmir in the region around Shahidullah and also those of his vassal, the Mir of Hunza. After the Mir's defeat in 1869 at the hands of the joint forces of the Maharaja and the British, the Chinese tried to co-opt him in their scheme while giving him refuge.

Till then, the Mir's authority, ranging in the Taghdumbash Pamirs till Dafdar and eastward in Raskam, had never been contested by the Chinese. The Chinese had started the practice of exchanging annual presents with the Mir of Hunza in recognition of his authority over the unruly nomadic tribes that inhabited these valleys. This tradition of exchanging gifts with the Mir was exploited to stake a retrospective claim to Hunza as a tributary of the Qing empire since 1762 AD. This chicanery is contradicted by China's own historical accounts and maps of the eighteenth and nineteenth centuries, which show the south-western frontiers of China extending barely up to the Kunlun Range.

By 1891, the Chinese had quietly moved south of the Kunlun Range to consolidate their presence at Shahidullah, which earlier marked the furthest outpost of the princely state of J&K. They then moved further south to Suget and thereafter showed up at the Karakoram pass. In 1936, the Mir of Hunza was asked by the British to abandon his rights in the Taghdumbash Pamirs as well as in the Raskam Valley, but the Shaksgam Valley to the southwest of Raskam and the Aghil Range remained with the Mir of Hunza. This remained the traditional frontier of British India until independence, inherited by India following J&K's accession in 1947.

The Pakistan connection

It is this border that was blatantly compromised by Pakistan in its so-called agreement with China on 2 March 1963. By giving in to China's expansionist designs and spurious claims to a boundary along the Karakoram Range, Pakistan not only compromised India's traditional frontier along the Kunlun Range to the northwest of the Karakoram Pass, but also enabled China to extrapolate a claim line eastwards along the Karakoram Range in Ladakh. This collusion allowed China to claim the whole of Aksai Chin in which it had no historical presence. After the Partition of the Indian subcontinent, from 1953, Chinese troops actively started transgressing the frontier in eastern Hunza. In October 1959, they rustled some livestock from the area, prompting an angry response from Pakistan that it was determined to defend its frontiers. However, President Ayub Khan, spotting an opportunity in the rapidly deteriorating India-China ties in the late 1950s, decided, instead, to pander to the Chinese. Pakistan deliberately chose to downgrade the historical claims of the Mir of Hunza and eventually signed away the Shaksgam Valley to China in 1963.

As party to the dispute

The provisional nature of the territorial settlement between China and Pakistan is evident in Article 6 of the 1963 agreement, which clearly states that 'the two Parties have agreed that after the settlement of the Kashmir dispute between Pakistan and India, the sovereign authority concerned will reopen negotiations with the Government of the People's Republic of China, on the boundary as described in Article Two of the present Agreement, so as to sign a formal Boundary Treaty to replace the present agreement'. In effect, this agreement has established China as a party to the dispute. It has a vested interest in legitimizing its illegitimate gains in the trans-Karakoram tract. The anniversary of the Instrument of Accession, on 26 October, is a reminder of China's illegal territorial occupation.

(The article was first published in *The Hindu*, 6 November 2020)

Chinese strategists forget that aggression against a large country like India will not work

It is extraordinary that in his seminal book, *On China*, published in 2011, former US national security advisor and later secretary of state, Henry Kissinger, thought it fit to add a prologue devoted to India-China relations. It is laced with factual inaccuracies and appears to be aimed solely at eulogizing Mao Zedong's great abilities as a military strategist. Mao, in fact, drew heavily from Chinese classics and history.

Based on his understanding of Chinese sources, Kissinger writes that in deciding to 'knock' India back 'to the negotiating table' through military action in 1962, Mao claimed to his commanders that he banked on strategic principles drawn from China's so-called historical experience of defeating India in 'one and a half' wars. Both the examples that Kissinger narrates are clearly ersatz, revealing Kissinger's insufficient scholarship on ancient India.

The fact is, there was no war between India and China during the Tang period (618-907 CE). There is a reference to a small event in *A History of Sino-Indian Relations* by Yukteshwar Kumar of Cheena Bhavana, Visva-Bharati University, Santiniketan. It involves a mention of Emperor Harshvardhan sending an emissary to China in 641 CE. After Harshvardhan's death and the decline of his empire, Wang Xuance, the Tang envoy to the court at Kannauj, and his entourage were reportedly attacked by a local feudal chieftain called Arunasa who had usurped power amidst the turmoil. Apparently, Wang fled to Tibet and sought to regroup before launching a campaign against Kannauj territory with the help of Tibetan mercenaries and Nepali horsemen. If this is the story that Mao was referring to, as he seems to have, it is apocryphal in terms of its scale and significance in India-China ties. Giving it an exaggerated spin reflects rather poorly on both the narrator and Kissinger, his eager audience.

Throughout history, the extreme fringes of all empires have often waxed and waned, and this was true of both Indian and Chinese empires. However, India and China did not share any border at the time. Tibet then was completely independent under a powerful Tibetan king, Srong-brtsan Sgam-po, and even the soldiers reportedly mustered by Wang Xuance to retaliate against Arunasa were obviously either Nepali or Tibetan mercenaries. Mao was clearly trying to reinterpret historical events in a manner through which Han Chinese chauvinism could lay a vicarious claim to a distant event in the past on the shoulders of mercenaries from third countries.[5]

Incidentally, the year 641 CE also coincides with the presence, in India, of the legendary Chinese monk Xuanzang who was still on his peregrinations in search of Buddhist scriptures and other religious

---

5   Tansen Sen, 'Changing Regimes: Two Episodes of Chinese Military Interventions in Medieval South Asia', in *Asian Encounters: Networks of Cross-Cultural Interactions*, eds Upinder Singh and Parul P. Dhar (New Delhi: Oxford University Press, 2014).

and philosophical texts. After nearly seventeen years of wandering, including a sojourn at Nalanda University, he carried back with him to Chang'an in China a rich trove to spread the teachings gathered in India among his fellow Han Chinese. This was no doubt an age marked by the absence of narrow nationalism, one that permitted Chinese monks such as Fa Xian, Xuanzang and Yi Jing from China, and Dharmaratna, Kasyapa Matanga and Bodhidharma from India to travel unfettered to exchange ideas and learnings. Xuanzang's journey has been recorded in detail in the classical Chinese text *Da Tang Xiyu Ji* (*Great Tang Records on the Western Regions*) and, eight centuries on, was immortalized by a Ming-era writer, Wu Cheng-en, in his fascinating fictionalized work, *Journey to the West*.

If Mao was referring to an 'Indian kingdom' that approached the Tang court to prevail over another 'Indian kingdom' during this period, he was probably referring to the ancient Buddhist kingdom of Kuche, home to the famous fifth-century Buddhist monk Kumarjiva, located on the northern Silk Road in modern-day Xinjiang. The small kingdom of Kuche was then populated by the Kushans and used the Indic script. It was one of the many kingdoms in the 'Western Regions' (Xiyu) against which the Tang Emperor Taizong waged military campaigns. Kuche, like many other neighbouring kingdoms in Central Asia, was influenced by Indian culture, religion and script, but was distinct from India, which lay south of the Himalayas.

That Kuche, which lay in modern-day Xinjiang, was in the ambit of Indic culture only highlights the limits of Han influence in the region, the alien nature of which the Uyghurs have resisted and challenged through the centuries to this day. Mao, like his Tang predecessors, could not really tell the difference between Tianzhu, as India was known in classical Chinese texts, and Xiyu, or Western Regions, which covered large parts of modern-day Xinjiang and Central Asia.

The second example unquestioningly quoted by Kissinger and attributed to Mao is equally specious. The 'half war' in which Mao takes credit for defeating India purportedly took place when Timur (Timur the Lame) sacked Delhi in 1398 CE. By no stretch of the imagination could that be claimed as a victory by the Han Chinese, who themselves had only recently overthrown the Mongol yoke of the Yuan dynasty in 1368 CE. The Yuan dynasty, established by Kublai Khan when he conquered Han China, had nothing to do with Timur, who was a member of the Turkicized Barlas tribe, a distant Mongol clan settled in Transoxania, in what is modern-day Uzbekistan.

In fact, Timur had planned to invade China next. In 1404 CE, he set off on an expedition against the Ming dynasty in China. Had he not died of illness in February 1405 CE at Faryab in contemporary Kazakhstan, not long into his campaign, he too would have been knocking at the gates of the Forbidden Palace in Beijing as many foreign military powers later did in 'China's century of humiliation' before the formation of the People's Republic of China.

It is a fairly common refrain for Chinese strategists to play up the Chinese People's Liberation Army (PLA) as some kind of an invincible force. In 1979, Deng Xiaoping had purportedly said that the Chinese PLA had crossed the southern border to 'teach Vietnam a lesson'. As it turned out, it was the gritty Vietnamese Army that taught the Chinese a lesson that they would not forget in a hurry.

Chinese writings often refer to the 1962 border conflict as China having 'taught India a lesson'. Of course, they conveniently ignore the drubbing received by the PLA in the military flare-up across Nathu La and Cho La in Sikkim in September 1967. In July 2017, during the Doklam crisis, the hard-line Communist Party mouthpiece *Global Times* had called for teaching India 'a bitter lesson' and had issued a thinly veiled warning that in a military conflict China would inflict 'greater losses than in 1962'. Following the unilateral actions by the PLA, which led to the ongoing stand-off in eastern Ladakh since April 2021, the indefatigable Hu Xijin, editor of the *Global Times*, warned India along the same lines.

Chinese strategists often forget that the age of teaching anyone a lesson is over. Unilateralism and military aggression, especially against a large country like India determined to defend its sovereignty and territorial integrity at any cost, will simply not work. The way forward, to resolve border tensions between India and China, is through dialogue and peaceful negotiations.

(The article was first published in *The Indian Express*, 13 January 2021)

CPEC: China designs, Pakistan's ambivalence and India's opposition

The China-Pakistan Economic Corridor (CPEC) is earmarked as a flagship project of the Belt and Road Initiative (BRI), which is a grand strategy aimed at restoring China's 'rightful' great-power status in the world. With an initial outlay of $46 billion, CPEC is envisaged as a hub with Gwadar's port, energy, transport infrastructure and industrial cooperation as its four main spokes. This project aims to create an alternative route to transport oil and gas to China and to accelerate economic growth and development across its remote western regions.

The CPEC cuts through Pakistan-occupied Kashmir (PoK) and the trans-Karakoram tract of Shaksgam, which was illegally ceded by Pakistan to China on 2 March 1963 under a provisional boundary settlement. The entire region of Gilgit-Baltistan through which the highway passes is located close to the Siachen Glacier as well as to Ladakh, the current flashpoint between India and China. Following the effective nullification of Article 370 of the Indian Constitution on 5 August 2019, India has reiterated its long-standing claim to Gilgit-Baltistan in PoK.

Economic motivation apart, China seeks to use the CPEC to consolidate its presence in a disputed region. If internal instability overwhelms Pakistan in the future, the CPEC affords China an opportunity to claim Hunza on the basis of specious historical records.

For China, the CPEC is a beachhead in South Asia, to facilitate a broader thrust in the Persian Gulf. It also provides a maritime connect to Djibouti and the littoral states.

The CPEC is viewed with ambivalence in Pakistan. It is regarded as a panacea for Pakistan's ailing economy. The road and rail networks, especially the energy transportation systems, have the potential to stretch across to Afghanistan, Tajikistan, Kyrgyzstan, Kazakhstan, Russia and even to Mongolia. The project is also expected to give a shot in the arm to Pakistan's debilitated power sector, with China committed to spending $35 billion to build up to nineteen new power plants.

But contrary to expectations that development in the wake of the CPEC project will bring peace to the insurgency-wracked province of Balochistan, the Chinese presence appears to have infused the Baloch nationalist movement with new energy. Chinese workers, seen as collaborators in the exploitation of the region's natural resources, have become a major target for insurgents. Even in the army's heartland of Punjab, media reports indicate clashes between Chinese workers and local police personnel.

The Pakistani military is determined to protect Chinese lives and investments, especially in the wake of serious incidents such as the attack on the Zaver Pearl Continental Hotel in Gwadar. A Special Security Division comprising 9,000 Pakistani soldiers and 6,000 paramilitary personnel has been set up as a dedicated force.

The colossal CPEC project has extracted a high cost across Pakistan. In the case of the Sahiwal coal power plant project in Pakistan's Punjab province, many people were forced to part with agricultural land. The police slapped terrorism charges against those who resisted. Some Sahiwal residents have reported health issues, attributed to water contamination caused by the coal-fired power plant. The prevalence of asthma, pneumonitis and chronic obstructive pulmonary disease (COPD) is on the rise in the area.

China realizes that India's support for the BRI, of which the CPEC is the linchpin, is crucial to its regional success. India's non-participation in the BRI is predicated on the unacceptability of the CPEC traversing parts of Jammu and Kashmir illegally occupied by Pakistan and China. It is, as stated by India's External Affairs Minister S. Jaishankar, a project initiated without consulting India. Besides, BRI, as a whole, lacks transparency and is geared to advancing China's interests through 'debt trap' financing. It should come as no surprise that India has maintained its consistent position in not endorsing the BRI.

(The article was first published in *Hindustan Times*,
19 January 2021)

A disengagement deal better than expected

The year 2021 has begun on an optimistic note for reduction of military tensions between India and China. Both sides announced on 11 February the simultaneous disengagement of their massive forward deployments in the Pangong Lake area, which have been cheek by jowl for the past ten months in eastern Ladakh. India's defence minister, Rajnath Singh, delivered a carefully worded statement in Parliament about the breakthrough, which envisages a pullback by both sides in 'a phased, coordinated and verified manner'. The headway in the impasse, achieved after lengthy talks between the two sides, surprised the doubting Thomases who questioned India's will and capacity for a military counterpoise that is essential for restoration of the situation as it prevailed before April 2020. It also caught off guard those who scoff at the notion of a peaceful resolution of territorial differences in keeping with the longer-term interests of both Asian giants.

Peaceful resolution

Tracing the genesis of the problem to April-May 2020, when the Chinese side suddenly positioned a large body of troops and armaments along the Line of Actual Control (LAC), the Indian defence minister also paid rich tribute to the armed forces and lauded their valiant sacrifices. Indeed, the intentions of the People's Liberation Army (PLA) were thwarted by India's robust military response guided by a resolute Indian government led by Prime Minister Narendra Modi.

Relations between India and China suffered a dramatic setback following the violation by China of the bilateral agreements and protocols, which ruptured peace and tranquillity. The bloody incident at Galwan on 15 June 2020, the first involving casualties since 1975, brought about the collapse of the prevailing consensus that bilateral ties could develop in parallel with efforts to resolve the boundary question and maintain peace and tranquillity. Since June 2020, India has consistently highlighted the view that peace is a fundamental prerequisite for the normal conduct of relations. The stand-off at Pangong Lake was but one of several in eastern Ladakh, but undoubtedly among the most significant. After China took steps to alter the ground situation between Fingers 4 and 8, the Indian Army carried out daring manoeuvres to take up advantageous positions along the Kailash Range on the southern bank, thereby dominating the key Chinese garrison at Moldo across the Spanggur Gap. Even on the northern bank, the Indian Army succeeded in offsetting any initial advantage that the PLA may have had along the spurs.

Message of endurance

Having acquired powerful leverage, Indian troops dug in for the long haul and mirrored the PLA's deployments. On its part, the government left no stone unturned to ensure that the Indian troops were provided with the necessary wherewithal to deal with any real or perceived asymmetry. The message was unambiguous. India was not going to cave in and stood ready to impose a harsh penalty if China engaged in any act of adventurism. The endurance of the Indian Army through the harsh winter months has been extraordinary. China appears to have realized that a prolonged stand-off, hardly a part of its original calculus and of little avail militarily or politically, was permanently impairing bilateral relations. The uncertainty associated with the law of unintended consequences, the high reputational costs to itself, the forward momentum in India-US relations and the Quadrilateral Security Dialogue (involving India, the US, Japan and Australia), better known as the Quad, may also have proved to be factors for China.

The disengagement at Pangong Lake is certainly a welcome development. This is an area in which the patrols of the two sides have been encountering one another for decades, whether on land or on the lake. The construction of a road by China from Finger 8 towards Fingers 5 and 4 many years ago had led to a spike in face-offs and gradually reduced access for Indian troops to their traditional patrolling point at Finger 8. Meanwhile, India too built better infrastructure all the way to its permanent presence at the Dhan Singh Thapa Post near Finger 3.

The disengagement deal is perhaps better than one might have expected under the circumstances. The Chinese have agreed to pull back forward deployments to their permanent base at Sirijap, east of Finger 8, and to dismantle all infrastructure created after April 2020. India's tough negotiators, both diplomatic and military, have ensured that our troops retain their presence at the permanent Indian post at Finger 3 even though China had earlier demanded that India fall back further. Moreover, all the Chinese posts atop the high spurs on the northern bank will also be dismantled, including those that overlooked the Dhan Singh Thapa Post. Of course, India will also fall back from its recently held positions along the Kailash Range to earlier positions.

With trust badly shattered after April 2020, one expects the Indian side to tread warily in implementing the deal at Pangong. Carrying out simultaneous disengagement in a phased and coordinated manner, with proper verification, is key to its success. There is little doubt that cautious diplomatic and military planning and hawk-like vigil will be called for throughout the implementation.

Faith in forces, negotiators

The government of Prime Minister Modi has amply demonstrated its willingness to take tough calls on matters pertaining to sovereignty and territorial integrity. It has demonstrated boldness in the face of a major military challenge. It has shown equal courage in grasping the nettle of peace. More importantly, the government has reposed full faith in its armed forces and negotiators. Mr Singh's statement, containing just the right blend of steel and velvet, generously acknowledged the unity of purpose among all departments of the government and highlighted the consistency with which India's unwavering position was put across. Both he and External Affairs Minister S. Jaishankar had engaged their Chinese counterparts in September 2020 and drawn the red lines. This no doubt strengthened the hand of the senior commanders and foreign ministry officials who hammered out the deal.

The progress at Pangong notwithstanding, the doubting Thomases will continue to raise questions. They run the risk of doing so without sufficient familiarity with either the facts or the military complexities on the ground. The truth is that India's tough military and diplomatic posture has paid off, resulting in an honourable disengagement. If tensions could be defused at Galwan, where much blood was shed, and at Pangong, it should be equally possible to fashion mutually acceptable terms for disengagement at Gogra/Hot Springs and for the resolution of patrolling issues in Depsang.

Over the next two to three weeks, both sides should be given a chance to implement the agreement. The temporary moratorium on military activities by both sides along the north bank, including on patrolling up to the traditional points, will improve the situation. That patrolling will be resumed only consequent to an agreement being reached in future diplomatic and military talks is also a step forward. Naturally, the pullback will prove to be a complex exercise involving meticulous planning of intricate details and scheduled withdrawals that must factor in the local terrain, the disposition of troops and a vast array of armaments. No doubt, one must also keep the powder dry.

(The article was first published in *The Hindu*, 15 February 2021)

Getting it right on the LAC disengagement

In the aftermath of the India-China agreement reached on 10 February 2021 for pullback in the Pangong Lake area, there has been much speculation about the gain and loss for India. Some have averred that the mutual withdrawal amounts to the creation of a 'buffer zone on Indian territory'. Others have alleged it to be a 'surrender of Indian territory'. Yet others have questioned the withdrawal of India's presence along the Kailash Range on the south bank of Pangong since it enabled India to dominate the Chinese garrison at Moldo.

Things are moving

Another charge has been levelled—of inadequate budgetary allocation for defence in the face of a 'two-front war'. The fact of the matter is that the increase in the outlay for capital procurement announced by the finance minister on 1 February for financial year 2021-22 represents a 18.75 per cent jump over the previous financial year, the highest in fifteen years. Moreover, the government has enhanced the delegated financial powers up to Rs 200 crore in senior ranks below the rank of vice chief as well, to facilitate procurement. Improved procedures and oversight have ensured better utilization with no surrendering of funds over the last four years.

The charge that India is not according proper priority to national security is baseless. Military modernization, indigenization and defence exports are top priorities. The building of long overdue roads, bridges, culverts and other infrastructure in the border areas, in mission mode, has spurred mobility and capacity for a rapid induction of forces. The Darbuk-Shyok-Daulat Beg Oldie Road has facilitated seamless access all the way up to Sub-Sector North, which abuts the Karakoram Pass and Siachen Glacier. It has provided an axis for developing lateral roads towards India's frontline in eastern Ladakh. Another example is the eponymous Atal Rohtang Tunnel, approved by the government of Atal Bihari Vajpayee. The tunnel, inaugurated in October 2020, makes for a much shorter logistics loop connecting the Middle and Western sectors of the India-China boundary on the Indian side.

Many defence reforms recommended by the Naresh Chandra Committee have been implemented in recent years. The creation of the Department of Military Affairs, the appointment of the Chief of Defence Staff and the soon-to-be-a-reality Theatre Commands are but a few examples.

The buffer zone stands

India has not surrendered any land in Galwan, Pangong or Depsang since the border crisis broke out in April-May 2020. The assumption that the disengagement implemented at Pangong, especially that the temporary moratorium on patrolling by both sides will result in a buffer zone entirely 'in our area', is incorrect. India has not accepted either the unilateral definition of China's so-called Line of Actual Control (LAC) of 1959 or its subsequent mutants. As such, a buffer zone on the other side of any so-called Chinese LAC is still a buffer zone on India's side, given that India regards the whole of Aksai Chin as an integral part of its territory. By using the benchmark of the so-called Chinese LAC to identify India's territory and China's, the naysayers are actually legitimizing the illegal Chinese presence across the LAC.

During the late 1950s and early 1960s, the idea of a mutual pullback by 20 km, which would have resulted in buffer zones, had been proposed by China and rejected by India. Later, India had accepted the modified 'Colombo Conference Proposals' mooted by six non-aligned countries in December 1962 after the war, which would have permitted Indian civilian administration to be present alongside the Chinese in the vacated areas. China had reservations and backed out in March 1963 after initially acquiescing. It was ready to consider them only as a basis for further bilateral negotiations. Much water may have flown down the Chip Chap, Galwan and Chang Chenmo rivers since then, but it is not as if pullbacks and buffer zones have never been considered before.

The pullback on the north bank of Pangong has resulted in the Chinese ceasing their patrolling between Fingers 4 and 8 for the first time in several decades. After the 1962 debacle, Indian patrols limited themselves to visiting Finger 8, which evolved as the de facto Indian line in this sector, but this access too was restricted by vehicle-mounted Chinese patrols along that stretch in recent decades. Given that China perceives its line to run further west of Finger 3, India has done well to maintain its permanent presence at the Dhan Singh Thapa Post near Finger 3 on what the Chinese regard as their side of the LAC.

As former Northern Army Commander Lieutenant General D.S. Hooda has stated in a recent opinion piece, by agreeing to relocate east of Finger 8, the PLA is pulling back from its claimed 'customary boundary line' and 'this is definitely not a minor concession'. It is, as he has pointed out, in line with India's consistent demand to restore the status quo ante that existed in April 2020.

Different implications

The word status quo ante with regard to the India-China boundary matters has different implications for the ground situation depending entirely on the timeline being referred to. In seeking a restoration of status quo ante on the north bank of Pangong with reference to April-May 2020, the advantage secured by India on the south bank was naturally a plus point, and put to good effect by Indian negotiators.

If the retention of the heights along the Kailash Range is deemed so important for leveraging concessions elsewhere, as some claim, why is it that no previous government acted to occupy the heights earlier, including during the face-off in Depsang in 2013? After all, differences over the LAC are hardly new. The fact is that Indian troops secured the heights on the south bank precisely to offset China's 'first-mover' advantage on the north bank. Moreover, if India's objective is to achieve status quo ante, India too would logically be required to revert to its pre-April 2020 status.

The potential linkage between the heights of the Kailash Range and Depsang, or for that matter Gogra and Hot Springs, cannot be arbitrarily conjured up. The situation in the pockets of differences is sui generis.

At the end of the tenth round of the India-China corps commander-level meetings, the two sides have positively appraised the smooth completion of disengagement at Pangong, acknowledging that it was a significant step that provided a good basis for resolving the remaining issues along the LAC.

Instead of commending our military and Ministry of External Affairs negotiators for their efforts in ensuring a successful disengagement at Pangong, some commentators have questioned the absence of 'iron-clad agreements' for resolving the differences at Depsang or Gogra/ Hot Spring, which are still being discussed. The negotiators ought to be given a chance. The truth is that there were no iron-clad guarantees in any of the agreements and protocols signed so far either, whether in 1993, 1996 or in 2005. Bilateral differences are best negotiated from a position of strength as has been done at Pangong, while maintaining high vigil and striving for positive outcomes elsewhere.

(The article was first published in *The Hindu*, 23 March 2021)

Tibet: The past haunts the future

The Chinese military entered Tibet in 1950. The Tibetans approached the United Nations following the entry of the People's Liberation Army (PLA) into their homeland. Apart from El Salvador, no other country showed much support in 1950. The UK, in keeping with the muddled policy of the British empire in the previous half-century, favoured deferring the matter till Tibet's legal position was clearer, and giving peaceful settlement a chance.

The US had historically outsourced Tibet policy to the British. It showed little interest in the blighted land. It has never questioned the sovereignty and territorial integrity of China. India waffled, with expression of hope for a peaceful settlement and continuation of traditional autonomy.

The seventeen-point Agreement on Measures for the Peaceful Liberation of Tibet was concluded under duress by Lhasa with Beijing on 23 May 1951. It provided for local autonomy and respect for Tibetan culture, and, more importantly, a commitment not to alter the established status, functions and powers of His Holiness the Dalai

Lama. The reality was different. A disillusioned Dalai Lama, as early as 1950, had thought of seeking refuge in India, but was discouraged by India. In the years that followed, matters got worse. The seventeen-point agreement failed to address the aspirations of the Tibetan people, and matters escalated in the face of a hard-line approach adopted by the authorities in Beijing. The land reform programmes impacted adversely on the land-owning Khampas and nomads of eastern Kham and Amdo regions who chose the path of armed resistance in 1956. These disturbances in eastern Tibet snowballed to a point of no return and had a fallout on the internal situation in Tibet. In March 1959, the Dalai Lama was obliged to flee Lhasa, after his advisors felt that he was on the verge of being detained by Chinese forces as part of a ruse during a cultural function at the local military headquarters. He entered India through the Bumla Pass in Arunachal Pradesh after an arduous two-week trek.

The decision to seek refuge in India was only natural, given Tibet's history, geography and close cultural and spiritual links with India, the land of Buddha and Padmasambhava, also known as Guru Rimpoche. The latter had founded Vajrayana Buddhism in Tibet in the eighth century.

Tibet's physical connectivity to India was far greater at that time than was the case with China. Even Chinese officials preferred to journey to Lhasa via Calcutta and the less arduous route along the Chumbi Valley. India has acted as a powerful lodestar for Tibet throughout its history.

Seeking refuge in India had precedents. In November 1956, when the Dalai Lama attended the 2,500th anniversary of the Buddha's attainment of salvation, he had to be encouraged to return to Tibet. Earlier, the thirteenth Dalai Lama had fled to India in 1910 when Manchu troops entered Lhasa.

The Tibetan issue was again half-heartedly considered by the United Nations in 1959. A resolution was jointly tabled by Malaya and Ireland, expressing grave concern at reports of violations of human rights and denial of freedom. Forty-five nations voted for the resolution and nine opposed it. What is interesting is that India was among the twenty-six nations that abstained. India got nothing in return from the Chinese, except further blame for alleged interference in Tibet.

Beginning in 1979, there was some hope for a settlement of the Tibet issue. Confidential talks between Beijing and the Dalai Lama's representatives in the 1980s failed. Thereafter, the international campaign for Tibet, the Dalai Lama's address to the European Parliament in Strasbourg in 1988, riots in Lhasa and the award of the Noble Prize to the Dalai Lama in 1989 widened the gulf between the Dalai Lama and Beijing.

The US policy is key to the future of Tibet. It appointed a Special Coordinator for Tibetan Issues in 1997. The Tibetan Policy Act of 2002 laid the foundation for renewed activism for further legislative measures to preserve the distinct heritage of the Tibetan people. The Reciprocal Access to Tibet Act of 2018 and the Tibetan Policy and Support Act of 2020 have helped put further pressure on China. The Tibetan Policy and Support Act of 2020 of the US categorically rejects any interference by China in the selection of the Dalai Lama.

An emboldened China no longer fears US sanctions. China has systematically eroded Tibetan culture and language. It has successfully absorbed Tibet by means of road, rail and air connectivity and weakened Tibetan Buddhism through a systematic proselytization of communist ideology.

The Dalai Lama has stated that he is not seeking independence for Tibet, only genuine autonomy. While there is great sympathy for the Tibetan people around the world, there appears to be scant appetite anywhere for Tibetan independence.

(The article was first published in *All India Radio*,
18 August 2021)

NAVIGATING INDIA'S NEIGHBOURHOOD

The compulsions of India's neighbourhood

India defines its neighbourhood both strategically and geographically. Strategically, India's neighbourhood stretches from the Strait of Hormuz in the west to the Strait of Malacca in the east. Developments in this region affect India in a major way. The Persian Gulf is significant for India's energy security and remittances as well as for religious linkages between Muslims in India and people in West Asia. On the eastern side, the Bay of Bengal acts as a critical link between India and Southeast Asia, which is a key pillar of India's Act East policy.

Geographically, the South Asian countries of Pakistan, Nepal, Bhutan, Bangladesh, Sri Lanka, Maldives, Afghanistan and Myanmar constitute the core of India's immediate neighbourhood.

South Asia has a population of 1.8 billion with a combined gross domestic product (GDP) of about $3.47 trillion, of which a very large part, about $2.72 trillion, is that of India. As a country accounting for about 70 per cent of the region's area, population, GDP and defence expenditure, India has a natural pre-eminence in South Asia and it has a special role to play in enabling regional integration. Its approach towards the region reflects this awareness and it is premised on non-reciprocity and commitment to develop friendly and mutually beneficial relationship with all its neighbours.

The greatest challenge facing various countries in the South Asian region is to develop a common front in their fight against poverty, climate change, natural disasters, pandemics and food and energy security. These issues are inter-related, indivisible and transcend borders. Cooperation on these issues will ensure their collective achievement of the Sustainable Development Goals (SDGs).

'Neighbourhood First' policy

India's 'Neighbourhood First' policy is mutually beneficial, consultative, broad-based, inclusive and sensitive to the priorities of India's neighbours. It has both developmental and security components. While there has been a basic continuity in India's neighbourhood policy since 2014, there is a much stronger focus on terror and unlike in previous governments, there is a greater emphasis on high-level exchanges, religious and cultural connectivity, people-to-people contacts at the grassroots level, subregional cooperation, maritime security, physical and multimodal connectivity (with Bangladesh) taking into account India's Act East policy and its Northeast states, and defence cooperation, especially in areas that previous governments were coy about.

India's initiatives over the last five years to build regional cooperation are anchored in its Neighbourhood First policy. From inviting the heads of all South Asian Association for Regional Cooperation (SAARC) states to Prime Minister Modi's swearing-in ceremony in 2014 to India's initiative to launch a South Asia satellite to improve communication and disaster response, India remains committed to its neighbourhood. India has always been the first off the block to provide relief in the wake of tsunamis, earthquakes and other natural disasters. Importantly, India does not seek reciprocity in the implementation of its Neighbourhood First policy.

Under the Neighbourhood First policy, intensifying bilateral developmental partnerships with countries in the region is likely to create the necessary impulse for regional cooperation in South Asia in the long run. Linkages established through connectivity initiatives undertaken by India with each of the neighbours in the region are not exclusive—they add to the network of communication, enabling connectivity and easy region-wide movement of goods, services, people and ideas. India has deep interest in enhancing intra-regional connectivity, which is evident from India's keenness to use the potential of South Asian countries to strengthen other regional and subregional groupings and partnerships such as the Bangladesh, Bhutan, India and Nepal (BBIN) initiative and the Bay of Bengal Initiative for Multisectoral Technical and Economic Cooperation (BIMSTEC). India is also committed to greater connectivity and cooperation with the Association for Southeast Asian Nations (ASEAN) region through its Act East policy.

India has invested in different states through credit lines, assistance programmes and waiver of loans in the areas of agriculture, education, culture, health, human resource development, drinking water and sanitation, disaster relief and rehabilitation, capacity-building, trade and investment as well as defence and security. India's efforts in this regard are geared towards generating impulses for greater regional cooperation to meet common challenges.

Cooperative security in any region is like a chain that is as strong as its weakest link. South Asia too has a weak link, with one country choosing to adopt terrorism as an instrument of state policy against its neighbours. The consequences of such a policy of nurturing radical jihadi groups have been felt across South Asia and globally too.

Connectivity is integral to regional security. Better connectivity can help nations overcome political differences by conceiving of their borders as bridges and not barriers. However, the efforts of SAARC to build a regional consensus have been undermined by one state as is evident in the case of the proposed SAARC motor vehicle agreement, which would have allowed region-wide movement of vehicles and promoted trade, commerce and people-to-people contacts.

Therefore, it is not without reason that intra-South Asian trade remains one of the lowest in the world. At the same time, it is a fact that rising powers need to build a regional consensus that facilitates their rise. Under Prime Minister Narendra Modi, India has expended considerable political and economic capital on building closer ties with its neighbours in South Asia. The policy has worked well with several countries, with the exception of Pakistan.

India has a special friendship with Bhutan. Bangladesh is a key pillar of India's regional engagement with which it has positively resolved long-pending maritime and boundary issues. India shares an open border with Nepal, which demonstrates mutual trust and confidence. Bilateral security cooperation with Myanmar has deepened in recent years. India is cooperating closely with both the friendly nations of Maldives and Sri Lanka to promote maritime security. As one of the biggest regional donors to Afghanistan's reconstruction efforts, India had established an air and maritime corridor with Afghanistan to strengthen bilateral ties. Notably, India had trained a large number of Afghan army officers— over a hundred—every year, before the Taliban's takeover.

The shared maritime interests in the extended neighbourhood remain anchored in developing a blue economy, particularly in the context of what Prime Minister Modi has termed SAGAR (Security and Growth for All in the Region). It is in the common interest of the region to ensure unimpeded commerce, protection of key sea lanes of communication and freedom of navigation and overflight.

An Afghanistan under the Taliban poses a fresh challenge for India. India has major stakes in Afghanistan, having spent over $3 billion in several flagship and high-impact developmental projects. It has trained thousands of Afghan cadets over the years, including figures like Sher Mohammad Abbas Stanikzai who emerged as one of the Taliban's top leaders. The Taliban spokesperson Suhail Shaheen's suggestion that India is welcome to continue its developmental projects in Afghanistan offers hope. At this stage, having evacuated the large majority of Indians in Afghanistan, India has adopted a wait-and-watch approach on the evolving security and political situation. Its status as a non-permanent member of the United Nations Security Council, particularly at a time when it chairs the Taliban Sanctions Committee and the Counter-Terrorism Committee, could be leveraged to put pressure on the Taliban regime to moderate its behaviour.

At the multilateral level, the press statement issued by UNSC on 16 August 2021 by India's Permanent Representative, in his capacity as its rotational President, inter alia called for the new Taliban regime in Afghanistan to be 'united, inclusive and representative'.

Obviously, the return of the Taliban to the helm of affairs in Afghanistan has security implications for India and the region at large. A spill-over of any chaos and instability in Afghanistan beyond its borders could give terrorism a shot in the arm.

Radical groups in Pakistan, Central Asia, China, Russia as also in Gaza, Syria and West Africa have unabashedly celebrated the victory of the Taliban. Jihadist groups, particularly those linked to al-Qaeda, have viewed the Taliban's return as a victory for Islamism and Jihadism, reviving hopes for imposition of Sharia law globally.

From India's point of view, it is a matter of concern that the Jaish-e-Mohammed (JeM) and Lashkar-e-Taiba (LeT) in the Khyber Pakhtunkhwa (KPK) province of Pakistan and in Pakistan-occupied Kashmir have held victory rallies since the Taliban's takeover.

The vacuum created by the departure of the US and allied forces from Afghanistan in August 2021 will undoubtedly encourage radical groups, militants and terrorists to reactivate their safe havens in that country. Pakistan will use its close nexus with the Haqqani network and the Islamic State-Khorasan Province (IS-K) to build new hideouts and training camps for India-centric terrorist groups in Afghanistan. This will enable Pakistan to deny the existence of terrorist camps on its soil.

There is also the possibility that radical fighters trained by the Inter-Services Intelligence (ISI) of Pakistan and long embedded in the Taliban, the Haqqani network and the IS-K could now be infiltrated into Kashmir. At the same time, Pakistan cannot rule out a blowback from its nexus with terrorists. The return of the Taliban has already strengthened the Tehreek-e-Taliban Pakistan (TTP), which is engaged in hostilities against the Pakistani state.

Much depends, though, on the hope and expectation that the Taliban 2.0 regime will not outsource Afghanistan's territory to any international jihadi group such as al-Qaeda. The latter, in any case, is much weaker today as compared to the past when it had Afghan territory available as its global base. After the massive US retaliation following the 9/11 attacks on New York City and Washington D.C., al-Qaeda splintered. Its regional franchisees were neither fully in sync with its ideology, nor necessarily under the full control of an al-Qaeda leadership on the run. In the intervening years, the global community has become far more vigilant. Advances in technological means of surveillance have restricted the nature and scope of jihadi activity, and better intelligence-sharing mechanisms have ensured that jihadis are often restricted to local attacks on softer targets, without either the means or the resources to coordinate another spectacular attack on the scale of the 9/11 attacks.

This, however, is of little comfort to the regional countries that share porous borders and ethnic footprints with Afghanistan. The

Central Asian countries are vulnerable. Iran has hosted the remnants of al-Qaeda, including bin Laden's family members in the aftermath of the US retaliation in 2001, but its relationship with al-Qaeda has been an uneasy one. A more radical and intolerant IS-K, driven by a purist Sunni/Salafi brand of Islam and seeking new pastures in Afghanistan's Pashtun heartland, may drive al-Qaeda elements closer to Iran out of mutual expediency and need for cooperation against a more virulent adversary.

The churn in Afghanistan, the return of the Taliban, even the complete overrunning of resistance in Panjshir, could not have been possible without the full political and military backing of Pakistan. For the moment, it appears that Pakistan is having the last laugh, with several members of the Haqqani network now occupying key ministries in the Taliban's government and Pakistan being wooed in every regional and global forum for consultations on Afghanistan. However, the global community is not giving the Taliban a free run after all. No country in the world has accorded recognition to the Taliban this time around, not even Pakistan, which was one of the first three countries, apart from Saudi Arabia and the UAE, to recognize the Taliban in their first incarnation in 1996. The UNSC resolution 2593, passed during India's presidency on 30 August 2021, inter alia demands that 'Afghan territory not be used to threaten or attack any country or to shelter or train terrorists, or to plan or to finance terrorist acts, and reiterates the importance of combating terrorism in Afghanistan, including those individuals and entities designated pursuant to resolution 1267 (1999), and notes the Taliban's relevant commitments'.

The major powers of the world have also not accorded recognition to the Taliban. The Taliban's feet are being held to the fire on matters such as their policies towards women and minorities, violation of human rights and freedom of the media. The Taliban are being watched on drug cultivation and trafficking. The US has frozen almost $10 billion in reserves belonging to the Afghan central bank. Afghanistan's coffers are empty, and this is not a tenable situation. Pleas for humanitarian assistance have generated global commitments of a paltry sum of less than $1 billion.

If the situation continues, the Taliban may expect Pakistan to rally to its assistance in terms of stopgap financial aid, food requirements and other immediate needs. Famine or other economic catastrophes could send millions across the border into Pakistan again. This burden could affect Pakistan even more than the danger posed through cohabitation with a regime committed to medieval policies and practices.

Regional perceptions of India's Neighbourhood First policy

India's neighbours have identified 'delivery deficit' as an important issue that interferes with India's efforts to fulfil their developmental aspirations. They do not doubt India's intentions but have genuine concerns about its ability to implement policies in an expeditious manner. The governments of the neighbouring countries are sensitive to India's security concerns, even if they are open to the idea of engaging China and other countries as alternative options for their development.

The larger question is whether connectivity in South Asia will be a key to uniting the regional countries or it will be the focus of a new 'Great Game'. India's sensitivities in this regard are well-known. But how does one address the ambivalence felt by some of India's neighbours with regard to the growing presence and activities of an extra-regional power like China?

While India may not seek strict reciprocity in its relations with neighbours, one of the fundamental requirements for building better cooperative architecture in the region is that neighbours remain sensitive to India's key concerns, while leveraging their own strategic autonomy.

Among the neighbours, there is a general appreciation of the significance India attaches to its large neighbourhood and the religious, cultural and civilizational linkages it shares with all its neighbours. There is a spontaneous desire among India's neighbours to harmonize their neighbourhood outlook with India's Neighbourhood First policy and a willingness to benefit from India's developmental diplomacy.

Bhutan and Maldives have responded to India's 'Neighbourhood First' policy with their 'India First' policies. While Maldivians believe that the potential for future cooperation will depend on internal developments in the Maldives and India's response to such developments, Bhutan continues to consider India as its closest and most important friend, which remains central to its unity, prosperity and success. The Bhutanese government is committed to the BBIN and to working towards generating a domestic consensus on the issue.

With the change of government in Maldives in November 2018, following the defeat of Abdullah Yameen Gayoom in the presidential elections of September 2018, there has been a dramatic upswing in the relationship between India and Maldives under the leadership of Mr Ibrahim Mohamed Solih, the current President of Maldives. The landslide win of the Maldives Democratic Party (MDP) in the subsequent parliamentary elections in April 2019 has further strengthened this relationship to the effect that Maldives has a declared 'India First' policy. The sense of trust, goodwill and cordiality is clearly visible in all the meetings that Indian delegations have with their Maldivian counterparts.

After the political changes in the island nation, there has been a visible interest in India's approach to the concept of the Indo-Pacific. There is a marked sense of relief in Maldivian circles that India does not view the 'Indo-Pacific' as a strategy aimed against any particular country, but instead regards it as an inclusive and open-ended concept. This appreciation comes in the wake of a false narrative peddled by certain vested interests in the Maldives that the concept of Indo-Pacific was being pushed by the US, including through India, to contain China.

Of greater interest to both India and the Maldives is the growing cooperation with regard to counterterrorism, especially issues such as deradicalization, terror financing, money laundering and drug trafficking. This mutual interest has opened up the possibility of Indian experts sharing their views with their counterparts in the Maldives to sensitize them to the insidious role played by Pakistan and entities in the Gulf to promote radical ideologies.

Many Maldivian officials aver that 'there is a natural and spontaneous urge among the people to have friendly relations with India'. Informal interactions that the author had with people in and around Male during his visits seemed to confirm such a view. High impact community development projects being implemented by India through local bodies are among the most popular. At the same time, there is also a contrarian view, including among officials and security forces, that friendship with India should not be at the cost of Maldives' relations with China. 'If Chinese assistance is only limited to developmental activities and does not have security implications, India need not worry', is a refrain that is also quite common. As in Sri Lanka, Chinese projects are seen as beneficial, without a full appreciation of their longer-term deleterious effects on the nation's sovereignty and financial independence.

Often, it is the pace at which connectivity projects are completed that creates a lasting impression. There is a popular belief in the Maldives that 'Indians are good wordsmiths, while the Chinese are work-smiths'. The Sinamalé Bridge, better known as 'China-Maldives Friendship Bridge', the first cross-sea bridge in the Maldives built by a Chinese company connecting Male with Hulhumalé, is cited as an example of Chinese capability and commitment to the Maldives.

Today, most Maldivians agree that President Yameen had unnecessarily antagonized India and crossed the redline by seeking to enhance cooperation with China in a manner that impinged on India's regional security calculus. There is a growing appreciation that security cooperation with India through the Coastal Surveillance Radar Network System provided by India will improve electronic surveillance, and enhance maritime domain awareness and coastal security in the Indian Ocean. India has provided similar systems to Mauritius, Seychelles and Sri Lanka as well.

With the growing instances of seizures of drugs and arms in the waters off the Lakshadweep islands, India has even more reason to secure the cooperation of both Sri Lanka and the Maldives in ensuring its own maritime security. All three countries need to work together to deal effectively with common threats such as maritime terrorism, piracy, human and contraband trafficking, illegal and unregulated fishing, arms running and poaching.

The Maldivian security forces are no doubt concerned about the expanding footprint of terrorism after the Easter bombing incident on 21 April 2019 in Sri Lanka and the growing radicalization in their own society in recent years. A large number of Maldivians, perhaps 172 or so, have joined ISIS in the Syrian war theatre, giving the Maldives the dubious and unwarranted distinction of making the highest per capita contribution among nations to the terror group.[6] Maldivian society is grappling with the fallout too, with the rehabilitation of the returnees. In some cases, the widows of Maldivian ISIS fighters wish to bring back children of the co-fighters of their husbands as their own. The Maldives has also not been very successful in arresting the flow of students to Pakistani religious establishments, especially Deobandi-Wahabi madrasas, despite being aware of the adverse consequences.

As an Islamic country with almost cent per cent Muslim population, the Maldives has followed a path of abundant caution in dealing with

---

6   The Indian Express, 'Maldives President Solih's visit came in a fraught moment in ties between the two countries. Delhi must tread carefully', *The Indian Express*, 5 August 2022; https://indianexpress.com/article/opinion/editorials/maldives-president-solihs-visit-came-in-a-fraught-moment-in-ties-between-the-two-countries-8071460/

the issue of religion and radical ideology at the ideational level. There is scope for India to help the Maldives in countering the ill effects of radical teachings radiating out of the Pakistan-Afghanistan region and the Levant.

The view from Bangladesh is that 'trust' and 'inclusiveness' are critical for the full realization of India's Neighbourhood First policy, and interdependence is key to a better neighbourhood approach. As a natural leader, India should continually work towards promoting interdependence, reducing the trust deficit and taking on a larger responsibility in creating a conducive environment for regional cooperation.

There is a view in Bangladesh that characterizing India as a net security provider and others as security recipients does not inspire trust and confidence. Security in the region should be a product of effective partnerships, with each country participating as both a provider and a recipient. The view from Maldives is in direct contrast to this— Maldives considers India as a net security provider.

India-Bangladesh relations are passing through their best phase in bilateral ties. However, a few people in Bangladesh believe that it is not a one-way traffic and that despite India's claim of non-reciprocity in its relationship with neighbours, Bangladesh is giving back more than it is receiving from India. Dhaka has taken measures to augment India's security and has also provided it an avenue for investment. Bangladesh expects India to deal with all outstanding contentious issues, including that of 'border firings', in a sensitive manner. Moreover, it was pointed out that the domestic discourse in India has often been 'less than friendly' towards Bangladesh in recent times, including pronouncements by some of the senior functionaries in the government, which should be avoided in the interest of better bilateral relations.

In recent years, the strategic community in Bangladesh has assessed the US as abdicating its international responsibilities, even as being unreliable and unpredictable, perhaps as a result of its experience during the Trump presidency. In contrast, China is increasingly perceived as being more outward-looking and willing to share its prosperity with other countries. China is viewed by many influential opinion-makers in Bangladesh as a generous provider of developmental finance and regional public goods through its ambitious projects such as the Belt and Road Initiative (BRI).

The competing themes of the BRI and the Indo-Pacific have created new pressures on Bangladesh, with many subscribing to a view that the Indian and Pacific Oceans are emerging as new theatres of great-power rivalry leading to the rise of a 'complex regional alliance system', which is forcing countries in the region to make difficult policy choices. To some extent, going by public perception and by the nature of their bilateral trade and economic engagement, it is clear that Bangladesh has already cast its lot with China. A senior advisor to the Bangladeshi Prime Minister, well-disposed towards India, told this author during a visit to Bangladesh that, 'Bangladesh cannot remain aloof from the BRI since there are several economic opportunities that Dhaka can avail of'. Such a sentiment runs through many other South Asian nations, including India's island neighbours. The bottom line is that while the relationship with India is important and central to Bangladesh's foreign policy, Dhaka will retain its autonomy in choosing its partners in the neighbourhood, and this is true of its dealings with China. This is also accompanied by a fear of strategic competition between India and China impeding Bangladesh's future engagement with Beijing, especially since India rejects the BRI.

The impact of the river water issue on bilateral relations between India and Bangladesh is often understated. The two countries share fifty-four rivers and there is heavy dependence on both sides on the vagaries of nature and the water flows. Lack of progress on the Teesta River sharing agreement, non-tariff barriers, trade deficit, the occasional killing of Bangladeshi smugglers at the borders and India's perceived apathetic stand on the Rohingya issue have prevented bilateral relations from being completely free of irritants. Together, these issues create a sense of distrust about Indian intentions. The National Register of Citizens (NRC) in Assam is also a matter of concern among intellectuals in Dhaka.

On the trade front, there is a general appreciation about the positive role played by border haats in promoting prosperity among the local border populace. These are local markets along the border which have been established through a bilateral Memorandum of Understanding (MOU) signed in 2010 covering trade at zero tariff in twenty-one items, largely agricultural and horticultural, using either nation's currency. There is a similar positive view about cross-border electricity flows. However, such sanguine views are laced with disproportionate (non-reciprocal) expectations of continued concessions from India including Indian initiatives to boost subregional cooperation, outsourcing production to Bangladesh through investments, and activating coastal shipping. Suggestions for improving trade include: (i) joint production and creation of global value chains; (ii) amendment of the Coastal Shipping Agreement to enable transport of goods to and from third countries; (iii) use of seaworthy vessels for coastal shipping and grant of permission to Bangladesh seamen to board them; (iv) technical support and investment by India to develop Bangladesh's tourism sector; (v) improvement of infrastructure and physical facilities in all the twenty-two land ports; (vi) institutionalization of business-to-business interactions; and (vii) greater integration of power and energy supply networks as well as developing energy-efficient technology.

On security cooperation, there is a prevailing view in Bangladesh about the potential for an 'open border' between the two countries, particularly since the Bangladesh government has addressed India's key security concerns.

The view from Sri Lanka is that India needs to focus on investing in the financial sector. Sri Lanka needs foreign investment and information technology to realize its plans to convert Colombo into a logistics hub.

There is no gainsaying the fact that despite some issues in the relationship, the current government in Colombo believes that 'India is at the heart of Sri Lanka's security and strategic policy'. As compared to a decade ago, there is greater sensitivity to India's security interests. There is acknowledgement of India's gesture of reserving the highest number of trainee slots (1,000 out of 1,700) in India's premier defence establishments for Sri Lankan armed forces personnel. There is palpable interest in Sri Lanka in deriving benefits by joining India's Sagarmala project and from enhanced connectivity, including ferry services between India and Sri Lanka. The Sagarmala Programme is an initiative by the Government of India aimed at 'bringing about a step change in India's logistics performance' and 'unlocking the full potential of India's coastline and waterways' through 'synergistic and coordinated port-led development' focusing on setting up 'logistics intensive industries', building efficient ports, developing the skill-base of the coastal community and ensuring seamless connectivity.

India and Sri Lanka can together tap many opportunities. After the Easter bombings, Colombo is keen to improve its investigative strategies and has welcomed Indian inputs on the investigation into the bombings. India and Sri Lanka need to strengthen counterterrorism cooperation through institutionalized interactions among concerned agencies dealing with issues related to terrorism. There is also a need for greater institutionalized intelligence-sharing under the trilateral dialogue (India-Sri Lanka-Maldives) at the level of the National Security Advisors (NSAs).

There is a common Sri Lankan perception that compared to arms and ammunition supplied by the US and China, Indian weaponry is cheaper and more useful. Cooperation in this area could be improved in future. Sri Lanka's geostrategic location is vital for implementing

Indian maritime strategies and the two navies need to scale up their cooperation to the strategic level.

As in Bangladesh, so also in Sri Lanka, there is a tug of war between China's BRI and the US' Millennium Challenge Corporation (MCC). The MCC was established by the US Congress in 2004 as an independent agency, separate from the State Department and USAID, to provide grants to countries for economic growth. The Sri Lankan response to this choice is more emotional than rational. The MCC would have granted $480 million to Sri Lanka for the improvement of land management and modernization of the transport system in the country. However, the then spokesperson of the government went on record saying that 'Sri Lanka will not sign MCC under any circumstance'. There are opponents in Sri Lanka who suspect that the MCC would result in international monitoring of the human rights situation in Sri Lanka through the backdoor which would provide a fillip to assertive minority groups to regroup and challenge the state. There are others, as in Nepal, who are convinced by the Chinese propaganda to regard the MCC as a policy directed against China's BRI projects.

The great irony amidst all this is the fact that India's generous and non-reciprocal offers of assistance in infrastructure and connectivity projects in Sri Lanka are unfairly tarred with the US brush, often seen as part of a US-led effort in the region to 'contain China'.

There are continuing misgivings about the Free Trade Agreement (FTA) with India in the shape of the Economic and Technical Cooperation Agreement (ETCA), which has replaced the earlier agreed Comprehensive Economic Partnership Agreement (CEPA). It is often viewed unfavourably by a section of the political dispensation. The sense of resistance tapers off as one engages with those who are either sympathetic towards the previous government which had negotiated the ETCA or those who have a rational approach to trade and economics. It appears virtually impossible to get the agreement through with the present government, which considers it to be against national interests. Those resisting the proposal argue that ETCA could open up the floodgates of unhindered trade and commerce, which would hurt the interests of Sri Lankan businessmen and lead to a lopsided trade balance in favour of India. Some in Sri Lanka suggest rather than pushing for ETCA, the two countries should evolve a new framework to discuss trade issues.

Nepal's views on geostrategic issues are increasingly tainted by its growing ties with China. There are, for instance, misgivings about the Indo-Pacific, which is regarded as being synonymous with the Quadrilateral Security Dialogue and suspected to be an American strategy to contain China. Some members of the strategic community in Nepal even call it a 'New Marshall Plan' or even an alliance, which poses a threat to the region in their assessment. India's opposition to the BRI has been frequently questioned in Nepal. The underlying assumption is that India is siding with the US in the global power struggle between China and the US.

It is clear that politicians, bureaucrats, media persons and scholars in Nepal are being consistently exposed to Chinese propaganda. The insidious nature of such propaganda has led to some extreme views wherein India's economic growth and progress is, ironically, viewed as a regional threat to its smaller neighbours, including Nepal. Some of these views originate among those with a pronounced leftist bias, but there are others too who have come under the spell of such false narratives promoted by select media houses and anchors under the influence of their northern neighbour, often acting in tandem with Pakistan's intelligence agencies. The adverse impact of such propaganda on public opinion can and must be countered through greater and regular exchange of views with Nepalese interlocutors to correct their bias.

The twin issues of Kalapani and Lipulekh have often been raised by vested interests in Nepal. The Sugauli Treaty ratified by the British East India Company and Nepal in 1816 states that the course of the Kali River, called the Mahakali in the downstream area, forms Nepal's western boundary. The treaty did not specify which of the two tributaries—the one originating around Lipukekh Pass and the other around Limpiyadhura—would be taken as the Kali River, and by extension, as Nepal's western extremity. Nepal claims the origin at Limpiyadhura, suggesting that territory east of the Kali River should go to Nepal. India's position is that the Kali River originates from around Lipulekh pass.

The map published by India in December 2019 (in the aftermath of the decision to abrogate Article 370 and the reorganization of the erstwhile state of Jammu and Kashmir) has been misconstrued by some elements in Nepal to spread canards about India's designs on so-called Nepalese territory. The India-Nepal Treaty of Peace and Friendship of 1950 provides for special relations between India and Nepal, giving Nepalese citizens facilities and job opportunities at par with Indian citizens in many instances. There is, therefore, a view in Nepal that since the 1950 treaty overrode all pre-existing treaties, the understanding between the British and Nepalese rulers on Kalapani (Treaty of Sugauli) was no longer relevant. There is inadequate appreciation in Nepal of the fact that there has been no change in the Indian position that Lipulekh pass is the origin of the Mahakali River, and that the Border Working Groups set up to demarcate the India-Nepal border are discussing the differences regarding border pillars following Nepal's unwillingness to accept the strip maps prepared by the Joint Technical Committee (JTC) led by Surveyors General of India and Nepal.

The 1950 treaty between India and Nepal elicits a mixed response across Nepal today. Some argue that it is an unequal treaty and should be revised. However, despite Indian assurances that it is open to this idea, there has been no progress on the issue. The Nepalese government has often used the issue as a stick to beat India with, with no real intention to sacrifice all the unilateral advantages that Nepal derives from the treaty.

There is no gainsaying the fact that the border blockade in 2015 by the Madhesis of Nepal, who felt betrayed by the ruling political dispensation in Kathmandu when it promulgated a new Constitution without incorporating provisions which they claimed had been discussed and agreed upon, to grant some advantages to them. The blockade lasted for 135 days, leaving a deep scar on Nepali public opinion. The dominant view is that the blockade was unofficially backed by India, and it pushed Nepal into the waiting arms of China. Unlike during the brief period of estrangement between India and Nepal in 1988, China no longer advises Nepal that it should not regard China as a substitute for India to overcome the limitations of its land-locked status. Today, China has redoubled efforts to create a maze of road and rail infrastructure to enmesh Nepal in its own regional connectivity plans in the context of the BRI, even offering access to its eastern seaports for Nepal's foreign trade.

There is a popular view in the public discourse in Nepal that 'China delivers, India only promises'. Yet, there is also a recognition that India is too important a country to be side-lined, despite Nepal's inclination to respond positively to China's overtures. To retain its pre-eminence in Nepal, India may have to expand its network of engagement, work with leaders of different political persuasions without getting too involved in the internal politics of Nepal, shed complacency, and speed up the implementation of its assistance programmes.

From Myanmar's perspective, India's role in maintaining peace and security in the region is praiseworthy and India can help its neighbours to grow economically as well. Myanmar appreciates Indian interest and investment in the Kaladan Multimodal Transit and Transport Project and BIMSTEC. These initiatives have the potential to significantly enhance bilateral trade from the current $1.7 billion. Myanmar is also interested in deepening military-to-military ties in areas of training, maritime security and joint surveillance. It has sought India's help to realize its plans of a blue-water navy. The transfer of an Indian submarine was greatly appreciated.

China factor

Most of India's neighbours seem to have a benign view of China. Even though Bhutan is not a signatory to the BRI, it believes that resolution of all outstanding issues between China and India—leading to more harmonious relations between the two countries—would benefit the neighbours, the region and the world. The informal Wuhan Summit (27-28 April 2018) and the Mamallapuram Summit (11-12 October 2019) meetings between the top leadership of India and China were regarded as positive steps that would lead to lowering of bilateral tensions and create a conducive environment for trade and cooperation among all countries in the neighbourhood.

It appears that Sri Lanka is not keen on hurting India's interests in the region and though Indian assistance and help is important. It will keep looking for other developmental opportunities and will develop its economic relations with China. Ironically, Sri Lankan leaders do not believe that Chinese loans can land the country in a debt trap because the size of the debt is a small percentage of the country's overall external debt.

Kathmandu will likely seek closer relations with China, while being cognizant of India's security interests. The economic blockade of 2015 affected the India-Nepal bilateral relationship adversely and forced Nepal to seek alternatives. In fact, Nepal signed a protocol on transit and transport agreement with China in March 2016. However, this is unlikely to help Nepal in the long run given the geographical terrain and the fact that many of the Chinese ports are far away from Nepal. Trade through such ports would not be cost-effective compared to ports in India. The Nepalese people know that India-Nepal economic relations are robust and China cannot replace India as an economic and developmental partner, especially when India remains committed to a robust Neighbourhood First policy.

India's neighbours are expected to continue to establish close relations with China, India's concerns in this regard notwithstanding. India should not be 'hypersensitive' about China's outreach to countries in the region. At the same time, India's neighbours would have to carefully weigh India's genuine and legitimate concerns while engaging China.

SAARC

The failure of SAARC is, in a way, being perceived as a failure of India's Neighbourhood First policy. There is a widely held perception that India should not abandon SAARC. Reactivating the defunct SAARC, mainly its secretariat, would be useful in speeding up connectivity programmes by generating intra-regional consensus on standardization, trade facilitation and monitoring mechanisms, and synchronization of customs. There is an appreciation of the fact that SAARC is deadlocked primarily due to Pakistan's non-cooperation. This has thwarted regional trade and connectivity.

Pakistan's role

Pakistan's attempt to stall the process of regional integration by refusing to sign the SAARC motor vehicles agreement has been criticized by several South Asian countries. They have expressed concerns about Pakistan's strategy to use terrorism as an instrument of state policy, which is spawning radicalism in the entire region. However, most neighbours, excluding Afghanistan but including Myanmar, believe that India needs to be more creative in dealing with Pakistan, even though it remains a known disruptive actor, and engage it at some level to promote regional cooperation.

Connectivity

Connectivity brings people closer, which in turn generates closeness. This shared closeness is expected to act as the basis of regional integration and shared regional identity in South Asia. Connectivity within the region has increased since 2010, with the exception of a lack of connectivity between India and Pakistan. Nonetheless, high costs and delays in implementing projects are major obstacles to strengthening connectivity networks in the region.

To improve connectivity, a new connectivity agenda should be developed based on the following: construction of economic corridors; coordinated border management; creation of a regional transport network; adoption of regional standards; and establishment of a single window for clearance of projects.

Terrorism and drug trafficking

India has transited from being a conduit to a major consumer of illegal drugs in the recent past. There has been a manifold increase in drug seizures during 2019-22, in the case of heroin, increasing from 237 kg in 2019 to 14,967 kg till September 2022. India faces this challenge on both its western and eastern borders. Drones have emerged as a preferred medium for sending drugs across from Pakistan. Apart from marijuana and heroin, synthetic drugs have emerged as a new menace in the Northeast of India, with growing local consumption. As the Dark Web is emerging as a new platform for drug trafficking, the region needs to invest in capacity-building exercises to secure itself from this menace. Since transborder terrorism cannot be tackled without bilateral or regional cooperation, there is a need for developing a regional approach to intelligence sharing, law enforcement and other forms of counterterrorism cooperation.

Energy cooperation

Energy cooperation among South Asian countries can be a win-win partnership for all the involved stakeholders. South Asian states have some of the lowest per capita energy consumption in the world, and they rely on fossil fuel-based energy sources for electricity generation. Regional cooperation in energy trade is essential to achieve environmentally sustainable economic growth in these countries.

Energy cooperation between India and Bhutan in the form of hydropower partnership is a unique win-win model for other countries. Bhutan benefits by earning much-needed revenue through the export of surplus power to India, which in turn benefits by importing clean energy to meet part of its growing energy demand.

Enhancing power-trading within South Asia would require investor-friendly policies, a harmonious regulatory framework, single-window clearances, standard contracts, unbundling of various activities, uniform rules and regulations and public-private partnership (PPP) mode of investments.

Recommendations

1. Given that intra-South Asian trade and investment flows are some of the lowest in the world, an evaluation of the cost and impact of disruption on region-wide economic growth should be undertaken to help countries in the region shed their differences in order to work towards regional economic integration.

2. To retain its credibility, India must address the issue of delivery-deficit, particularly at a time when its South Asian neighbours have other options.

3. An impact assessment exercise should be carried out to understand the effectiveness of Indian assistance. This can help to reformulate and recast the aid programme to address the developmental needs of India's neighbours.

4. With the introduction of democracy in Bhutan, India-Bhutan relations have been subjected to closer public scrutiny in Bhutan. Today, the challenge for India is to meet the demands of a changing Bhutan, especially the youth who are more conscious about global and regional issues than the previous generation. Other challenges include safeguarding Bhutan's communication lines that pass through India. While utilizing Bhutan's water resources for mutual benefit, India needs to be sensitive to Thimphu's climate change concerns.

5. India should offer to address Bangladesh's environmental concerns by focusing on clean energy projects.

6. Defence and security cooperation between India and Sri Lanka is a force multiplier for both states, especially when addressing maritime security threats and challenges in the India Ocean and across the Indo-Pacific. India should strengthen coastal shipping and maritime institutional frameworks in the region.

7. The region needs more PPP investments in large power projects. Private sector participation in cross-border electricity projects can be a tool to neutralize political risks.

8. Cyber threats to utility firms and energy infrastructure are key regional concerns. These need to be factored in by each country in the region in a much more focused way.

9. Expanding the areas under electrification is as important as ensuring quality of electricity. Uninterrupted power supply should be prioritized.

10. Infrastructure deficit, delays in implementing projects and revenue-sharing are significant challenges in improving connectivity in the region. The role of civil society, the business community, think tanks and the media is important for the sustainability of connectivity initiatives.

11. South Asians need to rise above their individual national identities and think like South Asians while discussing ways and means of boosting regional integration. Cross-country regional civil societies of South Asia also have a duty to encourage Track II dialogue such as the one held by the Manohar Parrikar Institute for Defence Studies and Analyses (MP-IDSA) every year. The Ministry of External Affairs could engage MP-IDSA even more and collaborate on various conferences that have a broad bearing on India's defence and security.

Know thy neighbour: Growth of India and China—sociocultural precepts and propositions

It is very important for large and populous neighbours such as India and China to have a better understanding of one another's history, culture and value systems. Perhaps no two peoples in the world are as similar as Indians and Chinese in terms of the agrarian foundations of our societies, our traditions with roots in Hindu-Buddhist rituals and philosophy and even the undue importance attached in the past to the male child. At the same time, we are also dissimilar: we use our hands to eat food, they use chopsticks; we use the slow flame to cook whereas they use a high flame; we are direct in speech and given to individualism whereas they are indirect and place group interests above that of the individual; the concept of 'loss of face' in China is much stronger than that of 'izzat' in India. We are a democracy. China has a centralized system that could not be more different. And how we achieved nationhood is also very different.

It goes without saying that good fences make good neighbours. The fact is that India and China have yet to build good fences. We have coexisted for millennia, amicably for the most part, except for the differences that surfaced in the twentieth century. India and China still have a long way to go to understand one another better, partly because both countries are changing so rapidly. Other variables in the mix are the narratives built up by the media and armchair specialists in India and in China's case, the Chinese Communist Party line, which unfortunately determine the bandwidth in which even academics operate.

The theme of this chapter has been divided into three distinct time frames in which India and China's perceptions of one another have evolved. The first covers our historical ties from the earliest links to the middle of the twentieth century. The second spans the period from the birth of the People's Republic of China in 1949 until the end of the last century. The third features the current period from the beginning of this century to the present.

The millennial ties between India and China revolve around the birth of Buddhism in India and its spread to neighbouring countries, including China, particularly during the Maurya and the Gupta dynasties. Much of what we know of the time is through the lens of the great travellers who went across boundaries that were yet only notional.

Great Buddhist monks such as Bodhidharma from India who founded the Dhyan ('Chan' in Chinese) school of meditation at the Shaolin Monastery in Henan around the fifth century, and the famous itinerant monks Fa Xian and Xuan Zang who travelled from China to India in the fourth and seventh centuries, respectively, in search of Buddhist scriptures, are part of the earliest impressions. These images of the other were benign, cultural and apolitical, bereft of ideological prejudice or the coloured lens of ethnic or national hubris. The Chinese travellers took back with them the real treasures of Indian thought and philosophy, and translated them from ancient Indian languages into

Chinese. These were preserved through the ages such that they left a deep and abiding mark on Chinese thought, philosophy and culture.

In the Ming period around 500 years ago, Zheng He's voyages brought Chinese ships to the shores of India (mainly around Calicut), but apart from the 'Chinese' fishing nets still in use there today, ceramics and a few other symbols of cultural contact, the footprint of Chinese culture in India was light. Thereafter, the Ming dynasty's maritime power shrank, giving way to the Qing dynasty's continental ambitions, which took nearly two centuries to consolidate in both Tibet and Xinjiang, finally bringing India and China face to face in the mid-twentieth century, for the first time as new nations in search of strong identities.

The nineteenth and twentieth century struggle against imperialism and colonialism in China and India, the marvels of modern travel and communication, and no doubt also the thrust provided by British trade interests, all edged us closer. Britain had a huge trade imbalance with China in the eighteenth and nineteenth centuries due to large imports of tea, silk and ceramics. Lord George Macartney's trade mission in 1793 had been roundly rebuffed by Emperor Qianlong who wrote to King George III of Britain that China had everything she needed, that China attached no value to Britain's manufactures and would never agree to give the trade privileges sought by Britain.

The Opium Wars that followed, the colonization of Hong Kong, even the sacking of the Old Summer Palace in 1860 and again by the Eight-Nation Alliance in 1900 after the Boxer Revolution all had, unfortunately, an Indian connection since the British exploited the colony that was India and often executed colonial reprisals throughout Asia using Indian troops.

The industrious Sikhs started the dairy industry in Shanghai in the 1920s and '30s. Indian traders and particularly the imposing Sikh soldiers and policemen were a commonplace and often a feared sight in Shanghai, Guangzhou and Hong Kong before 1949. As the third and fourth decades of the twentieth century unfolded, a number of Chinese refugees from the Civil War wound their way to settle in cities such as Kolkata, becoming restaurateurs, owners of shoe factories and salons. Intellectuals such as Tan Yunshan mingled with Rabindranath Tagore and other Indian intelligentsia at Visva-Bharati in Shantiniketan where he set up a centre for Sino-Indian studies in 1937, better known as Cheena Bhavana. During the second Sino-Japanese war in 1938, the Indian National Congress sent a five-member medical mission to assist the Chinese communists in response to a request for assistance by General Zhu De. The heroic assistance provided by India to the Chinese people during the medical mission led by Dr M. Atal, of which Dr Kotnis was a key member, remains etched in the collective memory and folklore in China. Dr Kotnis stayed back when the mission ended and the team returned to India. He continued to provide medical assistance to the communists, passing away in 1942 at a young age.

Gandhiji's non-violent path to Swaraj could not have provided a starker contrast to the path chosen by the Communist Party of China and Mao Zedong's advocacy of class struggle based on the firm belief that 'political power grows out of the barrel of a gun'. His other famous saying was that 'a revolution is not a dinner party, or writing an essay, or painting a picture, or doing embroidery; it cannot be so refined, so leisurely and gentle, so temperate, kind, courteous, restrained and magnanimous. A revolution is an insurrection, an act of violence by which one class overthrows another'. Contrast this with what Gandhiji said, 'I object to violence because when it appears to do good, the good is only temporary; the evil it does is permanent'.

This may well be taken as an early indication of how extremely differently India and China viewed their sociocultural contexts and the paths to the realization of their respective destinies. Also, one could say that the completely different models for achieving nationhood in India and China have also shaped the subsequent strategic culture in the two countries. China has since traditionally attached priority to hard power, and has unhesitatingly used it both internally to unify the country, and externally to define borders. India, on the other hand, has relied more on the notions of non-violence and coexistence and resorted to democratic processes and dialogue to resolve issues, though it has remained open to the exercise of hard power as a last resort as we showed during the Goa operation in December 1961 when the Indian Army evicted the Portuguese from the enclave through armed action after the latter declined to end its colonial rule.

Another difference is on account of the homogeneity of the people in China, which easily facilitates a monolithic view of the other, as against the plurality and diversity in India in which there is a great range of perceptions and opinions.

Unlike the case of India, the People's Republic of China was midwifed through revolutionary struggle by the Chinese Communist Party and its adjunct, the People's Liberation Army (PLA). In that sense, it is uniquely a state owned by an ideology backed by the PLA.

In the second half of the twentieth century, both India and China adopted very different paths to achieve somewhat similar objectives of alleviating poverty and improving the lives of millions of people. The consolidation of the Chinese presence in Tibet in the 1950s and simmering differences over the boundary between India and China, the discovery of the road (highway G219 connecting Xinjiang and Tibet) illegally built by the Chinese across Aksai Chin, and incidents in Barahoti in the Middle Sector and Hot Springs in the Western Sector of the Indo-China border region brought home the gap in perceptions and positions. Nehru's dream of unity in Asia was shattered. The Sino-Indian border conflict in 1962, of course, left deep and indelible scars in India, though hardly any of a lasting nature in the public imagination in China. The popular narrative in India since then is that after the perfidy of 1962, China cannot be trusted. This sense of betrayal has been cemented by China's unwavering moral and military support for Pakistan, including on issues such as Jammu and Kashmir and terrorism that directly affect India. China's inroads into South Asia, often at the cost of India's traditional goodwill and status, have also complicated matters. China is perceived as thwarting the rise of India. India's relations with other great powers, whether the Soviet Union in the past or the US now, have aroused deep unease in the Chinese mind.

Though scholars have not examined this aspect adequately, I believe that the absence of a formal ritualized religious foundation in Chinese society, notably the complete absence of it under communism, has also tempered Chinese thinking and perception in favour of the adage that 'the end justifies the means'. The 'here and now' of the material world has always been more important for the Chinese people. It would be true to say that the religious underpinnings of Indian society have led popular Indian thought to focus far more on notions of morality, karmic consequences in the 'hereafter' and even a sense of resignation to the inevitable, perhaps limiting the range and use of options available. The common Chinese is far more familiar with ancient strategists such as Sun Tzu and his *Art of War* or the medieval classic *Romance of the Three Kingdoms* than is the average Indian with either tactics or grand strategy of the type advocated by Kautilya in his masterful *Arthashastra*.

Traditionally, Indians have attached greater importance to individualism in thought, perception and even the path to salvation. India has valued 'soft power' attributes such as yoga, Bollywood songs and films, and Indian dance and cuisine. It gives us a sense of fulfilment to hear a Chinese sing Raj Kapoor's famous theme song from the film *Awara*. The Chinese derive much greater satisfaction when they see foreigners using Chinese products or Chinese-built infrastructure.

Chinese society has always favoured Confucian notions of authority, discipline and social harmony. In tandem with new-found economic power, it has made strategic use of the 'sharp power' of trade, investments and easy financing. This, though, is beginning to change gradually as India moves to a high growth trajectory that permits the use of more generous developmental finance, and China starts to appreciate the 'soft power' of Confucius Centres, mandarin language teaching and even Buddhism in the toolkit of external engagement as a means to smooth the rough edges of its rising and often disruptive power.

In the current phase, China's entry into the World Trade Organization in 2001, the US withdrawal from the Asia-Pacific post the 9/11 attacks on New York City and Washington D.C. and its focus on the international war on terror created tremendous opportunities for China, leading to its emergence today as the world's second-largest economy, with the ability to project unprecedented power on key issues relating to sovereignty and territorial claims. The ongoing US-China trade war, the push-back against the Belt and Road Initiative, and differences over data and technology theft have led to a new dynamic in which China is seeking, as are others, to stabilize ties with other regional powers.

Now the great question before us is whether India and China can live in peace in the future, our differences notwithstanding. One believes that stable and friendly ties are fundamentally important for the sake of our future generations. But to guarantee this also requires a change in mindsets and depends on how well we understand one another. The following recommendations would go a long way in enhancing mutual understanding:

1. Both countries need to fight stereotypes. Neither side should consider its political or economic system or sociocultural foundations to be superior. China's system is a choice made by the Chinese people; similarly, our parliamentary democracy is best suited to our needs. This requires a non-judgemental acceptance of one another for what each side represents. It would be unhelpful if Indians were to regard the Chinese state and systems of political and economic governance as doomed to failure in the

long run simply because they represent a different model from ours. We need to understand how discipline, unity of purpose and hard work have contributed to China's success, and how placing collective interest above the self actually helps the nation. Vicarious pleasure in the slowing down of the Chinese economy cannot be a substitute for proactive action on our own part to develop our economy. It does not help to bank on growing tensions in the US-China relationship. Equally, it would be counter-productive for Chinese public opinion to regard India as an obstreperous and relatively chaotic country with an unresolved 'class struggle', and a slower delivery in education, health and infrastructure. The Chinese understanding of India must go beyond casting India as a land of yoga, exotic superstition, rituals and practices, home to winners of beauty pageants and Bollywood films. China needs to understand how democracy works in India and how it has helped a large and populous nation do so well since independence without the internal upheavals, turmoil and bloodshed that China experienced.

2. For some in India to imagine that we would have made faster progress if we had some of the attributes and systems of the Chinese state is sheer naivety. Equally, it is unrealistic to expect that China will evolve into a democracy or relent on territorial differences or sever its close ties to Pakistan. The realities on both sides are far more complex.

3. It is not just India that has to adjust to the accretion in China's economic and strategic power; equally, China needs to adjust to the new reality of the rise of a big and civilizational power like India. India's determination and capacities during the stand-off at Doklam in 2017 have driven home this point. A broad-sweep division of the world by China, with the US at an aspirational level above China, a benign Europe laterally on the periphery, and the rest, particularly in Asia, all below China, simply will not work.

4. Both sides need to accommodate each other's interests and remain sensitive to one another's concerns. India remains deeply sensitive to China's traditional support for Pakistan; China's unhelpful positions on the boundary question, on India's membership of the Nuclear Suppliers Group (NSG), on Masood Azhar's designation as a terrorist by the United Nations Security Council 1267 Sanctions Committee, and the China-Pakistan Economic Corridor project that traverses Pakistan-occupied Kashmir are sources of concern, as is China's presence and activity in the Indian Ocean region. Just as India has respected the One China Policy on Tibet and Taiwan, China too must heed Indian sensitivities. China's misgivings on the question of Tibetans in India and India's relations with the US, particularly in the context of the evolving Indo-Pacific and the so-called Quadrilateral Security Dialogue are misplaced.

5. Post-Doklam, both sides have made laudable efforts to stabilize relations, with good results. The Wuhan informal summit (2019), the first of its kind aimed at establishing a frank dialogue between the leaders, has provided much needed strategic guidance at the highest level, and frequent summits between our leaders would be beneficial to ties. Other high-level exchanges have provided impetus, as has the recent India-China High Level Mechanism on Cultural and People-to-People Exchanges. These need to be pursued with vigour.

6. To avoid incidents such as the Doklam stand-off in 2017, both sides should strengthen dialogue, exchanges and confidence-building measures between the military establishments, on the border as well as off border. The importance of regular flag and border personnel meetings, use of hotlines and friendly exchanges such as the Hand-in-Hand Exercise held in December 2018 in Kunming, cannot be overstated. Similar confidence-building measures between the navies could contribute to allaying mutual apprehensions.

7. Trade needs to be balanced. Bilateral trade today stands in excess of $84 billion with India facing an adverse trade gap in excess of $63 billion. China must provide India with greater market access. A small beginning has been made with regard to soybean, sugar, non-basmati rice and some anti-cancer pharmaceuticals, but clearly this is not enough. Trade needs to be truly in the spirit of '*Hindi Chini Bhai Bhai*', and not just '*Hindi Chini Buy Buy*'.

8. The media, whether the *Global Times* in China or its equivalents in India, need to be sober and factual in reporting.

9. Above all, it is recommended that India and China should speak to one another with candour at all levels, including on prevailing differences, in order to address the trust deficit. Here, the importance of learning each other's languages cannot be overemphasized.

10. Competition and cooperation will continue to define India-China relations, but it is important to ensure that differences do not become disputes. Conflict between India and China is not inevitable. Both countries can work towards this objective by fostering better mutual understanding between their two peoples.

(The article was first published in *Strategic Analysis*, Vol. 43(2), April 2019)

Cooperative security in South Asia: A mirage?

Over the last few years, the concept of security has widened exponentially to include both traditional and non-traditional security threats such as economic and military competition, weapons of mass destruction (WMDs), climate change, piracy, radical ideology, cyberattacks, drug and human trafficking and energy and food security. The spectre of terrorism, especially cross-border terrorism, continues to challenge peace and prosperity.

Today, security is indivisible. Events in one region of the world have an impact, both positive and negative, on other regions. This highlights the necessity of combining strengths to forge new compacts that can appropriately deal with the emerging challenges.

India believes in the ancient Sanskrit saying of 'vasudhaiva kutumbakam', which means that the entire world is one family. India's family in South Asia comprises its several neighbours. Together, South Asia has a population of 1.8 billion people with a combined gross domestic product (GDP) of about $3.47 trillion, of which a very large part, about $2.72 trillion, is that of India. For family harmony, it is important that every member abide by certain common values and codes of behaviour.

Concept of cooperative security

As a concept, cooperative security implies that countries have, or seek, a degree of convergence with regard to threat perceptions, challenges and opportunities with a conviction that it is advantageous to their security, stability and prosperity. This implies a degree of conceptual clarity, which is increasingly difficult in a rapidly changing world. In an unpredictable era in which change is the only constant, power, both military and economic, stands fractured, and asymmetry in the absolute power quotient is increasingly bridged through exploitation of cyberspace, proliferation of WMDs, and misuse of internet of things (IoT) and social media platforms. This is true of state and non-state actors alike. Hedging and multi-alignment are the order of the day.

Cooperative security may logically begin with neighbours and the region but often transcends locational limitations. Cooperative security can be predicated on shared values, ideologies, religion or economic interests along multiple axes. The Cold War and North Atlantic Treaty Organization (NATO) implied cooperative security based on ideology. However, new constructs are emerging in the wake of the dramatic geostrategic changes in recent times. Germany has called for an integrated European Union (EU) military that would complement NATO. The uncertainty in the trans-Atlantic partnership suggests a greater shift towards reliance on shared geography and a common economic destiny as seen in the Eurasian Economic Union (EAEU) and the EU's nascent outreach to it.

Similarly, the Islamic Military Alliance to Fight Terrorism (IMAFT), headquartered in Riyadh, Saudi Arabia, seeks to address a global challenge but is narrowly based on a common faith. The Association of Southeast Asian Nations (ASEAN), the Shanghai Cooperation Organization (SCO), the Collective Security Treaty Organization (CSTO), the Commonwealth of Independent States (CIS), the Conference on Interaction and Confidence-Building Measures in Asia (CICA) and others such as the EU and the Organization for Security and Co-operation in Europe (OSCE) are variously glued together by geography, history and shifting regional security paradigms. Many of these structures are overlapping and multilayered. From alliance partnerships to client-state partnerships, the menu is vast and varied.

Significantly, developmental finance, much needed by many in the developing world, including in South Asia, has the potential to create economic dependence, erode sovereignty and weaken regional consensus on collective security. More often than not, it comes today steeped in strategic motives and with strings attached.

Cooperative security in South Asia

South Asia has a common history and celebrates its great cultural and linguistic overlap. South Asian nations came into their own at about the same time with the lifting of the colonial shadow. However, the South Asian experience in building cooperative security architecture has been mixed.

It can be argued that cooperative security in any region is like a chain that is as strong as its weakest link. The South Asian family, unfortunately, has its own black sheep. The weakest link in the chain continues to be Pakistan, which views security as a zero-sum game, and uses terrorism as an instrument of state policy against its neighbours. The consequences of such a policy pursued in one country in South Asia, aimed at systematically nurturing radical jihadi groups, have been felt in other South Asian countries as well—from Afghanistan to India and from Bangladesh to Sri Lanka.

South Asia can truly prosper only when it is free from the scourge of terrorism. The greatest challenges before South Asia are the fight against illiteracy and poverty, climate change and natural disasters and food and energy security issues. These are indivisible and transcend borders. Cooperation on these issues will ensure the achievement of the Sustainable Development Goals (SDGs).

One of the measures to improve regional security is to strengthen connectivity. Better connectivity can help nations overcome their political differences by conceiving of their borders as bridges and not as barriers. However, the efforts of the South Asian Association for Regional Cooperation (SAARC) to build a regional consensus have been undermined by one state's obstructionist policies. The SAARC motor vehicle agreement, which would have allowed region-wide movement of vehicles and promoted trade, commerce and people-to-people contacts, was, unfortunately, vetoed by one country.

Afghanistan, devastated by conflict, needs help. It requires the support of its neighbours to spur economic growth. Yet, India and Afghanistan have been denied overland transit by a common neighbour. It is not without reason that the intra-South Asian trade remains one of the lowest in the world.

India's commitment to cooperative security

As the world's second-most populous country with 1.25 billion people, India attaches great importance to strengthening cooperative security. India's initiatives over the last five years to build regional cooperation and security are anchored in its Neighbourhood First policy. From inviting the heads of all SAARC states to Prime Minister Narendra Modi's swearing-in ceremony in 2014 to India's initiative to launch a South Asia satellite to improve communication and disaster response, India remains committed to its neighbourhood. India has always been the first off the block to provide relief in the wake of tsunamis, earthquakes and other natural disasters.

Prime Minister Modi has emphasized the importance of shared prosperity with our neighbours through his clarion call of '*Sabka saath, sabka vikas, sabka vishwas*', the essence of which roughly translates as 'collective effort, inclusive growth and mutual trust'.

India remains optimistic about the future of South Asia at a time when it has emerged as one of the fastest-growing large economies in the world. India is the proverbial rising tide that can lift all boats in the region.

India is keen to strengthen other regional groupings and partnerships such as the Bangladesh, Bhutan, India and Nepal (BBIN) initiative and the Bay of Bengal Initiative for Multi-Sectoral Technical and Economic Cooperation (BIMSTEC), which includes Bangladesh, India, Myanmar, Sri Lanka, Thailand, Nepal and Bhutan. India is also committed to greater connectivity and cooperation with the ASEAN region through its Act East policy. India has also expanded its cooperation with the Shanghai Cooperation Organization (SCO), Indian Ocean Rim Association (IORA), ASEAN Regional Forum (ARF) and the East Asia Summit (EAS) in the extended neighbourhood.

These underlying principles have translated into India building excellent ties in its neighbourhood. India has a special friendship with Bhutan. Bangladesh is a key pillar of India's regional engagement. An open border with Nepal demonstrates mutual trust and confidence. Security cooperation with Myanmar has increased in recent years. India is cooperating closely with both the Maldives and Sri Lanka to promote maritime security. As one of the biggest regional donors to Afghanistan's reconstruction efforts, India has overcome hurdles and established an air and a maritime corridor with Afghanistan to strengthen bilateral ties. Notably, India trains a large number of Afghan army officers, over a hundred annually, and gives thousands of scholarships to the Afghan youth for studying and pursuing vocational training in India.

Similarly, the shared maritime interests in the extended neighbourhood remain anchored in developing a blue economy, particularly in the context of what Prime Minister Modi calls SAGAR (Security and Growth for All in the Region), and in ensuring unimpeded commerce, protection of key sea lanes of communication, and freedom of navigation and overflight. India believes that competition need not result in conflict, nor differences amount to disputes.

The one exception to this cooperative process in South Asia remains Pakistan. India has made clear that there can be no dialogue unless Pakistan halts its obsession with the use of terrorism against India and other countries in the region and brings the perpetrators of the Mumbai and other terrorist attacks who freely roam in Pakistan to book.

The Simla Agreement (1972) commits both sides to discussing all issues through a bilateral dialogue, but Pakistan continues to breach its commitment with growing frequency.

In conclusion, it can be argued that South Asia 'minus one' has achieved some measure of progress in strengthening regional cooperation, as observed by India's External Affairs Minister S. Jaishankar at the World Economic Forum's 33rd edition of the India Economic Summit held in New Delhi on 4 October 2019. Nevertheless, a lot more can be done. It is also hoped that the 'minus one' country will change its mindset, eschew terrorism and come around one day for the good of all in South Asia. Hopefully, Pakistan will one day support the growing developmental impulses in South Asia instead of irresponsibly brandishing the threat of nuclear weapons.

The roadmap for regional security, given by Prime Minister Modi at the SCO Summit in 2018, remains relevant. Better known by its acronym 'SECURE', its every letter is full of meaning.

- S stands for security of our citizens
- E stands for economic development for all

- C stands for connecting the region
- U stands for uniting our people
- R stands for respect for sovereignty and territorial integrity
- E stands for environmental protection

This year marks the 150th birth anniversary of Mahatma Gandhi, a great apostle of peace and votary of truth and non-violence. It would be a fitting tribute to him if countries can, one day, abjure the use of violence and force in favour of dialogue and cooperation to fully realize their destinies.

(The article was first published on the website of the Manohar Parrikar Institute for Defence Studies and Analyses, 23 October 2019)

Modi's neighbourhood policy is predicated on his 'Sabka saath, sabka vikas' vision for inclusive growth

The visit of Sri Lanka's Prime Minister Mahinda Rajapaksa to India in February 2020 marked the beginning of a new chapter in ties with a friendly neighbour, one with which India has close historical bonds straddling culture, religion, spirituality, art and language. More relevantly, there is a growing convergence against terrorism following the Easter attacks in Sri Lanka in 2019. Several infrastructure projects, direct flights between Chennai and Jaffna, resumption of ferry services, India's new lines of credit, and construction of houses for the internally displaced, homeless and landless people are indicative of a new warmth in relations. That both Mahinda Rajapaksa and his brother President Gotabaya chose India as the destination for their first overseas visit after assuming office bodes well.

Rajapaksa captured the sentiment well in a tweet on 8 February: 'PM @narendramodi's "Neighbourhood First" policy is much appreciated

& has led to a stronger relationship btw our nations'. There is deep appreciation in Sri Lanka for the free emergency services provided through 280 ambulances gifted by India, now operational in eight of the country's nine provinces. There are much better prospects today for trilateral cooperation between India, Japan and Sri Lanka in the development of the East Container Terminal at Colombo port and the proposed joint development of the Trincomalee oil storage tanks.

After the general elections in 2019, Prime Minister Modi's first foreign visit was to the Maldives in June 2019 to establish warm and friendly relations with President Ibrahim Solih, who has done much to promote closer relations with India through his India First policy. India was the first country that Solih visited in December 2018, a far cry from his predecessor Abdulla Yameen's brazen anti-India slant. Soon after assuming office, Solih's government annulled a controversial 2015 law that was meant to allow foreigners, particularly from China, to arbitrarily own islands. The inauguration during Modi's visit of two projects worth Rs 180 crore—the Coastal Surveillance Radar System and the Composite Training Center of the Maldivian National Defence Forces—has deep significance for the success of India's neighbourhood policy. India's offer of lines of credit worth about $800 million, and other capacity-building projects for water supply and sewerage are strong planks in our economic ties. Terrorism and radicalization are subjects of common concern.

The agreement to restart the trilateral DOSTI naval exercise as also the trilateral National Security Advisor-level dialogue between India, Maldives and Sri Lanka lay the ghost of the Yameen era to rest.

There are abundant signs of a fresh commitment by India to the neighbourhood in Modi's second term. In September 2019, India and Nepal jointly inaugurated South Asia's first cross-border petroleum products pipeline from Motihari in India to Amlekhgunj in Nepal. Prime Minister K.P. Oli himself acknowledged that the key connectivity project, which will provide Nepal with cleaner petroleum products at affordable cost, was completed well ahead of schedule, giving the lie to the notion that India's project delivery is tardy. India is also prioritizing the rebuilding of houses in Gorkha and Nuwakot districts, with 'Build Back Better' as the guiding principle in keeping with Modi's clarion call for a Coalition for Disaster Resilient Infrastructure (CDRI).

Geography plays a determining role in creating interdependence. Even as Nepal, like other South Asian countries, seeks closer ties with China, there is a much better appreciation today that India's role as a key economic and developmental partner is unique and indispensable.

India's relations with Bangladesh under Modi and Sheikh Hasina have evolved into a model partnership, consolidated by high-level exchanges, mutual trust and enhanced cooperation on security matters. Incidents of border firing, though rare, have an adverse fallout on public perception and need to be handled with sensitivity.

The India-Bhutan friendship runs deep, with growing cooperation in the vital hydropower sector providing it a fresh impetus. Notably, the centrepiece Mangdechhu project (750 MW) was completed on schedule last year. The introduction of the RuPay card in Bhutan and elsewhere in the neighbourhood will further cement economic and people-to-people ties. When India shortly hands over to Myanmar the INS Sindhuvir, a Kilo-class submarine, it will propel security cooperation to a higher pedestal. Close coordination with Myanmar was evident earlier in the cross-border strike on insurgents by Indian forces in 2015.

Modi's neighbourhood policy is predicated on his '*Sabka saath, sabka vikas*' vision for inclusive growth, development and prosperity. South Asia has 1.8 billion people and a combined GDP of nearly $3.47 trillion, with India's economy the largest by far. South Asia has great potential but has been held back by Pakistan, which has not only denied India and Afghanistan an overland transit route for trade, but has also thwarted Modi's efforts to place at centre stage the common struggle against poverty, illiteracy and natural disasters. It has held to ransom cooperation within the Southeast Asian Association for Regional Cooperation (SAARC) by raising extraneous matters, perpetuating terrorism and rejecting the ineluctable logic of intra-South Asian trade, which remains abysmally poor. Islamabad decided to opt out of the SAARC satellite project proposed by Modi, and it was finally launched in 2017 without Pakistan's participation. Pakistan also played the role of a spoiler at the 18th SAARC Summit in November 2014, preventing progress on the proposed motor vehicle agreement for the regulation of passenger and cargo vehicular traffic among SAARC member states.

Pakistan's intransigence on connectivity impairs Afghanistan's ability to link up with other countries in South Asia. The air corridor between India and Afghanistan cannot cater to the full potential of trade ties. Recent tensions between the US and Iran have cast a shadow on the sustainability of Chabahar port as an alternative maritime supply route to Afghanistan at a crucial juncture in its history. India's proactive role in recent years in building much-needed infrastructure and capacities in Afghanistan is widely recognized. Defence cooperation too has deepened under Modi, with India dropping its traditional coyness in such matters. Much more may have to be done, though, to help Afghanistan achieve stability through economic prosperity. Afghanistan's true destiny lies with South Asia.

India's External Affairs Minister S. Jaishankar has underscored some key aspects of the Neighbourhood First policy in Modi's second term. He spoke of India's willingness to respond to security challenges with new grit and to be an enthusiastic responder in providing humanitarian assistance and conducting disaster relief operations in Nepal, Sri Lanka, the Maldives and the extended neighbourhood. Even more important is the steady progress made by India to expand developmental assistance and improve project execution based on collaborative partnerships.

The stasis in SAARC is entirely due to Pakistan's recalcitrance. Even so, between 2014 and 2018, India's developmental assistance to six South Asian countries was over Rs 21,100 crore. The Bay of Bengal

Initiative for Multi-Sectoral Technical and Economic Cooperation (BIMSTEC), the other regional grouping, has done well. In February this year, delegates and rescue teams from India, Bangladesh, Nepal, Sri Lanka and Myanmar enthusiastically participated in disaster management exercises conducted at Ramachandi Beach at Puri in Odisha. The signing of the memorandum of understanding on the BIMSTEC grid interconnection at the fourth BIMSTEC Summit, attended by all seven member nations in Kathmandu in August 2018, provides a fillip to cross-border electricity trade.

India's focus on BIMSTEC and its Act East policy have served to highlight India's key role in promoting cooperative growth and development in several parts of South Asia. In a world increasingly characterized by a 'my country first' approach, India has endeavoured to harness the impulse for regional cooperation in a spirit of generosity, without insisting on reciprocity, to realize Modi's motto of Security and Growth for All in the Region (SAGAR).

If Pakistan were to shed its fetish for terrorism and malevolence, it too might join others one day as a responsible actor in regional cooperative efforts aimed at fulfilling the Sustainable Developmental Goals (SDGs), particularly eradication of poverty and hunger, and ensuring health, education, clean water, energy, gender equality and employment for South Asia's teeming millions by 2030.

(The article was first published in *The Indian Express*,
21 February 2020)

Trammelled Pashtun aspirations: The sad tale of another oppressed ethnic minority in Pakistan

Since inception, Pakistan has been wary of the Pashtuns' ethnic identity, brutally squashing their ethnocultural aspirations. Despite being the second largest ethnic community in the Pakistan Army, the Pashtuns have been viewed with suspicion on account of their cross-border ethnic ties in Afghanistan. No government in Afghanistan, not even the Taliban, has ever recognized the arbitrary Durand Line that divides the Pashtun nation between Afghanistan and Pakistan.

Pakistan's history is replete with examples of harsh military-led scorched earth campaigns to snuff out demands for provincial autonomy. After the army's horrific bloodletting in East Pakistan led to the birth of Bangladesh, Pakistan tried to inveigle the Pashtuns with false promises of provincial autonomy. However, the 1973 Constitution endorsed the idea of a centralized state. The National Awami Party, the legitimate conscience keeper of the Pashtuns, was denotified twice in succession, on 26 November 1971 and again on 10 February 1975.

The proud Pashtun nation has always resisted the military jackboot of a government and army dominated by the Punjabis. Ever since Pakistan turned their homeland into a nursery for radical indoctrination and militant training during the Afghan jihad in the 1980s, Pashtuns have been the worst victims of the transborder violence. Pakistan's policies have led to an influx of foreign radicals, who have created a lawless environment in which the local people have suffered immeasurably. Pakistan's misguided military operations have laid waste to the local economy, resulting in internal displacement of the tribal people and rising crime and drug abuse.

The Pashtun Tahafuz Movement (PTM), a non-violent group that seeks civil and political rights for the Pashtuns, was formed in January 2018 after the cold-blooded elimination of Naqeebullah Mehsud, a charismatic Pashtun, by the Karachi police in a fake encounter. A sociopolitical movement that openly challenges army excesses, PTM quickly gained in popularity, catching the imagination of the indignant Pashtuns who have been routinely subjected to second-class treatment in Punjabi-dominated institutions across Pakistan.

PTM organized a march of 5,000 followers from Waziristan to Islamabad in February 2018 and submitted a five-point memorandum to the government demanding an end to the profiling of Pashtuns, the clearing of Federally Administered Tribal Areas (FATA) of landmines, a time-bound judicial process for detainees, an inquiry commission to investigate extrajudicial killings, and the prosecution of Rao Anwar, the police officer accused of Mehsud's killing.

PTM regards the Pakistan Army as 'terrorists in uniform'. In reprisal, the state has launched a vigorous media campaign to malign the movement and suppress popular dissent. The recent killing of Arif Wazir, a prominent PTM leader and cousin of Ali Wazir, a member of the National Assembly, has added fuel to the fire. His assassination was a grim reminder of the state's capacity to silence dissidents.

PTM opposes the arbitrary and motivated army operations in the Khyber Pakhtunkhwa tribal areas, purportedly aimed at the Tehrik-e-Taliban Pakistan (TTP), also known as the Pakistani Taliban. TTP owes its allegiance to the Afghan Taliban, but powerful sections within it consider the Pakistan army and state to be un-Islamic. PTM alleges that a secret deal has been struck between Pakistan and the Afghan Taliban to draw an artificial distinction between the 'good' and 'bad' Taliban as a ploy to eliminate their respective opponents.

Sardar Arif Wazir was a votary of Pashtun rights and a vociferous opponent of state-sponsored violence until he was fatally shot in South Waziristan on 1 May 2020. His wanton killing, not surprisingly, was justified by the authorities. Arif's killing sparked an uproar. Tribesmen in the thousands congregated at his funeral in Wana.

PTM leader and North Waziristan member of the National Assembly Mohsin Dawar conveyed his party's resolve in a tweet on 2 May, stating that 'Arif Wazir was murdered by the "good" terrorists and our struggle against their masters will continue.' The hashtag #StateKilledArifWazir was trending on social media soon thereafter. Arif was the eighteenth member of his family to have been killed by state-sponsored militants.

Pakistan's systemic use of militant and terrorist proxies to wage so-called jihad, whether in Afghanistan or in Jammu and Kashmir in India or in the Khyber Pakhtunkhwa and FATA regions of Pakistan, is well-documented. It is a policy that promises a searing blowback on Pakistan.

(The article was first published in *The Times of India*,
11 June 2020)

Understanding the strategic flux and humanitarian crisis in Afghanistan

The world over, television screens are full of images of the extraordinary takeover of Afghanistan by the Taliban. This time, the Taliban have done it even faster than in 1996. An unfolding humanitarian tragedy has engulfed the country.

Thousands of Afghan citizens are fleeing in an attempt to put distance between themselves and the Taliban. With neighbouring countries still averse to admitting refugees from Afghanistan through overland routes, air travel out of Kabul seems the only option.

Chilling images of stampedes at Kabul airport, including of people running alongside a US Air Force plane and desperate stowaways plummeting to their deaths have shaken the global conscience.

The Afghan government and its defence forces have collapsed. Key leaders have fled the country. In staying on, Hamid Karzai, Abdullah Abdullah and Gulbuddin Hekmatyar are perhaps banking on their personal networks.

The US has expended much treasure, and shed much blood, over the last two decades. The original trigger for the US military intervention in Afghanistan was the 9/11 attacks on New York City and Washington D.C., orchestrated by the al-Qaeda. The objective then was to eliminate the al-Qaeda sanctuaries hosted by the Taliban. That goal was quickly attained, as was another one—the elimination of Osama bin Laden in Abbottabad, Pakistan, in 2011.

The US was thereafter sucked into a vortex in which its mission oscillated between counterterrorism and counter-insurgency. Even under four consecutive presidents, US policy towards Afghanistan remained in flux. The military presence in Afghanistan has been questioned by the US political firmament for a decade. The US has long been searching for an honourable exit. Meanwhile, the trillions of dollars pouring into Afghanistan for development and reconstruction programmes had led to vested interests in the form of private security contractors, service providers and non-governmental organizations.

Today, the rise of China is the main geostrategic threat for the US. In 2001, the US had taken its eye off the ball in diverting its attention to the global war on terror. Beginning with Afghanistan, it meandered through Iraq, Libya and Syria, with mixed results.

The US now regards China as its principal strategic competitor. The latter's muscle-flexing in the East and South China Seas calls for a renewed effort by the US to protect its stakes. China's recent ratcheting up of pressure on Taiwan has also sounded the alarm. The US can ill-afford the continued burden of a military presence in Afghanistan, that too of little avail, if it has to tackle China effectively in the Indo-Pacific in order to secure its interests.

China had shrewdly invited the Taliban leader Mullah Abdul Ghani Baradar in July 2021 in an attempt to secure assurances that Afghan territory would not be used to host Uyghur separatists.

In welcoming the latest developments, the spokesperson of the Chinese foreign ministry has expressed willingness to 'continue to develop friendly and cooperative relations with Afghanistan'. The engagement with the Taliban may pay dividends. At the same time, China cannot be unmindful of the fact that the US, having rid itself of the albatross of Afghanistan from around its neck, will have better options and greater resources in dealing with China.

It should come as no surprise if a Taliban government in Afghanistan were to be friendly towards China and Pakistan. The new regime in Kabul is likely to open the door to economic investments from China. At the geopolitical level, the Belt and Road Initiative (BRI) may well receive a boost, given China's interests in connectivity that could straddle the region, from Pakistan to Iran.

In 1996, Saudi Arabia, the UAE and Pakistan were quick to recognize the Islamic Emirate of Afghanistan established by the Taliban 1.0. This time around, too, Pakistan has shown alacrity in welcoming the change of guard in Kabul. Prime Minister Imran Khan's remarks about Afghans having freed themselves from the 'shackles of slavery' may irk the US.

At the multilateral level, the United Nations Security Council's press statement issued on 16 August 2021 by India's Permanent Representative, in his capacity as its rotational president, calls for 'an immediate cessation of all hostilities and the establishment, through inclusive negotiations of a new Government that is united, inclusive and representative'.

In recognition of the hard-earned gains made over the last two decades, it also underscores the need for the continued participation of women in governance. The statement also expresses concern about the violation of human rights and international humanitarian law.

The Taliban juggernaut is endeavouring to project a more moderate image of itself to a global audience that has vivid memories of its draconian rule in the 1990s. By announcing that there would be no reprisals, the Taliban have sent out a signal to this effect. However, the world will need more than just words by way of evidence in the coming months. The Taliban cannot afford to alienate the global community through a repeat of its retrograde policies, particularly on matters concerning safe havens for terrorists and the rights of women and minorities.

Taking over a country by force is one thing but governing it effectively is quite another matter. Through the recent campaign, the Taliban revealed a proclivity for violence. They will now have to demonstrate a capacity for governance. They will have to show moderation if they wish to be accepted as a member of the global community and to retain the talent nurtured in recent years.

Maintaining the vastly improved communications network, energy infrastructure, hospitals and healthcare facilities, and efficiently running the many community development projects in place will otherwise emerge as major challenges.

Obviously, the change in Afghanistan has security implications for India and the region at large. A spillover of any chaos and instability in Afghanistan beyond its borders could give terrorism a shot in the arm.

It could also singe Pakistan if it does not review its malevolent practices, which favour terror as an instrument of state policy.

India should prioritize the welfare of the Afghan people, whenever the opportunity presents itself. Currently, about 2,500 Afghan students are enrolled in educational and vocational institutions across India. They will no doubt wish to extend their scholarships. Hundreds of fresh students in Afghanistan may be waiting in the wings to come to India, having already secured admissions. One wonders if they will be able to leave Afghanistan under the present circumstances.

As a close neighbour, India has keen stakes in ensuring a stable, secure and developed Afghanistan. As the rotational president of the United Nations Security Council for August, India has an opportunity to engage important stakeholders on the way forward. Beyond that too, India's presence in the Security Council till the end of 2022 will provide a platform to explore options with greater flexibility.

(The article was first published in The Indian Express,
17 August 2021)

About the Author

Sujan Chinoy is the Director General of one of India's foremost think tanks, the Manohar Parrikar Institute for Defence Studies and Analyses (MP-IDSA), New Delhi, since 2019. He is the Chair of the Think20 engagement group for India's G20 Presidency. A career diplomat from 1981–2018, he held several important diplomatic assignments, including as Ambassador to Japan. He is a specialist on China, East Asia and the Indo-Pacific with a deep grasp of politico-military and security issues. He spent many years handling policy planning in the National Security Council Secretariat of India. As Consul General in Shanghai and Sydney, his hands-on experience covered trade, investment and economic issues. He is a prolific contributor to newspapers and journals and is a sought-after speaker in India and overseas. Besides English, he is fluent in Chinese (Mandarin) and speaks French, Spanish, German, Japanese, Arabic, Urdu and French-Creole. He is also well-versed in Hindi and his mother tongue, Gujarati.